BIG IDEAS
MATH.
Red Accelerated

Record and Practice Journal

- Fair Game Review Worksheets

- Activity Recording Journal

- Practice Worksheets

- Glossary

- Activity Manipulatives

BIG IDEAS LEARNING.

Erie, Pennsylvania

About the Record and Practice Journal

Fair Game Review

The Fair Game Review corresponds to the Pupil Edition Chapter Opener. Here you have the opportunity to practice prior skills necessary to move forward.

Activity Recording Journal

The Activity pages correspond to the Activity in the Pupil Edition. Here you have room to show your work and record your answers.

Practice Worksheets

Each section of the Pupil Edition has an additional Practice page with room for you to show your work and record your answers.

Glossary

This student-friendly glossary is designed to be a reference for key vocabulary, properties, and mathematical terms. Several of the entries include a short example to aid your understanding of important concepts

Activity Manipulatives

Manipulatives needed for the activities are included in the back of the Record and Practice Journal.

Big Ideas Learning and *Big Ideas Math* are registered trademarks of Larson Texts, Inc.

ISBN 13: 978-1-60840-462-9
ISBN 10: 1-60840-462-5

89-VLP-17 16 15

Contents

Chapter 1   Integers

Fair Game Review Worksheets 1

1.1   Integers and Absolute Value

Activity Recording Journal 3

Practice Worksheet 6

1.2   Adding Integers

Activity Recording Journal 7

Practice Worksheet 10

1.3   Subtracting Integers

Activity Recording Journal 11

Practice Worksheet 14

1.4   Multiplying Integers

Activity Recording Journal 15

Practice Worksheet 18

1.5   Dividing Integers

Activity Recording Journal 19

Practice Worksheet 22

Chapter 2   Rational Numbers

Fair Game Review Worksheets 23

2.1   Rational Numbers

Activity Recording Journal 25

Practice Worksheet 28

2.2   Adding Rational Numbers

Activity Recording Journal 29

Practice Worksheet 32

2.3   Subtracting Rational Numbers

Activity Recording Journal 33

Practice Worksheet 36

2.4   Multiplying and Dividing Rational Numbers

Activity Recording Journal 37

Practice Worksheet 40

Contents

Chapter 3   Expressions and Equations

Fair Game Review Worksheets..41

3.1   Algebraic Expressions

Activity Recording Journal..43

Practice Worksheet 46

3.2   Adding and Subtracting Linear Expressions

Activity Recording Journal..47

Practice Worksheet 50

Extension: Factoring Expressions

Practice Worksheet 51

3.3   Solving Equations Using Addition and Subtraction

Activity Recording Journal..53

Practice Worksheet 56

3.4   Solving Equations Using Multiplication and Division

Activity Recording Journal..57

Practice Worksheet 60

3.5   Solving Two-Step Equations

Activity Recording Journal..61

Practice Worksheet 64

Chapter 4   Inequalities

Fair Game Review Worksheets..65

4.1   Writing and Graphing Inequalities

Activity Recording Journal..67

Practice Worksheet 70

4.2   Solving Inequalities Using Addition or Subtraction

Activity Recording Journal..71

Practice Worksheet 74

4.3   Solving Inequalities Using Multiplication or Division

Activity Recording Journal..75

Practice Worksheet 78

4.4   Solving Two-Step Inequalities

Activity Recording Journal..79

Practice Worksheet 82

Contents

Chapter 5   Ratios and Proportions

Fair Game Review Worksheets 83

5.1   Ratios and Rates

Activity Recording Journal 85

Practice Worksheet 88

5.2   Proportions

Activity Recording Journal 89

Practice Worksheet 92

Extension: Graphing Proportional Relationships

Practice Worksheet 93

5.3   Writing Proportions

Activity Recording Journal 95

Practice Worksheet 98

5.4   Solving Proportions

Activity Recording Journal 99

Practice Worksheet 102

5.5   Slope

Activity Recording Journal 103

Practice Worksheet 106

5.6   Direct Variation

Activity Recording Journal 107

Practice Worksheet 110

Chapter 6   Percents

Fair Game Review Worksheets 111

6.1   Percents and Decimals

Activity Recording Journal 113

Practice Worksheet 116

6.2   Comparing and Ordering Fractions, Decimals, and Percents

Activity Recording Journal 117

Practice Worksheet 120

6.3   The Percent Proportion

Activity Recording Journal 121

Practice Worksheet 124

6.4   The Percent Equation

Activity Recording Journal 125

Practice Worksheet 128

Contents

6.5 **Percents of Increase and Decrease**

Activity Recording Journal 129

Practice Worksheet 132

6.6 **Discounts and Markups**

Activity Recording Journal 133

Practice Worksheet 136

6.7 **Simple Interest**

Activity Recording Journal 137

Practice Worksheet 140

Chapter 7 **Constructions and Scale Drawings**

Fair Game Review Worksheets 141

7.1 **Adjacent and Vertical Angles**

Activity Recording Journal 143

Practice Worksheet 146

7.2 **Complementary and Supplementary Angles**

Activity Recording Journal 147

Practice Worksheet 150

7.3 **Triangles**

Activity Recording Journal 151

Practice Worksheet 154

Extension: Angle Measures of Triangles

Practice Worksheet 155

7.4 **Quadrilaterals**

Activity Recording Journal 157

Practice Worksheet 160

7.5 **Scale Drawings**

Activity Recording Journal 161

Practice Worksheet 164

Chapter 8 **Circles and Area**

Fair Game Review Worksheets 165

8.1 **Circles and Circumference**

Activity Recording Journal 167

Practice Worksheet 170

8.2 **Perimeters of Composite Figures**

Activity Recording Journal 171

Practice Worksheet 174

Contents

8.3   Areas of Circles

Activity Recording Journal 175

Practice Worksheet 178

8.4   Areas of Composite Figures

Activity Recording Journal 179

Practice Worksheet 182

Chapter 9   Surface Area and Volume

Fair Game Review Worksheets 183

9.1   Surface Areas of Prisms

Activity Recording Journal 185

Practice Worksheet 188

9.2   Surface Areas of Pyramids

Activity Recording Journal 189

Practice Worksheet 192

9.3   Surface Areas of Cylinders

Activity Recording Journal 193

Practice Worksheet 196

9.4   Volumes of Prisms

Activity Recording Journal 197

Practice Worksheet 200

9.5   Volumes of Pyramids

Activity Recording Journal 201

Practice Worksheet 204

Extension: Cross Sections of Three-Dimensional Figures

Practice Worksheet 205

Chapter 10   Probability and Statistics

Fair Game Review Worksheets 207

10.1   Outcomes and Events

Activity Recording Journal 209

Practice Worksheet 212

10.2   Probability

Activity Recording Journal 213

Practice Worksheet 216

10.3   Experimental and Theoretical Probability

Activity Recording Journal 217

Practice Worksheet 220

Contents

10.4   **Compound Events**

Activity Recording Journal 221

Practice Worksheet 224

10.5   **Independent and Dependent Events**

Activity Recording Journal 225

Practice Worksheet 228

Extension: Simulations

Practice Worksheet 229

10.6   **Samples and Populations**

Activity Recording Journal 231

Practice Worksheet 234

Extension: Generating Multiple Samples

Activity Recording Journal 235

10.7   **Comparing Populations**

Activity Recording Journal 239

Practice Worksheet 242

Chapter 11   **Transformations**

Fair Game Review Worksheets 243

11.1   **Congruent Figures**

Activity Recording Journal 245

Practice Worksheet 248

11.2   **Translations**

Activity Recording Journal 249

Practice Worksheet 252

11.3   **Reflections**

Activity Recording Journal 253

Practice Worksheet 256

11.4   **Rotations**

Activity Recording Journal 257

Practice Worksheet 260

11.5   **Similar Figures**

Activity Recording Journal 261

Practice Worksheet 264

11.6   **Perimeters and Area of Similar Figures**

Activity Recording Journal 265

Practice Worksheet 268

Contents

11.7 **Dilations**
Activity Recording Journal 269
Practice Worksheet 272

Chapter 12 **Angles and Triangles**
Fair Game Review Worksheets 273

12.1 **Parallel Lines and Transversals**
Activity Recording Journal 275
Practice Worksheet 278

12.2 **Angles of Triangles**
Activity Recording Journal 279
Practice Worksheet 282

12.3 **Angles of Polygons**
Activity Recording Journal 283
Practice Worksheet 286

12.4 **Using Similar Triangles**
Activity Recording Journal 287
Practice Worksheet 290

Chapter 13 **Graphing and Writing Linear Equations**
Fair Game Review Worksheets 291

13.1 **Graphing Linear Equations**
Activity Recording Journal 293
Practice Worksheet 296

13.2 **Slope of a Line**
Activity Recording Journal 297
Practice Worksheet 300

Extension: Slopes of Parallel and Perpendicular Lines
Practice Worksheet 301

13.3 **Graphing Proportional Relationships**
Activity Recording Journal 303
Practice Worksheet 306

13.4 **Graphing Linear Equations in Slope-Intercept Form**
Activity Recording Journal 307
Practice Worksheet 310

13.5 **Graphing Linear Equation in Standard Form**
Activity Recording Journal 311
Practice Worksheet 314

Contents

13.6 **Writing Equations in Slope-Intercept Form**

Activity Recording Journal 315

Practice Worksheet 318

13.7 **Writing Equations in Point-Slope Form**

Activity Recording Journal 319

Practice Worksheet 322

Chapter 14 **Real Numbers and the Pythagorean Theorem**

Fair Game Review Worksheets 323

14.1 **Finding Square Roots**

Activity Recording Journal 325

Practice Worksheet 328

14.2 **Finding Cube Roots**

Activity Recording Journal 329

Practice Worksheet 332

14.3 **The Pythagorean Theorem**

Activity Recording Journal 333

Practice Worksheet 336

14.4 **Approximating Square Roots**

Activity Recording Journal 337

Practice Worksheet 340

Extension: Repeating Decimals

Practice Worksheet 341

14.5 **Using the Pythagorean Theorem**

Activity Recording Journal 343

Practice Worksheet 346

Chapter 15 **Volume and Similar Solids**

Fair Game Review Worksheets 347

15.1 **Volumes of Cylinders**

Activity Recording Journal 349

Practice Worksheet 352

15.2 **Volumes of Cones**

Activity Recording Journal 353

Practice Worksheet 356

15.3 **Volumes of Spheres**

Activity Recording Journal 357

Practice Worksheet 360

Contents

15.4 **Surface Areas and Volumes of Similar Solids**
Activity Recording Journal 361
Practice Worksheet 364

Chapter 16 **Exponents and Scientific Notation**
Fair Game Review Worksheets 365

16.1 **Exponents**
Activity Recording Journal 367
Practice Worksheet 370

16.2 **Product of Powers Property**
Activity Recording Journal 371
Practice Worksheet 374

16.3 **Quotient of Powers Property**
Activity Recording Journal 375
Practice Worksheet 378

16.4 **Zero and Negative Exponents**
Activity Recording Journal 379
Practice Worksheet 382

16.5 **Reading Scientific Notation**
Activity Recording Journal 383
Practice Worksheet 386

16.6 **Writing Scientific Notation**
Activity Recording Journal 387
Practice Worksheet 390

16.7 **Operations in Scientific Notation**
Activity Recording Journal 391
Practice Worksheet 394

Additional Topics

Topic 1 **Solving Multi-Step Equations**
Practice Worksheet 395

Topic 2 **Solving Equations with Variables on Both Sides**
Practice Worksheet 397

Topic 3 **Rewriting Equations and Formulas**
Practice Worksheet 399

Glossary **401**

Activity Manipulatives **425**

Name_____ Date_____

Simplify the expression. Explain each step.

1. $2 + (5 + y)$

2. $(c + 1) + 9$

3. $(2.3 + n) + 1.4$

4. $7 + (d + 5)$

5. $10(7t)$

6. $8(4k)$

Chapter 1 **Fair Game Review** (continued)

7. $13 \cdot 0 \cdot p$

8. $7 \cdot z \cdot 0$

9. $2.5 \cdot w \cdot 1$

10. $1 \cdot x \cdot 19$

11. $(t + 3) + 0$

12. $0 + (g + 4)$

1.1 Integers and Absolute Value
For use with Activity 1.1

Essential Question How can you use integers to represent the velocity and the speed of an object?

On these three pages, you will investigate vertical motion (up or down).

- Speed tells how fast an object is moving, but it does not tell the direction.

- Velocity tells how fast an object is moving, and it also tells the direction.

     When velocity is positive, the object is moving up.

     When velocity if negative, the object is moving down.

1 ACTIVITY: Falling Parachute

Work with a partner. You are gliding to the ground wearing a parachute. The table shows your height above the ground at different times.

Time (seconds)	0	1	2	3
Height (feet)	90	75	60	45

a. Describe the pattern in the table. How many feet do you move each second? After how many seconds will you land on the ground?

b. What integer represents your speed? Give the units.

c. Do you think your velocity should be represented by a positive or negative integer? Explain your reasoning.

d. What integer represents your velocity? Give the units.

1.1 **Integers and Absolute Value** (continued)

2 **ACTIVITY:** Rising Balloons

Work with a partner. You release a group of balloons. The table shows the height of the balloons above the ground at different times.

Time (seconds)	0	1	2	3
Height (feet)	8	12	16	20

a. Describe the pattern in the table. How many feet do the balloons move each second? After how many seconds will the balloons be at a height of 40 feet?

b. What integer represents the speed of the balloons? Give the units.

c. Do you think the velocity of the balloons should be represented by a positive or negative integer? Explain your reasoning.

d. What integer represents the velocity of the balloons? Give the units.

3 **ACTIVITY:** Firework Parachute

Work with a partner. The table shows the height of a firework's parachute above the ground at different times.

Time (seconds)	Height (feet)
0	480
1	360
2	240
3	120
4	0

a. Describe the pattern in the table. How many feet does the parachute move each second?

b. What integer represents the speed of the parachute? What integer represents the velocity? How are these integers similar in their relation to 0 on a number line?

4 **Big Ideas Math Red Accelerated**
Record and Practice Journal

Name_____ Date _____

Inductive Reasoning

4. Complete the table.

Velocity (feet per second)	−14	20	−2	0	25	−15
Speed (feet per second)						

5. Find two different velocities for which the speed is 16 feet per second.

6. Which number is greater: −4 or 3? Use a number line to explain your reasoning.

7. One object has a velocity of −4 feet per second. Another object has a velocity of 3 feet per second. Which object has the greater speed? Explain your answer.

8. **IN YOUR OWN WORDS** How can you use integers to represent the velocity and the speed of an object?

What Is Your Answer?

9. **LOGIC** In this lesson, you will study **absolute value**. Here are some examples:

Absolute value of $|-16| = 16$ Absolute value of $|16| = 16$

Absolute value of $|0| = 0$ Absolute value of $|-2| = 2$

Which of the following is a true statement? Explain your reasoning.

$$|\text{velocity}| = \text{speed}$$ $$|\text{speed}| = \text{velocity}$$

1.1 Practice
For use after Lesson 1.1

Find the absolute value.

1. $|-1|$

2. $|-14|$

3. $|0|$

4. $|6|$

Complete the statement using <, >, or =.

5. 6 ___ $|-2|$

6. -7 ___ $|-8|$

7. $|-9|$ ___ 5

8. $|-2|$ ___ 2

Order the values from least to greatest.

9. 4, $|7|$, -1, $|-3|$, -4

10. $|2|$, -3, $|-5|$, -1, 6

11. You download 12 new songs to your MP3 player. Then you delete 5 old songs. Write each amount as an integer.

1.2 Adding Integers
For use with Activity 1.2

Essential Question Is the sum of two integers *positive*, *negative*, or *zero*? How can you tell?

1 ACTIVITY: Adding Integers with the Same Sign

Work with a partner. Draw a picture to show how you use integer counters to find $-4 + (-3)$.

$-4 + (-3) = $ _____

2 ACTIVITY: Adding Integers with Different Signs

Work with a partner. Draw a picture to show how you use integer counters to find $-3 + 2$.

$-3 + 2 = $ _____

3 ACTIVITY: Adding Integers with Different Signs

Work with a partner. Show how to use a number line to find $5 + (-3)$.

$5 + (-3) = $ _____

1.2 Adding Integers (continued)

4 **ACTIVITY:** Adding Integers with Different Signs

**Work with a partner. Write the addition expression shown. Then find the sum.
How are the integers in the expression related to 0 on a number line?**

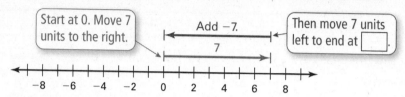

Start at 0. Move 7 units to the right.

Add −7.

7

Then move 7 units left to end at [ ].

7

−8 −6 −4 −2 0 2 4 6 8

Inductive Reasoning

Work with a partner. Use integer counters or a number line to complete the table.

	Exercise	Type of Sum	Sum	Sum: Positive, Negative, or Zero
1	**5.** −4 + (−3)			
2	**6.** −3 + 2			
3	**7.** 5 + (−3)			
4	**8.** 7 + (−7)			
	9. 2 + 4			
	10. −6 + (−2)			
	11. −5 + 9			
	12. 15 + (−9)			
	13. −10 + 10			
	14. −6 + (−6)			
	15. 13 + (−13)			

1.2 Adding Integers (continued)

What Is Your Answer?

16. **IN YOUR OWN WORDS** Is the sum of two integers *positive*, *negative*, or *zero*? How can you tell?

17. **STRUCTURE** Write a general rule for adding

  a. two integers with the same sign.

  b. two integers with different signs.

  c. two integers that vary in sign.

Name _____   Date _____

Add.

1. $-9 + 2$

2. $5 + (-5)$

3. $-12 + (-6)$

4. $-10 + 19 + 5$

5. $-11 + (-20) + 9$

6. $-7 + 7 + (-8)$

Use mental math to solve the equation.

7. $x + (-5) = 4$

8. $y + 6 = -2$

9. $-10 = -7 + z$

10. The table shows the change in your hair length over a year.

Month	January	February	August	September	December
Change in hair length (inches)	2	−1	3	−4	3

   a. What is the total change in your hair length at the end of the year?

   b. Is your hair longer in January or December? Explain your reasoning.

   c. When is your hair the longest? Explain your reasoning.

Name_____ Date _____

1.3 Subtracting Integers
For use with Activity 1.3

Essential Question How are adding integers and subtracting integers related?

---

1 ACTIVITY: Subtracting Integers

Work with a partner. Draw a picture to show how you use integer counters to find $4 - 2$.

$4 - 2 = $ _____

---

2 ACTIVITY: Adding Integers

Work with a partner. Draw a picture to show how you use integer counters to find $4 + (-2)$.

$4 + (-2) = $ _____

---

3 ACTIVITY: Subtracting Integers

Work with a partner. Show how to use a number line to find $-3 - 1$.

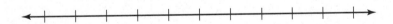

$-3 - 1 = $ _____

1.3 **Subtracting Integers** (continued)

4 **ACTIVITY:** Adding Integers

Work with a partner. Write the addition expression shown. Then find the sum.

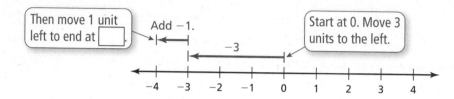

Inductive Reasoning

Work with a partner. Use integer counters or a number line to complete the table.

	Exercise	Operation: Add or Subtract	Answer
1	**5.** $4 - 2$		
2	**6.** $4 + (-2)$		
3	**7.** $-3 - 1$		
4	**8.** $-3 + (-1)$		
	9. $3 - 8$		
	10. $3 + (-8)$		
	11. $9 - 13$		
	12. $9 + (-13)$		
	13. $-6 - (-3)$		
	14. $-6 + 3$		
	15. $-5 - (-12)$		
	16. $-5 + 12$		

1.3 **Subtracting Integers** (continued)

What Is Your Answer?

17. **IN YOUR OWN WORDS** How are adding integers and subtracting integers related?

18. **STRUCTURE** Write a general rule for subtracting integers.

19. Use a number line to find the value of the expression $-4 + 4 - 9$. What property can you use to make your calculation easier? Explain.

1.3 Practice
For use after Lesson 1.3

Subtract.

1. $3 - 8$

2. $6 - (-7)$

3. $-10 - 9$

4. $-5 - (-4)$

Evaluate the expression.

5. $11 - (-2) + 14$

6. $-16 - (-12) + (-8)$

7. $6 - 17 - 4$

Use mental math to solve the equation.

8. $6 - x = 10$

9. $y - (-10) = 2$

10. $z - 17 = -14$

11. You begin a hike in Death Valley, California, at an elevation of -86 meters. You hike to a point of elevation at 45 meters. What is your change in elevation?

12. You sell T-shirts for a fundraiser. It costs $112 to have the T-shirts made. You make $98 in sales. What is your profit?

1.4 Multiplying Integers
For use with Activity 1.4

Essential Question Is the product of two integers *positive*, *negative*, or *zero*? How can you tell?

1 ACTIVITY: Multiplying Integers with the Same Sign

Work with a partner. Use repeated addition to find 3 • 2.

Recall that multiplication is repeated addition. 3 • 2 means to add 3 groups of 2.

3 • 2 = _____

2 ACTIVITY: Multiplying Integers with Different Signs

Work with a partner. Use repeated addition to find 3 • (−2).

3 • (−2) = _____

3 ACTIVITY: Multiplying Integers with Different Signs

Work with a partner. Use a table to find −3 • 2.

Describe the pattern of the products in the table. Then complete the table.

2	•	2	=
1	•	2	=
0	•	2	=
−1	•	2	=
−2	•	2	=
−3	•	2	=

−3 • 2 = _____

1.4 **Multiplying Integers** (continued)

4 **ACTIVITY: Multiplying Integers with the Same Sign**

Work with a partner. Use a table to find $-3 \cdot (-2)$.

Describe the pattern of the products in the table. Then complete the table.

-3	$\cdot$	3	$=$
-3	$\cdot$	2	$=$
-3	$\cdot$	1	$=$
-3	$\cdot$	0	$=$
-3	$\cdot$	-1	$=$
-3	$\cdot$	-2	$=$

$-3 \cdot (-2) =$ _____

Inductive Reasoning

Work with a partner. Complete the table.

	Exercise	Type of Product	Product	Product: Positive or Negative
1	**5.** $3 \cdot 2$			
2	**6.** $3 \cdot (-2)$			
3	**7.** $-3 \cdot 2$			
4	**8.** $-3 \cdot (-2)$			
	9. $6 \cdot 3$			
	10. $2 \cdot (-5)$			
	11. $-6 \cdot 5$			
	12. $-5 \cdot (-3)$			

1.4 **Multiplying Integers** (continued)

What Is Your Answer?

13. Write two integers whose product is 0.

14. IN YOUR OWN WORDS Is the product of two integers *positive*, *negative*, or *zero*? How can you tell?

15. STRUCTURE Write a general rule for multiplying

   a. two integers with the same sign.

   b. two integers with different signs.

Big Ideas Math Red Accelerated
Record and Practice Journal

Name _____ Date _____

Multiply.

1. $8 \cdot 9$

2. $7(-7)$

3. $-10 \cdot 4$

4. $-5(-6)$

5. $12 \cdot (-1) \cdot (-2)$

6. $-10(-3)(-7)$

7. $-20 \cdot 0 \cdot (-4)$

8. $-4 \cdot 8 \cdot 3$

Evaluate the expression.

9. $(-8)^2$

10. -11^2

11. $9 \cdot (-5)^2$

12. $(-2)^3 \cdot (-6)$

13. You lose 5 points for every wrong answer in a trivia game. What integer represents the change in your points after answering 8 questions wrong?

1.5 Dividing Integers
For use with Activity 1.5

Essential Question Is the quotient of two integers *positive*, *negative*, or *zero*? How can you tell?

1 ACTIVITY: Dividing Integers with Different Signs

Work with a partner. Draw a picture to show how you use integer counters to find $-15 \div 3$.

$-15 \div 3 =$ _____

2 ACTIVITY: Rewriting a Product as a Quotient

Work with a partner. Rewrite the product $3 \cdot 4 = 12$ as a quotient in two different ways.

First Way

12 is equal to 3 groups of _____.

$12 \div 3 =$ _____

Second Way

12 is equal to 4 groups of _____.

$12 \div 4 =$ _____

3 ACTIVITY: Dividing Integers with Different Signs

Work with a partner. Rewrite the product $-3 \cdot (-4) = 12$ as a quotient in two different ways. What can you conclude?

First Way

Second Way

1.5 **Dividing Integers** (continued)

4 **ACTIVITY:** Dividing Negative Integers

Work with a partner. Rewrite the product $3 \cdot (-4) = -12$ **as a quotient in two different ways. What can you conclude?**

First Way   *Second Way*

Inductive Reasoning

Work with a partner. Complete the table.

	Exercise	Type of Quotient	Quotient	Quotient: Positive, Negative, or Zero
1	**5.** $-15 \div 3$			
2	**6.** $12 \div 4$			
3	**7.** $12 \div (-3)$			
4	**8.** $-12 \div (-4)$			
	9. $-6 \div 2$			
	10. $-21 \div (-7)$			
	11. $10 \div (-2)$			
	12. $12 \div (-6)$			
	13. $0 \div (-15)$			
	14. $0 \div 4$			

1.5 **Dividing Integers** (continued)

What Is Your Answer?

15. IN YOUR OWN WORDS Is the quotient of two integers *positive*, *negative*, or *zero*? How can you tell?

16. STRUCTURE Write a general rule for dividing

    a. two integers with the same sign.

    b. two integers with different signs.

1.5 Practice
For use after Lesson 1.5

Divide, if possible.

1. $3 \div (-1)$

2. $8 \div 2$

3. $-10 \div 5$

4. $-21 \div (-7)$

5. $\dfrac{48}{-6}$

6. $\dfrac{-13}{-13}$

7. $\dfrac{0}{3}$

8. $\dfrac{-55}{11}$

Evaluate the expression.

9. $-63 \div (-7) + 6$

10. $-5 - 12 \div 3$

11. $-8 \bullet 7 + 33 \div (-11)$

12. The table shows the number of yards a football player runs in each quarter of a game. Find the mean number of yards the player runs per quarter.

Quarter	1	2	3	4
Yards	-2	14	-18	-6

Chapter 2 Fair Game Review

Write the decimal as a fraction.

1. 0.26

2. 0.79

3. 0.571

4. 0.846

Write the fraction as a decimal.

5. $\dfrac{3}{8}$

6. $\dfrac{4}{10}$

7. $\dfrac{11}{16}$

8. $\dfrac{17}{20}$

9. A quarterback completed 0.6 of his passes during a game. Write the decimal as a fraction.

Chapter 2 **Fair Game Review** (continued)

Evaluate the expression.

10. $\dfrac{1}{8} + \dfrac{1}{9}$

11. $\dfrac{2}{3} + \dfrac{9}{10}$

12. $\dfrac{7}{12} - \dfrac{1}{4}$

13. $\dfrac{6}{7} - \dfrac{4}{5}$

14. $\dfrac{5}{9} \bullet \dfrac{1}{3}$

15. $\dfrac{8}{15} \bullet \dfrac{3}{4}$

16. $\dfrac{7}{8} \div \dfrac{11}{16}$

17. $\dfrac{3}{10} \div \dfrac{2}{5}$

18. You have 8 cups of flour. A recipe calls for $\dfrac{2}{3}$ cup of flour. Another recipe

calls for $\dfrac{1}{4}$ cup of flour. How much flour do you have left after making

the recipes?

2.1 Rational Numbers
For use with Activity 2.1

Essential Question How can you use a number line to order rational numbers?

A **rational number** is a number that can be written as a ratio of two integers.

$$2 = \frac{2}{1} \qquad -3 = \frac{-3}{1} \qquad -\frac{1}{2} = \frac{-1}{2} \qquad 0.25 = \frac{1}{4}$$

1 ACTIVITY: Ordering Rational Numbers

Work in groups of five. Order the numbers from least to greatest.

- Use masking tape and a marker to make a number line on the floor similar to the one shown.

- Write the numbers on pieces of paper. Then each person should choose one piece of paper.

- Stand on the location of your number on the number line.

- Use your positions to order the numbers from least to greatest.

  The numbers from least to greatest are

  _____, _____, _____, _____, and _____.

a. $-0.5, 1.25, -\dfrac{1}{3}, 0.5, -\dfrac{5}{3}$

b. $-\dfrac{7}{4}, 1.1, \dfrac{1}{2}, -\dfrac{1}{10}, -1.3$

c. $-1.4, -\dfrac{3}{5}, \dfrac{9}{2}, \dfrac{1}{4}, 0.9$

d. $\dfrac{5}{4}, 0.75, -\dfrac{5}{4}, -0.8, -1.1$

2.1 Rational Numbers (continued)

2 ACTIVITY: The Game of Math Card War

Preparation:

- Cut index cards to make 40 playing cards.*

- Write each number in the table on a card.

$-\dfrac{3}{2}$	$\dfrac{3}{10}$	$-\dfrac{3}{4}$	-0.6	1.25	-0.15	$\dfrac{5}{4}$	$\dfrac{3}{5}$	-1.6	-0.3
$\dfrac{3}{20}$	$\dfrac{8}{5}$	-1.2	$\dfrac{19}{10}$	0.75	-1.5	$-\dfrac{6}{5}$	$-\dfrac{3}{5}$	1.2	0.3
1.5	1.9	-0.75	-0.4	$\dfrac{3}{4}$	$\dfrac{5}{4}$	-1.9	$\dfrac{2}{5}$	$-\dfrac{3}{20}$	$\dfrac{19}{10}$
$\dfrac{6}{5}$	$-\dfrac{3}{10}$	1.6	$-\dfrac{2}{5}$	0.6	0.15	$\dfrac{3}{2}$	-1.25	0.4	$-\dfrac{8}{5}$

To Play:

- Play with a partner.

- Deal 20 cards to each player facedown.

- Each player turns one card faceup. The player with the greater number wins. The winner collects both cards and places them at the bottom of his or her cards.

- Suppose there is a tie. Each player lays three cards facedown, then a new card faceup. The player with the greater of these new cards wins. The winner collects all ten cards and places them at the bottom of his or her cards.

- Continue playing until one player has all the cards. This player wins the game.

*Cut-outs are available in the back of the Record and Practice Journal.

2.1 **Rational Numbers** (continued)

What Is Your Answer?

3. **IN YOUR OWN WORDS** How can you use a number line to order rational numbers? Give an example.

The numbers are in order from least to greatest. Fill in the blank spaces with rational numbers.

4. $-\dfrac{1}{2}$, ⬚, $\dfrac{1}{3}$, ⬚, $\dfrac{7}{5}$, ⬚

5. $-\dfrac{5}{2}$, ⬚, -1.9, ⬚, $-\dfrac{2}{3}$, ⬚

6. $-\dfrac{1}{3}$, ⬚, -0.1, ⬚, $\dfrac{4}{5}$, ⬚

7. -3.4, ⬚, -1.5, ⬚, 2.2, ⬚

2.1 Practice
For use after Lesson 2.1

Write the rational number as a decimal.

1. $-\dfrac{9}{10}$

2. $-4\dfrac{2}{3}$

3. $1\dfrac{7}{16}$

Write the decimal as a fraction or mixed number in simplest form.

4. -0.84

5. 5.22

6. -1.716

Order the numbers from least to greatest.

7. $\dfrac{1}{5}, 0.1, -\dfrac{1}{2}, -0.25, 0.3$

8. $-1.6, \dfrac{5}{2}, -\dfrac{7}{8}, 0.9, -\dfrac{6}{5}$

9. $-\dfrac{2}{3}, \dfrac{5}{9}, 0.5, -1.3, -\dfrac{10}{3}$

10. The table shows the position of each runner relative to when the first place finisher crossed the finish line. Who finished in second place? Who finished in fifth place?

Runner	A	B	C	D	E	F
Meters	-1.264	$-\dfrac{5}{4}$	-1.015	-0.480	$-\dfrac{14}{25}$	$-\dfrac{13}{8}$

Name_____ Date_____

2.2 Adding Rational Numbers
For use with Activity 2.2

Essential Question How can you use what you know about adding integers to add rational numbers?

---

1 ACTIVITY: Adding Rational Numbers

Work with a partner. Use a number line to find the sum.

a. $2.7 + (-3.4)$

$2.7 + (-3.4) =$ _____

b. $1.3 + (-1.5)$ **c.** $-2.1 + 0.8$

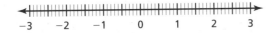   

d. $-1\dfrac{1}{4} + \dfrac{3}{4}$ **e.** $\dfrac{3}{10} + \left(-\dfrac{3}{10}\right)$

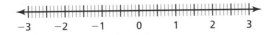   

---

2 ACTIVITY: Adding Rational Numbers

Work with a partner. Use a number line to find the sum.

a. $-1\dfrac{2}{5} + \left(-\dfrac{4}{5}\right)$

$-1\dfrac{2}{5} + \left(-\dfrac{4}{5}\right) =$ _____

2.2 **Adding Rational Numbers** (continued)

b. $-\dfrac{7}{10} + \left(-1\dfrac{7}{10}\right)$

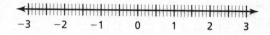

c. $-1\dfrac{2}{3} + \left(-1\dfrac{1}{3}\right)$

d. $-0.4 + (-1.9)$

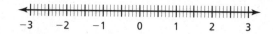

e. $-2.3 + (-0.6)$

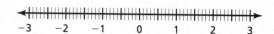

3 **ACTIVITY: Writing Expressions**

Work with a partner. Write the addition expression shown. Then find the sum.

a.

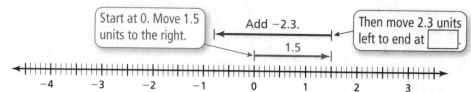

b.

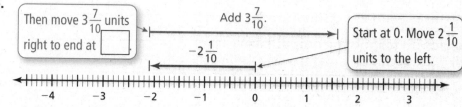

2.2 **Adding Rational Numbers** (continued)

c.

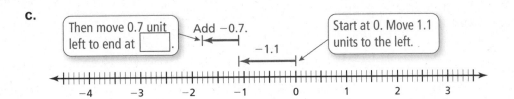

What Is Your Answer?

4. **IN YOUR OWN WORDS** How can you use what you know about adding integers to add rational numbers?

PUZZLE **Find a path through the table so that the numbers add up to the sum. You can move horizontally or vertically.**

5. Sum: $\dfrac{3}{4}$

Start →

$\dfrac{1}{2}$	$\dfrac{2}{3}$	$-\dfrac{5}{7}$
$-\dfrac{1}{8}$	$-\dfrac{3}{4}$	$\dfrac{1}{3}$

← End

6. Sum: -0.07

Start →

2.43	1.75	-0.98
-1.09	3.47	-4.88

← End

2.2 Practice
For use after Lesson 2.2

Add. Write fractions in simplest form.

1. $-\dfrac{4}{5} + \dfrac{3}{20}$

2. $-8 + \left(-\dfrac{6}{7}\right)$

3. $1\dfrac{2}{15} + \left(-3\dfrac{1}{2}\right)$

4. $-\dfrac{1}{6} + \left(-\dfrac{5}{12}\right)$

5. $\dfrac{9}{10} + (-3)$

6. $-5\dfrac{3}{4} + \left(-4\dfrac{5}{6}\right)$

7. $0.46 + (-0.642)$

8. $0.13 + (-5.7)$

9. $-2.57 + (-3.48)$

10. Before a race, you start $4\dfrac{5}{8}$ feet behind your friend. At the halfway point, you are $3\dfrac{2}{3}$ feet ahead of your friend. What is the change in distance between you and your friend from the beginning of the race?

Name_____ Date_____

2.3 Subtracting Rational Numbers
For use with Activity 2.3

Essential Question How can you use what you know about subtracting integers to subtract rational numbers?

---

1 ACTIVITY: Subtracting Rational Numbers

Work with a partner. Use a number line to find the difference.

a. $-1\dfrac{1}{2} - \dfrac{1}{2}$

$-1\dfrac{1}{1} - \dfrac{1}{2} = $ _____

b. $\dfrac{6}{10} - 1\dfrac{3}{10}$

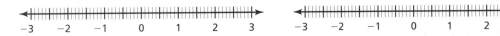

c. $-1\dfrac{1}{4} - 1\dfrac{3}{4}$

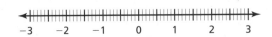

d. $-1.9 - 0.8$

e. $0.2 - 0.7$

---

2 ACTIVITY: Finding Distances on a Number Line

Work with a partner.

a. Plot -3 and 2 on the number line. Then find $-3 - 2$ and $2 - (-3)$. What do you notice about your results?

2.3   **Subtracting Rational Numbers** (continued)

b. Plot $\frac{3}{4}$ and 1 on the number line. Then find $\frac{3}{4} - 1$ and $1 - \frac{3}{4}$. What do you notice about your results?

c. Choose any two points a and b on a number line. Find the values of $a - b$ and $b - a$. What do the absolute values of these differences represent? Is this true for any pair of rational numbers? Explain.

3   **ACTIVITY:** Financial Literacy

Work with a partner. The table shows the balance in a checkbook.

- Deposits and interest are amounts added to the account.
- Amounts shown in parentheses are taken from the account.

Date	Check #	Transaction	Amount	Balance
--	--	Previous Balance	--	100.00
1/02/2013	124	Groceries	(34.57)	
1/07/2013		Check deposit	875.50	
1/11/2013		ATM withdrawal	(40.00)	
1/14/2013	125	Electric company	(78.43)	
1/17/2013		Music store	(10.55)	
1/18/2013	126	Shoes	(47.21)	
1/22/2013		Check deposit	125.00	
1/24/2013		Interest	2.12	
1/25/2013	127	Cell phone	(59.99)	
1/26/2013	128	Clothes	(65.54)	
1/30/2013	129	Cable company	(75.00)	

2.3 **Subtracting Rational Numbers** (continued)

You can find the balance in the second row two different ways.

$$100.00 - 34.57 = 65.43$$ Subtract 34.57 from 100.00.

$$100.00 + (-34.57) = 65.43$$ Add −34.57 to 100.00.

a. Complete the balance column of the table on the previous page.

b. How did you find the balance in the twelfth row?

c. Use a different way to find the balance in part (b).

What Is Your Answer?

4. IN YOUR OWN WORDS How can you use what you know about subtracting integers to subtract rational numbers?

5. Give two real-life examples of subtracting rational numbers that are not integers.

2.3 Practice
For use after Lesson 2.3

Subtract. Write fractions in simplest form.

1. $\dfrac{4}{9} - \left(-\dfrac{2}{9}\right)$

2. $-2\dfrac{3}{7} - 1\dfrac{2}{3}$

3. $-2.35 - (-1.27)$

Find the distance between the two numbers on a number line.

4. $-3\dfrac{1}{4},\ -6\dfrac{1}{2}$

5. $-1.5,\ 2.8$

6. $-4,\ -7\dfrac{1}{3}$

Evaluate.

7. $2\dfrac{1}{2} + \left(-\dfrac{7}{6}\right) - 1\dfrac{3}{4}$

8. $2.37 - (-1.55) - 2.48$

9. Your friend drinks $\dfrac{2}{3}$ of a bottle of water. You drink $\dfrac{5}{7}$ of a bottle of water. Find the difference of the amounts of water left in each bottle.

2.4 Multiplying and Dividing Rational Numbers
For use with Activity 2.4

Essential Question Why is the product of two negative rational numbers positive?

1 ACTIVITY: Showing $(-1)(-1) = 1$

Work with a partner. How can you show that $(-1)(-1) = 1$?

To begin, assume that $(-1)(-1) = 1$ is a true statement. From the Additive Inverse Property, you know that $1 + (-1) = 0$. So, substitute $(-1)(-1)$ for 1 to get $(-1)(-1) + (-1) = 0$. If you can show that $(-1)(-1) + (-1) = 0$ is true, then you have shown that $(-1)(-1) = 1$.

Justify each step.

$$
\begin{aligned}
(-1)(-1) + (-1) &= (-1)(-1) + 1(-1) \quad \underline{\hspace{5cm}} \\
&= (-1)\big[(-1) + 1\big] \quad \underline{\hspace{4.5cm}} \\
&= (-1)0 \quad \underline{\hspace{5cm}} \\
&= 0 \quad \underline{\hspace{5cm}}
\end{aligned}
$$

$(-1)(-1) = $ _____

2 ACTIVITY: Multiplying by -1

Work with a partner.

a. Graph each number below on three different number lines. Then multiply each number by -1 and graph the product on the appropriate number line.

$$2 \qquad\qquad 8 \qquad\qquad -1$$

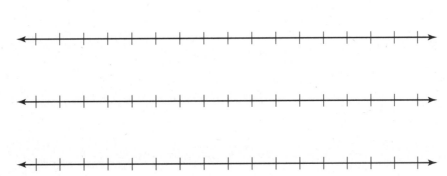

2.4 **Multiplying and Dividing Rational Numbers** (continued)

b. How does multiplying by –1 change the location of the points in part (a)? What is the relationship between the number and the product?

c. Graph each number below on three different number lines. Where do you think the points will be after multiplying by –1? Plot the points. Explain your reasoning.

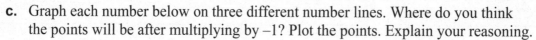

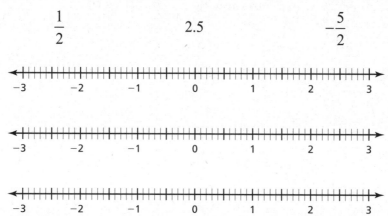

d. What is the relationship between a rational number $-a$ and the product $-1(a)$? Explain your reasoning.

3 **ACTIVITY:** Understanding the product of Rational Numbers

Work with a partner. Let a and b be positive rational numbers.

a. Because a and b are positive, what do you know about $-a$ and $-b$?

b. Justify each step.

$$(-a)(-b) = (-1)(a)(-1)(b) \quad \rule{5cm}{0.4pt}$$
$$= (-1)(-1)(a)(b) \quad \rule{5cm}{0.4pt}$$
$$= (1)(a)(b) \quad \rule{5cm}{0.4pt}$$
$$= ab \quad \rule{5cm}{0.4pt}$$

c. Because a and b are positive, what do you know about the product ab?

2.4 **Multiplying and Dividing Rational Numbers** (continued)

d. What does this tell you about products of rational numbers? Explain.

---

4 **ACTIVITY:** Writing a Story

Work with a partner. Write a story that uses addition, subtraction, multiplication, or division of rational numbers.

- At least one of the numbers in the story has to be negative and *not* an integer.

- Draw pictures to help illustrate what is happening in the story.

- Include the solution of the problem in the story.

If you are having trouble thinking of a story, here are some common uses of negative numbers:

- A profit of −$15 is a loss of $15.

- An elevation of −100 feet is a depth of 100 feet below sea level.

- A gain of −5 yards in football is a loss of 5 yards.

- A score of −4 in golf is 4 strokes under par.

What Is Your Answer?

5. IN YOUR OWN WORDS Why is the product of two negative rational numbers positive?

6. PRECISION Show that $(-2)(-3) = 6$.

7. How can you show that the product of a negative rational number and a positive rational number is negative?

Name _____ Date _____

2.4 Practice

For use after Lesson 2.4

Multiply or divide. Write fractions in simplest form.

1. $-\dfrac{8}{9}\left(-\dfrac{18}{25}\right)$

2. $-4\left(\dfrac{9}{16}\right)$

3. $-3\dfrac{3}{7} \times 2\dfrac{1}{2}$

4. $-\dfrac{2}{3} \div \dfrac{5}{9}$

5. $\dfrac{7}{13} \div (-2)$

6. $-5\dfrac{5}{8} \div \left(-4\dfrac{7}{12}\right)$

7. $-1.39 \times (-6.8)$

8. $-10 \div 0.22$

9. $-12.166 \div (-1.54)$

10. In a game of tug of war, your team changes $-1\dfrac{3}{10}$ feet in position every 10 seconds. What is your change in position after 30 seconds?

Name_____ Date _____

Evaluate the expression when $x = \dfrac{1}{2}$ **and** $y = -3$.

1. $-4xy$

2. $6x - 3y$

3. $-5y + 8x + 1$

4. $-x^2 - y + 2$

5. $2x + 4\left(x + \dfrac{1}{2}\right) + 7$

6. $2(4x - 1)^2 - 3$

7. Find the area of the garden when $x = 2$ feet.

3x ft

2x ft

Chapter 3 Fair Game Review (continued)

Write the phrase as an algebraic expression.

8. the sum of eight and a number y

9. six less than a number p

10. the product of seven and a number m

11. eight less than the product of eleven and a number c

12. a number r decreased by the quotient of a number r and two

13. the product of nine and the sum of a number z and four

3.1 Simplifying Algebraic Expressions
For use with Activity 3.1

Essential Question How can you simplify an algebraic expression?

1 ACTIVITY: Simplifying Algebraic Expressions

Work with a partner.

a. Evaluate each algebraic expression when $x = 0$ and when $x = 1$. Use the results to match each expression in the left table with its equivalent expression in the right table.

	Expression	Value When $x = 0$	Value When $x = 1$
A.	$3x + 2 - x + 4$		
B.	$5(x - 3) + 2$		
C.	$x + 3 - (2x + 1)$		
D.	$-4x + 2 - x + 3x$		
E.	$-(1 - x) + 3$		
F.	$2x + x - 3x + 4$		
G.	$4 - 3 + 2(x - 1)$		
H.	$2(1 - x + 4)$		
I.	$5 - (4 - x + 2x)$		
J.	$5x - (2x + 4 - x)$		

	Expression	Value When $x = 0$	Value When $x = 1$
a.	4		
b.	$-x + 1$		
c.	$4x - 4$		
d.	$2x + 6$		
e.	$5x - 13$		
f.	$-2x + 10$		
g.	$x + 2$		
h.	$2x - 1$		
i.	$-2x + 2$		
j.	$-x + 2$		

b. Compare each expression in the left table with its equivalent expression in the right table. In general, how do you think you obtain the equivalent expression in the right table?

3.1 **Algebraic Expressions** (continued)

2 **ACTIVITY:** Writing a Math Lesson

Work with a partner. Use your results from Activity 1 to write a lesson on simplifying an algebraic expression.

Simplifying an Algebraic Expression

Key Idea   Use the following steps to simplify an algebraic expression.

    1.

    2.

    3.

> Describe steps you can use to simplify an expression.

Examples   ←   Write 3 examples. Use expressions from Activity 1.

    a.

    b.

    c.

Exercises   ←   Write 3 exercises. Use expressions different from the ones in Activity 1.

Simplify the expression.

    1.

    2.

    3.

3.1 **Algebraic Expressions** (continued)

What Is Your Answer?

3. **IN YOUR OWN WORDS** How can you simplify an algebraic expression? Give an example that demonstrates your procedure.

4. **REASONING** Why would you want to simplify an algebraic expression? Discuss several reasons.

3.1 Practice

For use after Lesson 3.1

Identify the terms and like terms in the expression.

1. $3x + 4 - 7x - 6$

2. $-9 + 2.5y - 0.7y + 1 + 6.4y^2$

Simplify the expression.

3. $5a - 2a + 9$

4. $m - \dfrac{1}{6} - 4m + \dfrac{5}{6}$

5. $2.3w - 7 + 8.1 - 3w$

6. $7(d - 1) + 2$

7. $13g + 2(4k - g)$

8. $20(p + 2) + 16(-3 - p)$

9. Write an expression in simplest form that represents the cost for shampooing and cutting w women's hair and m men's hair.

	Women	Men
Cut	$15	$7
Shampoo	$5	$2

3.2 Adding and Subtracting Linear Expressions
For use with Activity 3.2

Essential Question How can you use algebra tiles to add or subtract algebraic expressions?

Key: [+] = variable   [−] = −variable   [+][−] = zero pair

[+] = 1   [−] = −1   [+][−] = zero pair

---

1 ACTIVITY: Writing Algebraic Expressions

Work with a partner. Write an algebraic expression shown by the algebra tiles.

a. [+][+][+][+]

b. [+][−][−]
    [+]

c. [+][+][+][+][+]
    [+][−][−]

d. [+][+][+][+]
    [+][−][−][−][−]
    [+][−][−]

---

2 ACTIVITY: Adding Algebraic Expressions

Work with a partner. Write the sum of two algebraic expressions modeled by the algebra tiles. Then use the algebra tiles to simplify the expression.

a. ([+][+][+]) + ([+][+][+][+][+])

b. ([+][−][−][−][−][−]) + ([+][−][−])

3.2 **Adding and Subtracting Linear Expressions** (continued)

c. $\left(\boxed{+} \; \boxed{+}\boxed{+}\boxed{+}\boxed{+} \right) + \left(\boxed{\begin{array}{c}+\\+\end{array}} \; \boxed{-}\boxed{-}\boxed{-} \right)$

d. $\left(\boxed{\begin{array}{c}+\\+\end{array}} \; \boxed{-}\boxed{-}\boxed{-}\boxed{-}\boxed{-} \right) + \left(\boxed{\begin{array}{c}+\\+\\+\end{array}} \; \begin{array}{c}\boxed{+}\boxed{+}\boxed{+}\\ \boxed{+}\boxed{+}\end{array} \right)$

---

3 **ACTIVITY:** Subtracting Algebraic Expressions

Work with a partner. Write the difference of two algebraic expressions modeled by the algebra tiles. Then use the algebra tiles to simplify the expression.

a. $\left(\boxed{+} \; \boxed{+}\boxed{+}\boxed{+} \right) - \left(\boxed{+} \; \boxed{+} \right)$

b. $\left(\boxed{+} \; \boxed{-}\boxed{-}\boxed{-} \right) - \left(\boxed{+} \; \boxed{-}\boxed{-}\boxed{-} \right)$

c. $\left(\boxed{\begin{array}{c}+\\+\end{array}} \; \boxed{+}\boxed{+}\boxed{+}\boxed{+}\boxed{+} \right) - \left(\boxed{+} \; \boxed{-} \right)$

3.2 **Adding and Subtracting Linear Expressions** (continued)

d. $\left(\begin{array}{} + \\ + \\ + \end{array} \boxed{-}\boxed{-}\boxed{-}\boxed{-}\boxed{-} \right) - \left(\begin{array}{} + \\ + \end{array} \boxed{+}\boxed{+}\boxed{+} \right)$

4 **ACTIVITY:** Adding and Subtracting Algebraic Expressions

Work with a partner. Use algebra tiles to model the sum or difference. Then use the algebra tiles to simplify the expression.

a. $(2x + 1) + (x - 1)$

b. $(2x - 6) + (3x + 2)$

c. $(2x + 4) - (x + 2)$

d. $(4x + 3) - (2x - 1)$

What Is Your Answer?

5. **IN YOUR OWN WORDS** How can you use algebra tiles to add or subtract algebraic expressions?

6. Write the difference of two algebraic expressions modeled by the algebra tiles. Then use the algebra tiles to simplify the expression.

$\left(\boxed{-}\boxed{+}\boxed{+}\boxed{+} \right) - \left(\boxed{-}\boxed{-}\boxed{-}\boxed{-} \right)$

3.2 Practice
For use after Lesson 3.2

Find the sum or difference.

1. $(x - 2) + (x + 6)$

2. $(2n - 4) - (4n - 3)$

3. $2(-3y - 1) + (2y + 7)$

4. $(1 - 3k) - 4(2 + 2.5k)$

5. $(6g - 9) + \dfrac{1}{3}(15 - 9g)$

6. $\dfrac{1}{2}(2r + 4) - \dfrac{1}{4}(16 - 8r)$

7. You earn $(4x + 12)$ points after completing x levels of a video game and then lose $(2x - 5)$ points. Write an expression that represents the total number of points you have now.

Name_____ Date _____

Factor the expression using the GCF.

1. $7 + 28$

2. $25 + 50$

3. $7b - 7$

4. $8a - 16$

5. $8x + 12$

6. $12y + 24t$

7. $10w + 50z$

8. $10v + 12u$

9. $9a + 15b$

Factor out the coefficient of the variable.

10. $\dfrac{1}{2}a - \dfrac{1}{2}$

11. $\dfrac{1}{4}d - \dfrac{3}{4}$

12. $\dfrac{5}{6}s + \dfrac{2}{3}$

**Extension
3.2** **Practice** (continued)

Factor out the coefficient of the variable.

13. $\dfrac{3}{10}y - \dfrac{2}{5}$

14. $1.1x + 9.9$

15. $3.4c + 10.2$

16. Factor -2 out of $-6x + 10$.

17. Factor $-\dfrac{1}{3}$ out of $\dfrac{1}{3}y - \dfrac{3}{2}$.

18. A square window has a perimeter of $(8x + 12)$ feet. Write an expression that represents the side length of the window (in feet).

Name_____ Date_____

3.3 Solving Equations Using Addition or Subtraction
For use with Activity 3.3

Essential Question How can you use algebra tiles to solve addition or subtraction equations?

1 ACTIVITY: Solving Equations

Work with a partner. Use algebra tiles to model and solve the equation.

a. $x - 3 = -4$

Model the equation $x - 3 = -4$. Draw a sketch of your tiles.

To get the variable tile by itself, remove the _____ tiles on the left side by adding _____ tiles to each side.

How many *zero pairs* can you remove from each side? Circle them.

The remaining tiles show the value of x.

$x = $ _____

b. $z - 6 = 2$

c. $p - 7 = -3$

d. $-15 = t - 5$

3.3 Solving Equations Using Addition or Subtraction (continued)

2 ACTIVITY: Solving Equations

Work with a partner. Use algebra tiles to model and solve the equation.

a. $-5 = n + 2$

b. $y + 10 = -5$

c. $7 + b = -1$

d. $8 = 12 + z$

3 ACTIVITY: Writing and Solving Equations

Work with a partner. Write an equation shown by the algebra tiles. Then solve.

a.

b.

c.

d.

3.3 Solving Equations Using Addition or Subtraction (continued)

4 ACTIVITY: Using a Different Method to Find a Solution

Work with a partner. The *melting point* **of a solid is the temperature at which the solid melts to become a liquid. The melting point of the element bromine is about 19°F. This is about 57°F more than the melting point of mercury.**

a. Which of the following equations can you use to find the melting point of mercury? What is the melting point of mercury?

| $x + 57 = 19$ | $x - 57 = 19$ | $x + 19 = 57$ | $x + 19 = -57$ |

b. **CHOOSE TOOLS** How can you solve this problem without using an equation? Explain. How are these two methods related?

What Is Your Answer?

5. **IN YOUR OWN WORDS** How can you use algebra tiles to solve addition or subtraction equations? Give an example of each.

6. **STRUCTURE** Explain how you could use inverse operations to solve addition or subtraction equations without using algebra tiles.

7. What makes the cartoon funny?

"**Dear Sir: Yesterday you said x = 2. Today you are saying x = 3. Please make up your mind.**"

8. The word *variable* comes from the word *vary*. For example, the temperature in Maine varies a lot from winter to summer. Write two other English sentences that use the word *vary*.

Name _____ Date _____

Solve the equation. Check your solution.

1. $y + 12 = -26$

2. $15 + c = -12$

3. $-16 = d + 21$

4. $n + 12.8 = -0.3$

5. $1\dfrac{1}{8} = g - 4\dfrac{2}{5}$

6. $-5.47 + k = -14.19$

Write the word sentence as an equation. Then solve.

7. 42 less than x is -50.

8. 32 is the sum of a number z and 9.

9. A clothing company makes a profit of \$2.3 million. This is \$4.1 million more than last year. What was the profit last year?

10. A drop on a wooden roller coaster is $-98\dfrac{1}{2}$ feet. A drop on a steel roller coaster is $100\dfrac{1}{4}$ feet lower than the drop on the wooden roller coaster. What is the drop on the steel roller coaster?

3.4 Solving Equations Using Multiplication or Division
For use with Activity 3.4

Essential Question How can you use multiplication or division to solve equations?

1 ACTIVITY: Using Division to Solve Equations

Work with a partner. Use algebra tiles to model and solve the equation.

a. $3x = -12$

Model the equation $3x = -12$. Draw a sketch of your tiles.

Your goal is to get one variable tile by itself. Because there are _____ variable tiles, divide the _____ tiles into _____ equal groups. Circle the groups.

Keep one of the groups. This shows the value of x. Draw a sketch of the remaining tiles.

$x = $_____.

b. $2k = -8$

3.4 Solving Equations Using Multiplication or Division (continued)

c. $-15 = 3t$

d. $-20 = 5m$

e. $4h = -16$

---

2 **ACTIVITY:** Writing and Solving Equations

Work with a partner. Write an equation shown by the algebra tiles. Then solve.

a.

b.

c.

d.

3.4 **Solving Equations Using Multiplication or Division** (continued)

3 **ACTIVITY:** Using a Different Method to Find a Solution

Work with a partner. Choose the equation you can use to solve each problem. Solve the equation. Then explain how to solve the problem without using an equation. How are the two methods related?

a. For the final part of a race, a handcyclist travels 32 feet each second across a distance of 400 feet. How many seconds does it take for the handcyclist to travel the last 400 feet of the race?

$$32x = 400$$

$$400x = 32$$

$$\frac{x}{32} = 400$$

$$\frac{x}{400} = 32$$

b. The melting point of the element radon is about −96°F. The melting point of nitrogen is about 3.6 times the melting point of radon. What is the melting point of nitrogen?

$$3.6x = -96$$

$$x + 96 = 3.6$$

$$\frac{x}{3.6} = -96$$

$$-96x = 3.6$$

c. This year, a hardware store has a profit of −\$6.0 million. This profit is $\frac{3}{4}$ of last year's profit. What is last year's profit?

$$\frac{x}{-6} = \frac{3}{4}$$

$$-6x = \frac{3}{4}$$

$$\frac{3}{4} + x = -6$$

$$\frac{3}{4}x = -6$$

What Is Your Answer?

4. **IN YOUR OWN WORDS** How can you use multiplication or division to solve equations? Give an example of each.

3.4 Practice
For use after Lesson 3.4

Solve the equation. Check your solution.

1. $\dfrac{d}{5} = -6$

2. $8x = -6$

3. $-15 = \dfrac{z}{-2}$

4. $3.2n = -0.8$

5. $-\dfrac{3}{10}h = 15$

6. $-1.1k = -1.21$

Write the word sentence as an equation. Then solve.

7. A number divided by -8 is 7.

8. The product of -12 and a number is 60.

9. You earn $0.85 for every cup of hot chocolate you sell. How many cups do you need to sell to earn $55.25?

3.5 Solving Two-Step Equations
For use with Activity 3.5

Essential Question How can you use algebra tiles to solve a two-step equation?

---

1 ACTIVITY: Solving a Two-Step Equation

Work with a partner. Use algebra tiles to model and solve $2x - 3 = -5$.

Model the equation $2x - 3 = -5$.
Draw a sketch of your tiles.

Remove the _____ red tiles on the left side by
adding _____ yellow tiles to each side.

How many *zero pairs* can you remove from each side?
Circle them.

Because there are _____ green tiles, divide
the red tiles into _____ equal groups.
Circle the groups.

Keep one of the groups. This shows the value of x.
Draw a sketch of the remaining tiles.

$x =$ _____.

---

2 ACTIVITY: The Math behind the Tiles

Work with a partner. Solve $2x - 3 = -5$ without using algebra tiles.
Complete each step. Then answer the questions.

   a. Which step is first, adding 3 to each side or dividing each side by 2?

   b. How are the above steps related to the steps in Activity 1?

3.5 **Solving Two-Step Equations** (continued)

3 ACTIVITY: Solving Equations Using Algebra Tiles

Work with a partner.

- **Write an equation shown by the algebra tiles.**

- **Use algebra tiles to model and solve the equation.**

- **Check your answer by solving the equation without using algebra tiles.**

a.

b.

4 ACTIVITY: Working Backwards

Work with a partner.

a. Your friend pauses a video game to get a drink. You continue the game. You double the score by saving a princess. Then you lose 75 points because you do not collect the treasure. You finish the game with –25 points. How many points did you have when you started?

One way to solve the problem is to work backwards. To do this, start with the end result and retrace the events.

You started the game with _____ points.

3.5 **Solving Two-Step Equations** (continued)

b. You triple your account balance by making a deposit. Then you withdraw $127.32 to buy groceries. Your account is now overdrawn by $10.56. By working backwards, find your account balance before you made the deposit.

What Is Your Answer?

5. **IN YOUR OWN WORDS** How can you use algebra tiles to solve a two-step equation?

6. When solving the equation $4x + 1 = -11$, what is the first step?

7. **REPEATED REASONING** Solve the equation $2x - 75 = -25$. How do your steps compare with the strategy of working backwards in Activity 4?

3.5 Practice
For use after Lesson 3.5

Solve the equation. Check your solution.

1. $3a - 5 = -14$

2. $10 = -2c + 22$

3. $18 = -5b - 17$

4. $-12 = -8z + 12$

5. $1.3n - 0.03 = -9$

6. $-\dfrac{5}{11}h + \dfrac{7}{9} = \dfrac{2}{9}$

7. The length of a rectangle is 3 meters less than twice its width.

   a. Write an equation to find the length of the rectangle.

   b. The length of the rectangle is 11 meters. What is the width of the rectangle?

Chapter 4 — Fair Game Review

Graph the inequality.

1. $x < -3$

2. $x \geq -5$

3. $x \leq 2$

4. $x > 7$

5. $x \leq -2.3$

6. $x > \dfrac{2}{5}$

7. The deepest free dive by a human in the ocean is 417 feet. The depth humans have been in the ocean can be represented by the inequality $x \leq 417$. Graph the inequality.

Chapter 4 **Fair Game Review** (continued)

Complete the number sentence with < or >.

8. $\dfrac{3}{4}$ _____ 0.2

9. $\dfrac{7}{8}$ _____ 0.7

10. -0.6 _____ $-\dfrac{2}{3}$

11. -1.76 _____ 1.75

12. $\dfrac{17}{3}$ _____ 6

13. 1.8 _____ $\dfrac{31}{16}$

14. Your height is 5 feet and $1\dfrac{5}{8}$ inches. Your friend's height is 5.6 feet. Who is taller? Explain.

4.1 Writing and Graphing Inequalities
For use with Activity 4.1

Essential Question How can you use a number line to represent solutions of an inequality?

---

1 ACTIVITY: Understanding Inequality Statements

Work with a partner. Read the statement. Circle each number that makes the statement true, and then answer the questions.

a. "You are in **at least** 5 of the photos."

$$-3 \quad -2 \quad -1 \quad 0 \quad 1 \quad 2 \quad 3 \quad 4 \quad 5 \quad 6$$

- What do you notice about the numbers that you circled?

- Is the number 5 included? Why or why not?

- Write four other numbers that make the statement true.

b. "The temperature is **less than** -4 degrees Fahrenheit."

$$-7 \quad -6 \quad -5 \quad -4 \quad -3 \quad -2 \quad -1 \quad 0 \quad 1 \quad 2$$

- What do you notice about the numbers that you circled?

- Can the temperature be exactly -4 degrees Fahrenheit? Explain.

- Write four other numbers that make the statement true.

c. "**More than** 3 students from our school are in the chess tournament."

$$-3 \quad -2 \quad -1 \quad 0 \quad 1 \quad 2 \quad 3 \quad 4 \quad 5 \quad 6$$

- What do you notice about the numbers that you circled?

4.1 **Writing and Graphing Inequalities** (continued)

- Is the number 3 included? Why or why not?

- Write four other numbers that make the statement true.

d. "The balance in a yearbook fund is **no more than** −$5."

$$-7 \quad -6 \quad -5 \quad -4 \quad -3 \quad -2 \quad -1 \quad 0 \quad 1 \quad 2$$

- What do you notice about the numbers that you circled?

- Is the number −5 included? Why or why not?

- Write four other numbers that make the statement true.

2 **ACTIVITY:** Understanding Inequality Symbols

Work with a partner.

a. Consider the statement "x is a number such that $x > -1.5$."

- Can the number be exactly −1.5? Explain.

- Make a number line. Shade the part of the number line that shows the numbers that make the statement true.

- Write four other numbers that are not integers that make the statement true.

b. Consider the statement "x is a number such that $x \le \dfrac{5}{2}$."

- Can the number be exactly $\dfrac{5}{2}$? Explain.

4.1 **Writing and Graphing Inequalities** (continued)

- Make a number line. Shade the part of the number line that shows the numbers that make the statement true.

- Write four other numbers that are not integers that make the statement true.

3 **ACTIVITY:** Writing and Graphing Inequalities

Work with a partner. Write an inequality for each graph. Then, in words, describe all the values of x that make the inequality true.

a.

b.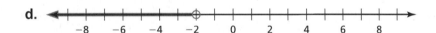

c.

d.

What Is Your Answer?

4. **IN YOUR OWN WORDS** How can you use a number line to represent solutions of an inequality?

5. **STRUCTURE** Is $x \geq -1.4$ the same as $-1.4 \leq x$? Explain.

4.1 Practice
For use after Lesson 4.1

Write the word sentence as an inequality.

1. A number t is less than or equal to 5.

2. A number g subtracted from 6 is no more than $\dfrac{3}{4}$.

Tell whether the given value is a solution of the inequality.

3. $r - 3 \leq 9; r = 8$

4. $4h > -12; h = -5$

Graph the inequality on a number line.

5. $y > -1$

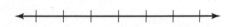

6. $d \leq 2.5$

7. $s \geq 3\dfrac{3}{4}$

8. $p < 9$

9. You have at most 30 games on your smart phone. Write an inequality that represents this situation.

4.2 Solving Inequalities Using Addition or Subtraction
For use with Activity 4.2

Essential Question How can you use addition or subtraction to solve an inequality?

1 ACTIVITY: Writing an Inequality

Work with a partner. Members of the Boy Scouts must be less than 18 years old. In 4 years, your friend will still be eligible to be a scout.

a. Which of the following represents your friend's situation? What does x represent? Explain your reasoning.

| $x + 4 > 18$ | $x + 4 < 18$ | $x + 4 \geq 18$ | $x + 4 \leq 18$ |

b. Graph the possible ages of your friend on a number line. Explain how you decided what to graph.

2 ACTIVITY: Writing an Inequality

Work with a partner. Supercooling is the process of lowering the temperature of a liquid or a gas below its freezing point without it becoming a solid. Water can be supercooled to 86°F below its normal freezing point (32°F) and still not freeze.

a. Let x represent the temperature of water. Which inequality represents the temperature at which water can be a liquid or a gas? Explain your reasoning.

| $x - 32 > -86$ | $x - 32 < -86$ | $x - 32 \geq -86$ | $x - 32 \leq -86$ |

4.2 **Solving Inequalities Using Addition or Subtraction** (continued)

b. On a number line, graph the possible temperatures at which water can be a liquid or a gas. Explain how you decided what to graph.

3 **ACTIVITY:** Solving Inequalities

Work with a partner. Complete the following steps for Activity 1. Then repeat the steps for Activity 2.

- Use your inequality from part (a). Replace the inequality symbol with an equal sign.

- Solve the equation.

- Replace the equal sign with the original inequality symbol.

- Graph this new inequality.

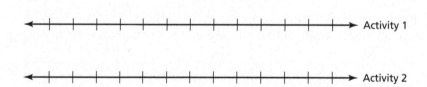

- Compare the graph with your graph in part (b). What do you notice?

Name_____ Date _____

4 ACTIVITY: Temperatures of Continents

Work with a partner. The table shows the lowest recorded temperature on each continent. Write an inequality that represents each statement. Then solve and graph the inequality.

Continent	Lowest Temperature
Africa	−11°F
Antarctica	−129°F
Asia	−90°F
Australia	−9.4°F
Europe	−67°F
North America	−81.4°F
South America	−27°F

a. The temperature at a weather station in Asia is more than 150°F greater than the record low in Asia.

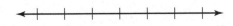

b. The temperature at a research station in Antarctica is at least 80°F greater than the record low in Antarctica.

What Is Your Answer?

5. IN YOUR OWN WORDS How can you use addition or subtraction to solve an inequality?

6. Describe a real-life situation that you can represent with an inequality. Write the inequality. Graph the solution on a number line.

Big Ideas Math Red Accelerated   **73**
Record and Practice Journal

4.2 **Practice**
For use after Lesson 4.2

Solve the inequality. Graph the solution.

1. $y - 3 \geq -12$

2. $-14 \leq 8 + x$

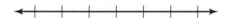

3. $t - 4 < -4$

4. $-9 \geq 2 + d$

5. $-3.4 > c - 1.2$

6. $j + \dfrac{5}{12} < -\dfrac{3}{4}$

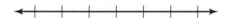

7. A bounce house can hold 15 children. Seven children go in the bounce house. Write and solve an inequality that represents the additional number of children that can go in the bounce house.

4.3 Solving Inequalities Using Multiplication or Division
For use with Activity 4.3

Essential Question How can you use multiplication or division to solve an inequality?

1 **ACTIVITY:** Using a Table to Solve an Inequality

Work with a partner.

- **Complete the table.**
- **Decide which graph represents the solution of the inequality.**
- **Write the solution of the inequality.**

a. $4x > 12$

x	−1	0	1	2	3	4	5
4x							
4x $\overset{?}{>}$ 12							

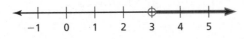

b. $-3x \leq 9$

x	−5	−4	−3	−2	−1	0	1
−3x							
−3x $\overset{?}{\leq}$ 9							

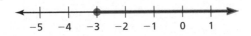 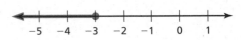

4.3 **Solving Inequalities Using Multiplication or Division** (continued)

2 **ACTIVITY:** Solving an Inequality

Work with a partner.

a. Solve $-3x \leq 9$ by adding $3x$ to each side of the inequality first. Then solve the resulting inequality.

b. Compare the solution in part (a) with the solution in Activity 1(b).

3 **ACTIVITY:** Using a Table to Solve an Inequality

Work with a partner.

- **Complete the table.**
- **Decide which graph represents the solution of the inequality.**
- **Write the solution of the inequality.**

a. $\dfrac{x}{3} < 1$

x	-1	0	1	2	3	4	5
$\dfrac{x}{3}$							
$\dfrac{x}{3} \overset{?}{<} 1$							

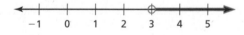   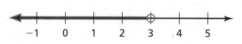

Name_____ Date _____

b. $\dfrac{x}{-4} \geq \dfrac{3}{4}$

x	-5	-4	-3	-2	-1	0	1
$\dfrac{x}{-4}$							
$\dfrac{x}{-4} \overset{?}{\geq} \dfrac{3}{4}$							

4 **ACTIVITY:** Writing Rules

Work with a partner. Use a table to solve each inequality.

a. $-2x \leq 10$ **b.** $-6x > 0$ **c.** $\dfrac{x}{-4} < 1$ **d.** $\dfrac{x}{-8} \geq \dfrac{1}{8}$

x										
$-2x$										
$-6x$										
$\dfrac{x}{-4}$										
$\dfrac{x}{-8}$										

Write a set of rules that describes how to solve inequalities like those in Activities 1 and 3. Then use your set of rules to solve each of the four inequalities above.

What Is Your Answer?

5. IN YOUR OWN WORDS How can you use multiplication or division to solve an inequality?

4.3 Practice
For use after Lesson 4.3

Solve the inequality. Graph the solution.

1. $6n < 90$

2. $\dfrac{x}{4} \leq -18$

3. $-20t > -80$

4. $-3q \geq 91.5$

5. $-4p < \dfrac{2}{3}$

6. $-8 \geq 1.6m$

7. $-\dfrac{r}{4} \leq -10$

8. $-\dfrac{t}{5} > 2.5$

9. $-2 \geq \dfrac{q}{-0.3}$

10. To win a game, you need at least 45 points. Each question is worth 3 points. Write and solve an inequality that represents the number of questions you need to answer correctly to win the game.

Name_____ Date_____

4.4 Solving Two-Step Inequalities
For use with Activity 4.4

Essential Question How can you use an inequality to describe the dimensions of a figure?

1 **ACTIVITY:** Areas and Perimeters of Figures

Work with a partner.

- **Use the given condition to choose the inequality that you can use to find the possible values of the variable. Justify your answer.**

- **Write four values of the variable that satisfy the inequality you chose.**

a. You want to find the values of x so that the area of the rectangle is more than 22 square units.

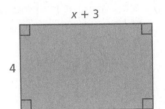

$4x + 12 > 22$ $4x + 3 > 22$

$4x + 12 \geq 22$ $2x + 14 > 22$

b. You want to find the values of x so that the perimeter of the rectangle is greater than or equal to 28 units.

$x + 7 \geq 28$ $4x + 12 \geq 28$ $2x + 14 \geq 28$ $2x + 14 \leq 28$

4.4 **Solving Two-Step Inequalities** (continued)

c. You want to find the values of y so that the area of the parallelogram is fewer than 41 square units.

| $5y + 7 < 41$ | $5y + 35 < 41$ |
| $5y + 7 \leq 41$ | $5y + 35 \leq 41$ |

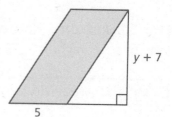

d. You want to find the values of z so that the area of the trapezoid is at most 100 square units.

| $5z + 30 \leq 100$ | $10z + 30 \leq 100$ |
| $5z + 30 < 100$ | $10z + 30 < 100$ |

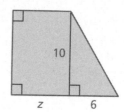

2 **ACTIVITY:** Volumes of Rectangular Prisms

Work with a partner.

- Use the given condition to choose the inequality that you can use to find the possible values of the variable. Justify your answer.

- Write four values of the variable that satisfy the inequality you chose.

a. You want to find the values of x so that the volume of the rectangular prism is at least 50 cubic units.

| $15x + 30 > 50$ | $x + 10 \geq 50$ |
| $15x + 30 \geq 50$ | $15x + 2 \geq 50$ |

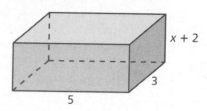

4.4 Solving Two-Step Inequalities (continued)

b. You want to find the values of x so that the volume of the rectangular prism is no more than 36 cubic units.

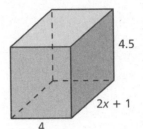

| $8x + 4 < 36$ | $36x + 18 < 36$ |

| $2x + 9.5 \leq 36$ | $36x + 18 \leq 36$ |

4.5

$2x + 1$

4

What Is Your Answer?

3. IN YOUR OWN WORDS How can you use an inequality to describe the dimensions of a figure?

4. Use what you know about solving equations and inequalities to describe how you can solve a two-step inequality. Give an example to support your explanation.

4.4 Practice

For use after Lesson 4.4

Solve the inequality. Graph the solution.

1. $5 - 3x > 8$

2. $-4x - 7 \leq 9$

3. $3 + 4.5x \geq 21$

4. $-2y - 5 > \dfrac{5}{2}$

5. $2(y - 4) < -18$

6. $-6 \geq -6(y - 3)$

7. You borrow $200 from a friend to help pay for a new laptop computer. You pay your friend back $12 per week. Write and solve an inequality to find when you will owe your friend less than $60.

Name_____ Date _____

Chapter 5 Fair Game Review

Simplify.

1. $\dfrac{3}{18}$

2. $\dfrac{4}{6}$

3. $\dfrac{12}{60}$

4. $\dfrac{14}{28}$

5. $\dfrac{16}{36}$

6. $\dfrac{40}{50}$

Are the fractions equivalent?

7. $\dfrac{3}{8} \overset{?}{=} \dfrac{6}{11}$

8. $\dfrac{4}{10} \overset{?}{=} \dfrac{16}{40}$

9. $\dfrac{22}{32} \overset{?}{=} \dfrac{11}{16}$

10. $\dfrac{63}{72} \overset{?}{=} \dfrac{7}{9}$

11. You see 58 birds while on a bird watching tour. Of those birds, you see 12 hawks. Write and simplify the fraction of hawks you see.

Chapter 5 **Fair Game Review** (continued)

Solve the equation. Check your solution.

12. $\dfrac{d}{12} = -4$

13. $-7 = \dfrac{x}{-3}$

14. $\dfrac{1}{8}n = 5$

15. $6a = -54$

16. $10 = -2k$

17. $2.7 = -0.9y$

18. $-23.4 = -1.3w$

19. $\dfrac{1}{15}z = 6$

20. You and three friends spend $35 on tickets at the movies. Write and solve an equation to find the price p of one ticket.

Name_____ Date_____

5.1 Ratios and Rates
For use with Activity 5.1

Essential Question How do rates help you describe real-life problems?

1 ACTIVITY: Finding Reasonable Rates

Work with a partner.

a. Match each description with a verbal rate.

b. Match each verbal rate with a numerical rate.

c. Give a reasonable numerical rate for each description. Then give an unreasonable rate.

Description	*Verbal Rate*	*Numerical Rate*
Your running rate in a 100-meter dash	Dollars per year	$= \dfrac{\boxed{} \text{ in.}}{\text{yr}}$
The fertilization rate for an apple orchard	Inches per year	$= \dfrac{\boxed{} \text{ lb}}{\text{acre}}$
The average pay rate for a professional athlete	Meters per second	$= \dfrac{\$\boxed{}}{\text{yr}}$
The average rainfall rate in a rainforest	Pounds per acre	$= \dfrac{\boxed{} \text{ m}}{\text{sec}}$

2 ACTIVITY: Simplifying Expressions That Contain Fractions

Work with a partner. Describe a situation where the given expression may apply. Show how you can rewrite each expression as a division problem. Then simplify and interpret your result.

a. $\dfrac{\frac{1}{2}\,c}{4\text{ fl oz}}$

b. $\dfrac{2\text{ in.}}{\frac{3}{4}\text{ sec}}$

5.1 **Ratios and Rates** (continued)

c. $\dfrac{\frac{3}{8} \text{ c sugar}}{\frac{3}{5} \text{ c flour}}$

d. $\dfrac{\frac{5}{6} \text{ gal}}{\frac{2}{3} \text{ sec}}$

---

3 **ACTIVITY:** Using Ratio Tables to Find Equivalent Rates

Work with a partner. A communications satellite in orbit travels about 18 miles every 4 seconds.

a. Identify the rate in this problem.

b. Recall that you can use *ratio tables* to find and organize equivalent ratios and rates. Complete the ratio table below.

Time (seconds)	4	8	12	16	20
Distance (miles)					

c. How can you use a ratio table to find the speed of the satellite in miles per minute? miles per hour?

d. How far does the satellite travel in 1 second? Solve this problem (1) by using a ratio table and (2) by evaluating a quotient.

e. How far does the satellite travel in $\dfrac{1}{2}$ second? Explain your steps.

5.1 **Ratios and Rates** (continued)

4 **ACTIVITY:** Unit Analysis

Work with a partner. Describe a situation where the product may apply. Then find each product and list the units.

a. $10 \text{ gal} \times \dfrac{22 \text{ mi}}{\text{gal}}$

b. $\dfrac{7}{2} \text{ lb} \times \dfrac{\$3}{\frac{1}{2} \text{lb}}$

c. $\dfrac{1}{2} \sec \times \dfrac{30 \text{ ft}^2}{\sec}$

What Is Your Answer?

5. **IN YOUR OWN WORDS** How do rates help you describe real-life problems? Give two examples.

6. To estimate the annual salary for a given hourly pay rate, multiply by 2 and insert "000" at the end.

Sample: $10 per hour is about $20,000 per year.

a. Explain why this works. Assume the person is working 40 hours a week.

b. Estimate the annual salary for an hourly pay rate of $8 per hour.

c. You earn $1 million per month. What is your annual salary?

"We had someone apply for the job. He says he would like $1 million a month, but will settle for $8 an hour."

d. Why is the cartoon funny?

Name _____ Date _____

5.1 Practice

For use after Lesson 5.1

Write the ratio as a fraction in simplest form.

1. 8 to 14

2. 36 even : 12 odd

3. 42 vanilla to 48 chocolate

Find the unit rate.

4. $2.50 for 5 ounces

5. 15 degrees in 2 hours

6. 183 miles in 3 hours

Use the ratio table to find the unit rate with the specified units.

7. pounds per box

Boxes	0	1	2	3
Pounds	0	30	60	90

8. cost per notebook

Notebooks	0	5	10	15
Cost (dollars)	0	9.45	18.90	28.35

9. You create 15 centerpieces for a party in 5 hours.

   a. What is the unit rate?

   b. How long will it take you to make 42 centerpieces?

Name_____ Date_____

5.2 Proportions
For use with Activity 5.2

Essential Question How can proportions help you decide when things are "fair"?

---

1 ACTIVITY: Determining Proportions

Work with a partner. Tell whether the two ratios are equivalent. If they are not equivalent, change the next day to make the ratios equivalent. Explain your reasoning.

a. On the first day, you pay $5 for 2 boxes of popcorn. The next day, you pay $7.50 for 3 boxes.

First Day   Next Day

$$\frac{\$5.00}{2 \text{ boxes}} \overset{?}{=} \frac{\$7.50}{3 \text{ boxes}}$$

b. On the first day, it takes you $3\frac{1}{2}$ hours to drive 175 miles. The next day, it takes you 5 hours to drive 200 miles.

First Day   Next Day

$$\frac{3\frac{1}{2} \text{ h}}{175 \text{ mi}} \overset{?}{=} \frac{5 \text{ h}}{200 \text{ mi}}$$

c. On the first day, you walk 4 miles and burn 300 calories. The next day, you walk $3\frac{1}{3}$ miles and burn 250 calories.

First Day   Next Day

$$\frac{4 \text{ mi}}{300 \text{ cal}} \overset{?}{=} \frac{3\frac{1}{3} \text{ mi}}{250 \text{ cal}}$$

d. On the first day, you paint 150 square feet in $2\frac{1}{2}$ hours. The next day, you paint 200 square feet in 4 hours.

First Day   Next Day

$$\frac{150 \text{ ft}^2}{2\frac{1}{2} \text{ h}} \overset{?}{=} \frac{200 \text{ ft}^2}{4 \text{ h}}$$

5.2 Proportions (continued)

2 **ACTIVITY:** Checking a Proportion

Work with a partner.

a. It is said that "one year in a dog's life is equivalent to seven years in a human's life." Explain why Newton thinks he has a score of 105 points. Did he solve the proportion correctly?

$$\frac{1 \text{ year}}{7 \text{ years}} \overset{?}{=} \frac{15 \text{ points}}{105 \text{ points}}$$

"I got 15 on my online test. That's 105 in dog points! Isn't that an A+?"

b. If Newton thinks his score is 98 points, how many points does he actually have? Explain your reasoning.

3 **ACTIVITY:** Determining Fairness

Work with a partner. Write a ratio for each sentence. Compare the ratios. If they are equal, then the answer is "It is fair." If they are not equal, then the answer is "It is not fair." Explain your reasoning.

a.

| You pay $184 for 2 tickets to a concert. | & | I pay $266 for 3 tickets to the same concert. | ➡️ **Is this fair?** |

5.2 **Proportions** (continued)

b.

| You get 75 points for answering 15 questions correctly. | **&** | I get 70 points for answering 14 questions correctly. |

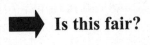 **Is this fair?**

c.

| You trade 24 football cards for 15 baseball cards. | **&** | I trade 20 football cards for 32 baseball cards. |

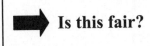 **Is this fair?**

What Is Your Answer?

4. Find a recipe for something you like to eat. Then show how two of the ingredient amounts are proportional when you double or triple the recipe.

5. IN YOUR OWN WORDS How can proportions help you decide when things are "fair"? Give an example.

5.2 Practice
For use after Lesson 5.2

Tell whether the ratios form a proportion.

1. $\dfrac{1}{5}, \dfrac{5}{15}$

2. $\dfrac{2}{3}, \dfrac{12}{18}$

3. $\dfrac{15}{2}, \dfrac{4}{30}$

4. $\dfrac{56}{21}, \dfrac{8}{3}$

5. $\dfrac{5}{8}, \dfrac{62.5}{100}$

6. $\dfrac{17}{20}, \dfrac{90.1}{106}$

7. $\dfrac{3.2}{4}, \dfrac{16}{24}$

8. $\dfrac{34}{50}, \dfrac{6.8}{10}$

Tell whether the two rates form a proportion.

9. 28 points in 3 games;
   112 points in 12 games

10. 32 notes in 4 measures;
    12 notes in 2 measures

11. You can type 105 words in two minutes. Your friend can type 210 words in four minutes. Are these rates proportional? Explain.

Extension 5.2 Practice

For use after Extension 5.2

Use a graph to tell whether *x* and *y* are in a proportional relationship.

1.

x	2	3	4	5
y	5	7	9	11

2.

x	1	2	3	4
y	3	6	9	12

3.

x	1	2	3	4
y	2.4	4.8	7.2	9.6

4.

x	2	4	6	8
y	2	3	4	5

Extension 5.2 Practice (continued)

Interpret each plotted point in the graph of the proportional relationship.

5.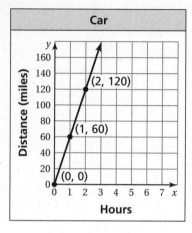

6.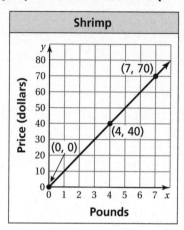

7.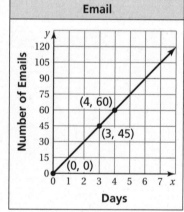

8.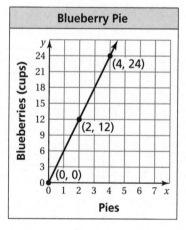

Name_____ Date_____

5.3 Writing Proportions
For use with Activity 5.3

Essential Question How can you write a proportion that solves a problem in real life?

1 ACTIVITY: Writing Proportions

Work with a partner. A rough rule for finding the correct bat length is "the bat length should be half of the batter's height." So, a 62-inch tall batter uses a bat that is 31 inches long. Write a proportion to find the bat length for each given batter height.

    a. 58 inches   **b.** 60 inches   **c.** 64 inches

2 ACTIVITY: Bat Lengths

Work with a partner. Here is a more accurate table for determining the bat length for a batter. Find all the batter heights and corresponding weights for which the rough rule in Activity 1 is exact.

| | Height of Batter (inches) | | | | | | | |
	45–48	49–52	53–56	57–60	61–64	65–68	69–72	Over 72
Under 61	28	29	29					
61–70	28	29	30	30				
71–80	28	29	30	30	31			
81–90	29	29	30	30	31	32		
91–100	29	30	30	31	31	32		
101–110	29	30	30	31	31	32		
111–120	29	30	30	31	31	32		
121–130	29	30	30	31	32	33	33	
131–140	30	30	31	31	32	33	33	
141–150	30	30	31	31	32	33	33	
151–160	30	31	31	32	32	33	33	33
161–170		31	31	32	32	33	33	34
171–180				32	33	33	34	34
Over 180					33	33	34	34

(Left side label: Weight of Batter (pounds))

5.3 **Writing Proportions** (continued)

3 **ACTIVITY:** Writing Proportions

Work with a partner. The batting average of a baseball player is the number of "hits" divided by the number of "at bats."

$$\text{batting average} = \frac{\text{hits } (H)}{\text{at Bats } (A)}$$

A player whose batting average is 0.250 is said to be "batting 250."

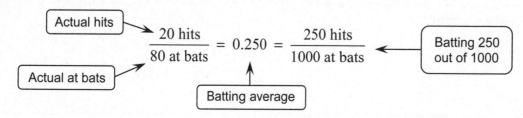

Write a proportion to find how many hits H a player needs to achieve the given batting average. Then solve the proportion.

a. 50 times at bat;
batting average is 0.200.

b. 84 times at bat;
batting average is 0.250.

c. 80 times at bat;
batting average is 0.350.

d. 1 time at bat;
batting average is 1.000.

5.3 Writing Proportions (continued)

What Is Your Answer?

4. **IN YOUR OWN WORDS** How can you write a proportion that solves a problem in real life?

5. Two players have the same batting average.

	At Bats	Hits	Batting Average
Player 1	132	45	
Player 2	132	45	

Player 1 gets four hits in the next five at bats. Player 2 gets three hits in the next three at bats.

a. Who has the higher batting average?

b. Does this seem fair? Explain your reasoning.

Name _____ Date _____

5.3 Practice
For use after Lesson 5.3

Write a proportion to find how many points a student needs to score on the test to get the given score.

1. test worth 50 points; test score of 84%
2. test worth 75 points; test score of 96%

Use the table to write a proportion.

3.

	Trip 1	Trip 2
Miles	104	78
Gallons	4	g

4.

	Tree 1	Tree 2
Inches	15	x
Years	4	3

Solve the proportion.

5. $\dfrac{1}{3} = \dfrac{x}{12}$

6. $\dfrac{5}{9} = \dfrac{25}{y}$

7. $\dfrac{26}{z} = \dfrac{13}{22}$

8. $\dfrac{b}{30} = \dfrac{2.6}{1.5}$

9. A local Humane Society houses 300 animals. The ratio of cats to all animals is 7 : 15.

   a. Write a proportion that gives the number of cats c.

   b. How many cats are in the Humane Society?

5.4 Solving Proportions
For use with Activity 5.4

Essential Question How can you use ratio tables and cross products to solve proportions?

---

1 **ACTIVITY:** Solving a Proportion in Science

Work with a partner. You can use ratio tables to determine the amount of a compound (like salt) that is dissolved in a solution. Determine the unknown quantity. Explain your procedure.

  a. **Salt Water**

Salt Water	1 L	3 L
Salt	250 g	x g

1 liter   3 liters

There are _____ grams of salt in the 3-liter solution.

  b. **White Glue Solution**

Water	$\frac{1}{2}$ cup	1 cup
White Glue	$\frac{1}{2}$ cup	x cups

  c. **Borax Solution**

Borax	1 tsp	2 tsp
Water	1 cup	x cups

5.4 **Solving Proportions** (continued)

d. **Slime** (See recipe.)

Borax Solution	$\frac{1}{2}$ cup	1 cup
White Glue Solution	y cups	x cups

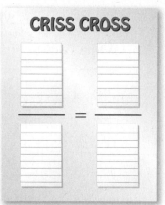

Recipe for SLIME

1. Add ½ cup of water and ½ cup white glue. Mix thoroughly. This is your white glue solution.

2. Add a couple drops of food coloring to the glue solution. Mix thoroughly.

3. Add 1 teaspoon of borax to 1 cup of water. Mix thoroughly. This is your borax solution (about 1 cup).

4. Pour the borax solution and the glue solution into a separate bowl.

5. Place the slime that forms in a plastic bag and squeeze the mixture repeatedly to mix it up.

2 **ACTIVITY:** The Game of Criss Cross

Preparation:

- Cut index cards to make 48 playing cards.

- Write each number on a card.
  1, 1, 1, 2, 2, 2, 3, 3, 3, 4, 4, 4, 5, 5, 5, 6, 6, 6, 7, 7,
  7, 8, 8, 8, 9, 9, 9, 10, 10, 10, 12, 12, 12, 13, 13,
  13, 14, 14, 14, 15, 15, 15, 16, 16, 16, 18, 20, 25

- Make a copy of the game board.

CRISS CROSS

=

To play:

- Play with a partner.

- Deal 8 cards to each player.

- Begin by drawing a card from the remaining cards. Use four of your cards to try and form a proportion.

- Lay the four cards on the game board. If you form a proportion, then say "Criss Cross." You earn 4 points. Place the four cards in a discard pile. Now it is your partner's turn.

- If you cannot form a proportion, then it is your partner's turn.

- When the original pile of cards is empty, shuffle the cards in the discard pile. Start again.

- The first player to reach 20 points wins.

5.4 **Solving Proportions** (continued)

What Is Your Answer?

3. **IN YOUR OWN WORDS** How can you use ratio tables and cross products to solve proportions? Give an example.

4. **PUZZLE** Use each number once to form three proportions.

1	2	10	4	12	20

15	5	16	6	8	3

5.4 Practice
For use after Lesson 5.4

Use multiplication to solve the proportion.

1. $\dfrac{a}{40} = \dfrac{3}{10}$

2. $\dfrac{6}{11} = \dfrac{c}{77}$

3. $\dfrac{b}{65} = \dfrac{7}{13}$

Use the Cross Products Property to solve the proportion.

4. $\dfrac{k}{6} = \dfrac{8}{16}$

5. $\dfrac{5.4}{7} = \dfrac{27}{h}$

6. $\dfrac{8}{11} = \dfrac{4}{y+2}$

Write and solve a proportion to complete the statement.

7. 42 in. = _____ cm

8. 12.6 kg ≈ _____ lb

9. 3 oz ≈ _____ g

10. A cell phone company charges \$5 for 250 text messages. How much does the company charge for 300 text messages?

Name_____ Date _____

5.5 Slope
For use with Activity 5.5

Essential Question How can you compare two rates graphically?

1 **ACTIVITY:** Comparing Unit Rates

Work with a partner. The table shows the maximum speeds of several animals.

a. Find the missing speeds. Round your answers to the nearest tenth.

b. Which animal is fastest? Which animal is slowest?

c. Explain how you convert between the two units of speed.

Animal	Speed (miles per hour)	Speed (feet per second)
Antelope	61.0	
Black mamba snake		29.3
Cheetah		102.6
Chicken		13.2
Coyote	43.0	
Domestic pig		16.0
Elephant		36.6
Elk		66.0
Giant tortoise	0.2	
Giraffe	32.0	
Gray fox		61.6
Greyhound	39.4	
Grizzly bear		44.0
Human		41.0
Hyena	40.0	
Jackal	35.0	
Lion		73.3
Peregrine falcon	200.0	
Quarter horse	47.5	
Spider		1.76
Squirrel	12.0	
Thomson's gazelle	50.0	
Three-Toed sloth		0.2
Tuna	47.0	

5.5 **Slope** (continued)

2 **ACTIVITY:** Comparing Two Rates Graphically

Work with a partner. A cheetah and a Thomson's gazelle run at maximum speeds.

   a. Use the table in Activity 1 to calculate the missing distances.

	Cheetah	Gazelle
Time (seconds)	**Distance (feet)**	**Distance (feet)**
0		
1		
2		
3		
4		
5		
6		
7		

   b. Use the table to write ordered pairs. Then plot the ordered pairs and connect the points for each animal. What do you notice about the graphs?

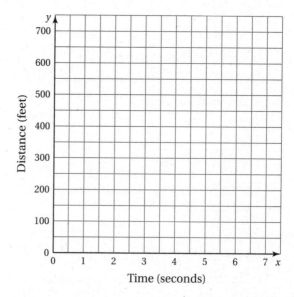

   c. Which graph is steeper? The speed of which animal is greater?

5.5 **Slope** (continued)

What Is Your Answer?

3. **IN YOUR OWN WORDS** How can you compare two rates graphically? Explain your reasoning. Give some examples with your answer.

4. **REPEATED REASONING** Choose 10 animals from Activity 1.

   a. Make a table for each animal similar to the table in Activity 2.

   b. Sketch a graph of the distances for each animal.

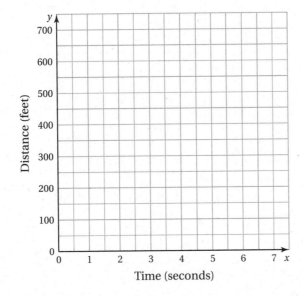

   c. Compare the steepness of the 10 graphs. What can you conclude?

Name _____ Date _____

Find the slope of the line.

1.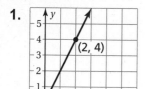

2.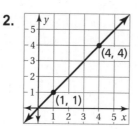

3.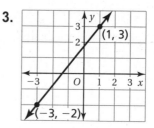

Graph the data. Then find and interpret the slope of the line through the points.

4.

Minutes, x	0	1	3	5
Pages, y	0	1.5	4.5	7.5

5.

Miles, x	0	1	2	3
Calories, y	0	135	270	405

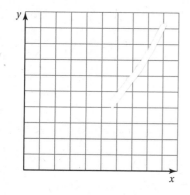

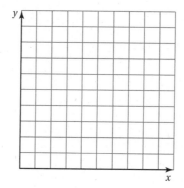

6. By law, the maximum slope of a wheelchair ramp is $\dfrac{1}{12}$.

   a. A ramp is designed that is 4 feet high and has a horizontal length of 50 feet. Does this ramp meet the law? Explain.

   b. What could be adjusted on an unacceptable ramp so that it meets the law?

Name_____ Date_____

5.6 Direct Variation
For use with Activity 5.6

Essential Question How can you use a graph to show the relationship between two quantities that vary directly? How can you use an equation?

1 ACTIVITY: Math in Literature

Gulliver's Travels was written by Jonathan Swift and published in 1726. Gulliver was shipwrecked on an island in Lilliput, where the people were only 6 inches tall. When the Lilliputians decided to make a shirt for Gulliver, a Lilliputian tailor stated that he could determine Gulliver's measurements by simply measuring the distance around Gulliver's thumb. He said "Twice around the thumb equals once around the wrist. Twice around the wrist is once around the neck. Twice around the neck is once around the waist."

Work with a partner. Use the tailor's statement to complete the table.

Thumb, *t*	Wrist, *w*	Neck, *n*	Waist, *x*
0 in.			
1 in.			
	4 in.		
		12 in.	
			32 in.
	10 in.		

5.6 **Direct Variation** (continued)

2 **ACTIVITY:** Drawing a Graph

Work with a partner. Use the information from Activity 1.

a. In your own words, describe the relationship between t and w.

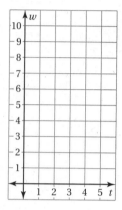

b. Use the table to write ordered pairs (t, w). Then plot the ordered pairs.

c. What do you notice about the graph of the ordered pairs?

d. Choose two points and find the slope of the line between them.

e. The quantities t and w are said to *vary directly*. An equation that describes the relationship is $w =$ _____ t.

3 **ACTIVITY:** Drawing a Graph and Writing an Equation

Work with a partner. Use the information from Activity 1 to draw a graph of the relationship. Write an equation that describes the relationship between the two quantities.

a. Thumb t and neck n

$$\left(n = \boxed{} \; t \right)$$

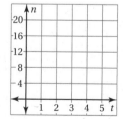

b. Wrist w and waist x

$$\left(x = \boxed{} \; w \right)$$

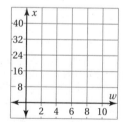

5.6 **Direct Variation** (continued)

c. Wrist w and thumb t

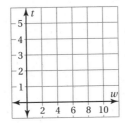

d. Waist x and wrist w

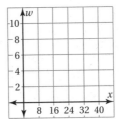

What Is Your Answer?

4. IN YOUR OWN WORDS How can you use a graph to show the relationship between two quantities that vary directly? How can you use an equation?

5. STRUCTURE How are all the graphs in Activity 3 alike?

6. Give a real-life example of two variables that vary directly.

7. Work with a partner. Use string to find the distance around your thumb, wrist, and neck. Do your measurements agree with the tailor's statements in *Gulliver's Travels*? Explain your reasoning.

Name _____ Date _____

Tell whether x and y show direct variation. Explain your reasoning. If so, find k.

1.

x	1	2	3	4
y	3	6	9	12

2.

x	−1	0	1	2
y	1	3	7	13

3.

x	0	2	4	6
y	8	5	2	−1

4. $y + 2 = x$

5. $3y = x$

6. $\dfrac{y}{x} = 4$

The variables x and y vary directly. Use the values to find the constant of proportionality and write an equation that relates x and y.

7. $y = 8; x = 2$

8. $y = 14, x = 16$

9. $y = 25, x = 35$

10. The table shows the cups c of dog food needed to feed a dog that weighs p pounds. Graph the data. Tell whether p and c show direct variation. If so, write an equation that represents the line.

Pounds, p	10	20	40	70
Food, c	$\dfrac{3}{4}$	$1\dfrac{1}{4}$	2	$2\dfrac{3}{4}$

Name_____ Date_____

Write the percent as a fraction or mixed number in simplest form.

1. 25%

2. 65%

3. 110%

4. 250%

5. 15%

6. 6%

7. A store marks up a pair of sneakers 30%. Write the percent as a fraction or mixed number in simplest form.

Chapter 6 **Fair Game Review** (continued)

Write the fraction or mixed number as a percent.

8. $\dfrac{1}{5}$

9. $\dfrac{1}{4}$

10. $\dfrac{21}{25}$

11. $1\dfrac{2}{5}$

12. $2\dfrac{13}{20}$

13. $1\dfrac{1}{2}$

14. You own $\dfrac{3}{5}$ of the coins in a collection. What percent of the coins do you own?

Name_____ Date_____

Essential Question How does the decimal point move when you rewrite a percent as a decimal and when you rewrite a decimal as a percent?

1 **ACTIVITY:** Writing Percents as Decimals

Work with a partner. Write the percent shown by the model. Write the percent as a decimal.

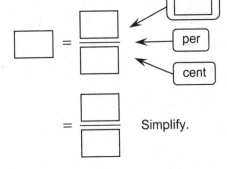

per

cent

$$\Box = \frac{\Box}{\Box}$$

$$= \frac{\Box}{\Box}$$ Simplify.

$$= \Box$$ Write fraction as a decimal.

a.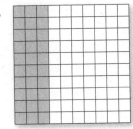

b.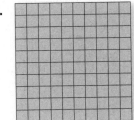

c.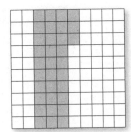

d.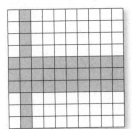

e.

6.1 **Percents and Decimals** (continued)

f. 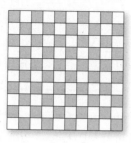   **g.**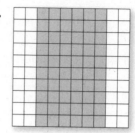

2 **ACTIVITY:** Writing Percents as Decimals

Work with a partner. Write the percent as a decimal.

a. $13.5\% = \dfrac{\boxed{}}{\boxed{}}$ $\boxed{}$ ← per ← cent

$= \dfrac{\boxed{}}{\boxed{}}$ Multiply numerator and denominator by 10.

$= \boxed{}$ Write fraction as a decimal.

b. 12.5%

c. 3.8%

d. 0.5%

6.1 Percents and Decimals (continued)

3 ACTIVITY: Writing Decimals as Percents

Work with a partner. Draw a model to represent the decimal. Write the decimal as a percent.

a. 0.1

b. 0.24

c. 0.58

d. 0.05

What Is Your Answer?

4. **IN YOUR OWN WORDS** How does the decimal point move when you rewrite a percent as a decimal and when you rewrite a decimal as a percent?

5. Explain why the decimal point moves when you rewrite a percent as a decimal and when you rewrite a decimal as a percent.

6.1 Practice
For use after Lesson 6.1

Write the percent as a decimal.

1. 35%   **2.** 160%   **3.** 74.8%   **4.** 0.3%

Write the decimal as a percent.

5. 1.23   **6.** 0.49   **7.** 0.024   **8.** 0.881

Write the percent as a fraction in simplest form and as a decimal.

9. 48%   **10.** 15.5%   **11.** 84.95%

12. People with severe hearing loss were given a sentence and word recognition test six months after they got implants in their ears. The patients scored an average of 82% on the test. Write this percent as a decimal.

6.2 Comparing and Ordering Fractions, Decimals, and Percents For use with Activity 6.2

Essential Question How can you order numbers that are written as fractions, decimals, and percents?

---

1 ACTIVITY: Using Fractions, Decimals, and Percents

Work with a partner. Decide which number form (fraction, decimal, or percent) is more common. Then find which is greater.

a. 7% sales tax or $\frac{1}{20}$ sales tax

b. 0.37 cup of flour or $\frac{1}{3}$ cup of flour

c. $\frac{5}{8}$-inch wrench or 0.375-inch wrench

d. $12\frac{3}{5}$ dollars or 12.56 dollars

e. 93% test score or $\frac{7}{8}$ test score

f. $5\frac{5}{6}$ fluid ounces or 5.6 fluid ounces

---

2 ACTIVITY: Ordering Numbers

Work with a partner to order the following numbers.

$\frac{1}{8}$ 11% $\frac{3}{20}$ 0.172   0.32   43%   7%   0.7 $\frac{5}{6}$

a. Decide on a strategy for ordering the numbers. Will you write them all as fractions, decimals, or percents?

b. Use your strategy and a number line to order the numbers from least to greatest. (Note: Label the number line appropriately.)

6.2 **Comparing and Ordering Fractions, Decimals, and Percents** (continued)

3 **ACTIVITY:** The Game of Math Card War

Preparation:

- Cut index cards to make 40 playing cards.*

- Write each number in the table onto a card.

75%	$\frac{3}{4}$	$\frac{1}{3}$	$\frac{3}{10}$	0.3	25%	0.4	0.25	100%	0.27
0.75	$66\frac{2}{3}\%$	12.5%	40%	$\frac{1}{4}$	4%	0.5%	0.04	$\frac{1}{100}$	$\frac{2}{3}$
0	30%	5%	$\frac{27}{100}$	0.05	$33\frac{1}{3}\%$	$\frac{2}{5}$	0.333...	27%	1%
1	0.01	$\frac{1}{20}$	$\frac{1}{8}$	0.125	$\frac{1}{25}$	$\frac{1}{200}$	0.005	0.666...	0%

To Play:

- Play with a partner.

- Deal 20 cards to each player facedown.

- Each player turns one card faceup. The player with the greater number wins. The winner collects both cards and places them at the bottom of his or her cards.

- Suppose there is a tie. Each player lays three cards facedown, then a new card faceup. The player with the greater of these new cards wins. The winner collects all 10 cards and places them at the bottom of his or her cards.

- Continue playing until one player has all the cards. This player wins the game.

*Cut-outs are available in the back of the Record and Practice Journal.

6.2 **Comparing and Ordering Fractions, Decimals, and Percents** (continued)

What Is Your Answer?

4. IN YOUR OWN WORDS How can you order numbers that are written as fractions, decimals, and percents? Give an example with your answer.

5. All but one of the U.S. coins shown has a name that is related to its value. Which one is it? How are the names of the others related to their values?

Name_____ Date _____

6.2 Practice
For use after Lesson 6.2

Circle the number that is greater.

1. 0.06, 60%

2. 78%, $\dfrac{19}{25}$

3. $\dfrac{23}{20}$, 110%

4. 0.23, 2.3%

Use a number line to order the numbers from least to greatest.

5. 44.5%, 0.4445, $\dfrac{4}{9}$, 0.44

6. $\dfrac{5}{12}$, 0.4, 42%, 0.416

7. The table shows the portion of each age group that recycles plastic. Order the groups by the portion that recycle from least to greatest.

Age Group	Echo Boomers	Gen X	Baby Boomers	Matures
Portion that Recycle	51%	0.57	0.61	$\dfrac{6}{10}$

Name_____ Date_____

6.3 The Percent Proportion
For use with Activity 6.3

Essential Question How can you use models to estimate percent questions?

1 ACTIVITY: Estimating a Part

The statement "25% of 12 is 3" has three numbers. In real-life problems, any one of these can be unknown.

Question	Which number is missing?	Type of Question
What is 25% of 12?	_____	Find a part of a number.
3 is what percent of 12?	_____	Find a percent.
3 is 25% of what?	_____	Find the whole.

Work with a partner. Use a model to estimate the answer to each question.

a. What number is 50% of 30?

b. What number is 75% of 30?

c. What number is 40% of 30?

d. What number is 6% of 30?

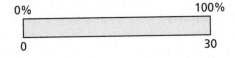

e. What number is 65% of 30?

6.3 **The Percent Proportion** (continued)

2 **ACTIVITY:** Estimating a Percent

Work with a partner. Use a model to estimate the answer to each question.

a. 15 is what percent of 75?

b. 5 is what percent of 20?

c. 18 is what percent of 40?

d. 50 is what percent of 80?

e. 75 is what percent of 50?

3 **ACTIVITY:** Estimating a Whole

Work with a partner. Use a model to estimate the answer to each question.

a. 24 is $33\frac{1}{3}\%$ of what number?

b. 13 is 25% of what number?

c. 110 is 20% of what number?

6.3 **The Percent Proportion** (continued)

d. 75 is 75% of what number?

0%   100%

e. 81 is 45% of what number?

0%   100%

4 **ACTIVITY:** Using Ratio Tables

Work with a partner. Use a ratio table to answer each question. Then compare your answer to the estimate you found using the model.

1d **a.** What number is 6% of 30?

Part	6	
Whole	100	30

1e **b.** What number is 65% of 30?

Part	65	
Whole	100	30

2c **c.** 18 is what percent of 40?

Part	18	
Whole	40	100

3e **d.** 81 is 45% of what number?

Part	45	81
Whole	100	

What Is Your Answer?

5. IN YOUR OWN WORDS How can you use models to estimate percent questions? Give examples to support your answer.

6. Complete the proportion below using the given labels.

percent	whole
100	part

$$\frac{\boxed{}}{\boxed{}} = \frac{\boxed{}}{\boxed{}}$$

Name_____ Date _____

Write and solve a proportion to answer the question.

1. 40% of 60 is what number?

2. 17 is what percent of 50?

3. 38% of what number is 57?

4. 44% of 25 is what number?

5. 52 is what percent of 50?

6. 150% of what number is 18?

7. You put 60% of your paycheck into your savings account. Your paycheck is $235. How much money do you put in your savings account?

Name_____ Date_____

6.4 The Percent Equation
For use with Activity 6.4

Essential Question How can you use an equivalent form of the percent proportion to solve a percent problem?

1 ACTIVITY: Solving Percent Problems Using Different Methods

Work with a partner. The circle graph shows the number of votes received by each candidate during a school election. So far, only half the students have voted.

Votes Received by Each Candidate

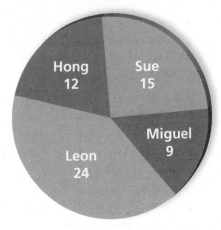

a. Complete the table.

b. Find the percent of students who voted for each candidate. Explain the method you used to find your answers.

Candidate	Number of votes received / Total number of votes
Sue	
Miguel	
Leon	
Hong	

c. Compare the method you used in part (b) with the methods used by other students in your class. Which method do you prefer? Explain.

6.4 **The Percent Equation** (continued)

2 **ACTIVITY:** Finding Parts Using Different Methods

Work with a partner. The circle graph shows the final results of the election.

a. Find the number of students who voted for each candidate. Explain the method you used to find your answers.

Final Results

b. Compare the method you used in part (a) with the methods used by other students in your class. Which method do you prefer? Explain.

3 **ACTIVITY:** Deriving the Percent Equation

Work with a partner. In Section 6.3, you used the percent proportion to find the missing percent, part, or whole. You can also use the _percent equation_ to find these missing values.

a. Complete the steps below to find the percent equation.

$$\frac{\text{part}}{\text{whole}} = \text{percent}$$ Definition of percent

$$\frac{\text{part}}{\text{whole}} \cdot \boxed{} = \boxed{} \cdot \boxed{}$$ Multiply each side by the $\boxed{}$.

$$\text{part} = \boxed{} \cdot \boxed{}$$ Divide out common factors. This is the percent equation.

b. You used two methods in Activity 2 to find the number of students who voted for each candidate. Do you prefer the percent proportion or the percent equation method?

6.4 The Percent Equation (continued)

4 ACTIVITY: Identifying Different Equations

Work with a partner. Without doing any calculations, choose the equation that you cannot use to answer each question.

a. What number is 55% of 80?

$$a = 0.55 \cdot 80$$

$$a = \frac{11}{20} \cdot 80$$

$$80a = 0.55$$

$$\frac{a}{80} = \frac{55}{100}$$

b. 24 is 60% of what number?

$$\frac{24}{w} = \frac{60}{100}$$

$$24 = 0.6 \cdot w$$

$$\frac{24}{60} = w$$

$$24 = \frac{3}{5} \cdot w$$

What Is Your Answer?

5. IN YOUR OWN WORDS How can you use an equivalent form of the percent proportion to solve a percent problem?

6. Write a percent proportion and a percent equation that you can use to answer the question below.

16 is what percent of 250?

Name _____ Date _____

Write and solve an equation to answer the question.

1. What number is 35% of 80?

2. 8 is what percent of 5?

3. What percent of 125 is 50?

4. 12% of what number is 48?

5. 12 is what percent of 50?

6. What percent of 12 is 3?

7. You receive 15% of the profit from a car wash. How much money do you receive from a profit of $300?

Percents of Increase and Decrease
For use with Activity 6.5

Essential Question What is a percent of decrease? What is a percent of increase?

---

1 **ACTIVITY:** Percent of Decrease

Work with a partner.

Each year in the Columbia River Basin, adult salmon swim upriver to streams to lay eggs and hatch their young.

To go up river, the adult salmon use fish ladders. But to go down the river, the young salmon must pass through several dams.

At one time, there were electric turbines at each of the eight dams on the main stem of the Columbia and Snake Rivers. About 88% of the young salmon passed through these turbines unharmed.

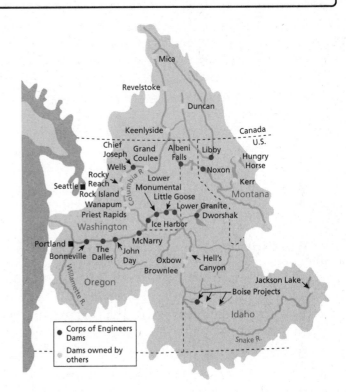

a. Complete the table to show the number of young salmon that made it through the dams.

Dam	0	1	2	3	4	5	6	7	8
Salmon	1000								

6.5 Percents of Increase and Decrease (continued)

b. Display the data in a bar graph.

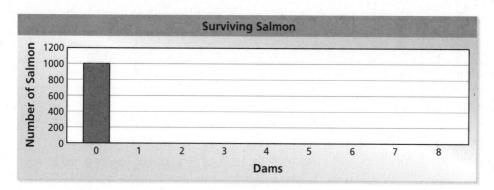

c. By what percent did the number of young salmon decrease when passing through each dam?

---

2 ACTIVITY: Percent of Increase

Work with a partner. In 2013, the population of a city was 18,000 people.

a. An organization projects that the population will increase by 2% each year for the next 7 years. Complete the table to find the populations of the city for 2014 through 2020. Then display the data in a bar graph.

For 2014: 2% of 18,000 = 0.02 • 18,000 = 360

$$18,000 + 360 = 18,360 \longleftarrow \boxed{\text{2014 Population}}$$

$$\boxed{\text{2013 Population}} \quad \boxed{\text{Increase}}$$

Year	Population
2013	18,000
2014	18,360
2015	
2016	
2017	
2018	
2019	
2020	

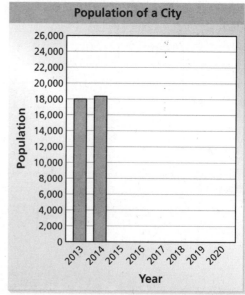

6.5 **Percents of Increase and Decrease** (continued)

b. Another organization projects that the population will increase by 3% each year for the next 7 years. Repeat part (a) using this percent.

Year	Population
2013	
2014	
2015	
2016	
2017	
2018	
2019	
2020	

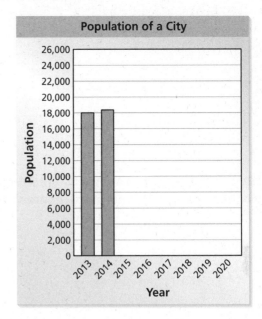

c. Which organization projects the larger populations? How many more people do they project for 2020?

What Is Your Answer?

3. IN YOUR OWN WORDS What is a percent of decrease? What is a percent of increase?

4. Describe real-life examples of a percent of decrease and a percent of increase.

6.5 Practice
For use after Lesson 6.5

Find the new amount.

1. 120 books increased by 55%

2. 80 members decreased by 65%

Identify the percent of change as an *increase* or *decrease*. Then find the percent of change. Round to the nearest tenth of a percent, if necessary.

3. 25 points to 50 points

4. 125 invitations to 75 invitations

5. 32 pages to 28 pages

6. 7 players to 10 players

7. One week, 72 people got a speeding ticket. The next week, only 36 people got a speeding ticket. What is the percent of change in speeding tickets?

6.6 Discounts and Markups
For use with Activity 6.6

Essential Question How can you find discounts and selling prices?

1 ACTIVITY: Comparing Discounts

Work with a partner. The same pair of sneakers is on sale at three stores.
Which one is the best buy? Explain.

a. Regular Price: $45   **b.** Regular Price: $49   **c.** Regular Price: $39

a.

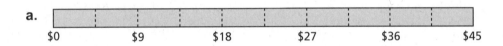

$0 $9 $18 $27 $36 $45

b.

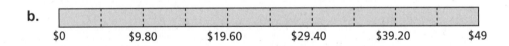

$0 $9.80 $19.60 $29.40 $39.20 $49

c.

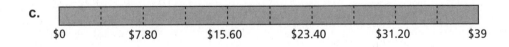

$0 $7.80 $15.60 $23.40 $31.20 $39

6.6 **Discounts and Markups** (continued)

2 **ACTIVITY:** Finding the Original Price

Work with a partner.

a. You buy a shirt that is on sale for 30% off. You pay $22.40. Your friend wants to know the original price of the shirt. Show how you can use the model to find the original price.

$0 $22.40   Original
                                                              Price

b. Explain how you can use the percent proportion to find the original price.

3 **ACTIVITY:** Finding Selling Prices

You own a small jewelry store. You increase the price of jewelry by 125%.

Work with a partner. Use a model to estimate the selling price of the jewelry. Then use a calculator to find the selling price.

a. Your cost is $250.

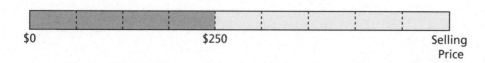

$0 $250   Selling
                                                 Price

6.6 **Discounts and Markups** (continued)

b. Your cost is $50.

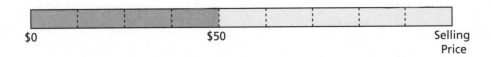

c. Your cost is $170.

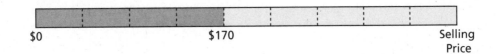

What Is Your Answer?

4. IN YOUR OWN WORDS How can you find discounts and selling prices?
Give examples of each.

6.6 Practice

For use after Lesson 6.6

Complete the table.

	Original Price	Percent of Discount	Sale Price
1.	$20	20%	
2.	$95	35%	
3.		75%	$55.50
4.		40%	$78

Find the selling price.

5. Cost to store: $20

   Markup: 15%

6. Cost to store: $56

   Markup: 80%

7. Cost to store: $110

   Markup: 140%

8. A store buys an item for $10. To earn a profit of $25, what percent does the store need to markup the item?

Name_____ Date _____

6.7 Simple Interest
For use with Activity 6.7

Essential Question How can you find the amount of simple interest earned on a savings account? How can you find the amount of interest owed on a loan?

Simple interest is money earned on a savings account or an investment. It can also be money you pay for borrowing money.

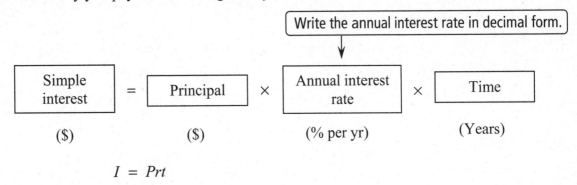

Write the annual interest rate in decimal form.

| Simple interest | = | Principal | × | Annual interest rate | × | Time |

($) ($) (% per yr) (Years)

$$I = Prt$$

---

1 ACTIVITY: Finding Simple Interest

Work with a partner. You put $100 in a savings account. The account earns 6% simple interest per year. (a) Find the interest earned and the balance at the end of 6 months. (b) Complete the table. Then make a bar graph that shows how the balance grows in 6 months.

a. $I = Prt$

b.

Time	Interest	Balance
0 month		
1 month		
2 months		
3 months		
4 months		
5 months		
6 months		

Account Balance

Balance (dollars): 103.50, 103.00, 102.50, 102.00, 101.50, 101.00, 100.50, 100.00, 99.50, 99.00, 98.50, 0

Months: 0 1 2 3 4 5 6

6.7 Simple Interest (continued)

2 ACTIVITY: Financial Literacy

Work with a partner. Use the following information to write a report about credit cards. In the report, describe how a credit card works. Include examples that show the amount of interest paid each month on a credit card.

U.S. Credit Card Data

- A typical household with credit card debt in the United States owes about $16,000 to credit card companies.

- A typical credit card interest rate is 14% to 16% per year. This is called the annual percentage rate.

3 ACTIVITY: The National Debt

Work with a partner. In 2012, the United States owed about $16 trillion in debt. The interest rate on the national debt is about 1% per year.

a. Write $16 trillion in decimal form. How many zeros does this number have?

6.7 Simple Interest (continued)

b. How much interest does the United States pay each year on its national debt?

c. How much interest does the United States pay each day on its national debt?

d. The United States has a population of about 314 million people. Estimate the amount of interest that each person pays per year toward interest on the national debt.

What Is Your Answer?

4. IN YOUR OWN WORDS How can you find the amount of simple interest earned on a savings account? How can you find the amount of interest owed on a loan? Give examples with your answer.

6.7 Practice
For use after Lesson 6.7

An account earns simple interest. (a) Find the interest earned. (b) Find the balance of the account.

1. $400 at 7% for 3 years

2. $1200 at 5.6% for 4 years

Find the annual interest rate.

3. $I = \$18$, $P = \$200$, $t = 18$ months

4. $I = \$310$, $P = \$1000$, $t = 5$ years

Find the amount of time.

5. $I = \$60$, $P = \$750$, $r = 4\%$

6. $I = \$825$, $P = \$2500$, $r = 5.5\%$

7. You put $500 in a savings account. The account earns $15.75 simple interest in 6 months. What is the annual interest rate?

Chapter 7 **Fair Game Review**

Use a protractor to find the measure of the angle. Then classify the angle as *acute*, *obtuse*, *right*, or *straight*.

1.

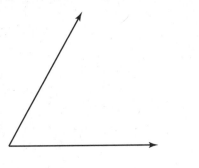

2.

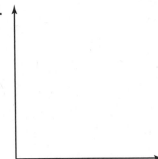

3.

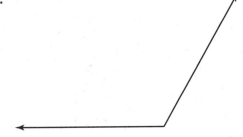

4.

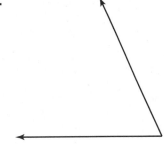

5.

6.

Chapter 7 **Fair Game Review** (continued)

Use a protractor to draw an angle with the given measure.

7. 80°

8. 35°

9. 100°

10. 175°

11. 57°

12. 122°

7.1 Adjacent and Vertical Angles
For use with Activity 7.1

Essential Question What can you conclude about the angles formed by two intersecting lines?

Classification of Angles

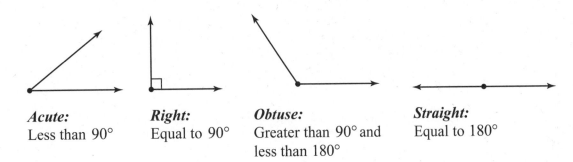

Acute:
Less than 90°

Right:
Equal to 90°

Obtuse:
Greater than 90° and less than 180°

Straight:
Equal to 180°

---

1 **ACTIVITY:** Drawing Angles

Work with a partner.

    a. Draw the hands of the clock to represent the given type of angle.

        Acute   Straight   Right   Obtuse

    b. What is the measure of the angle formed by the hands of the clock at the given time?

        9:00   6:00   12:00

7.1 Adjacent and Vertical Angles (continued)

2 ACTIVITY: Naming Angles

Work with a partner. Some angles, such as $\angle A$, **can be named by a single
letter. When this does not clearly identify an angle, you should use three
letters, as shown.**

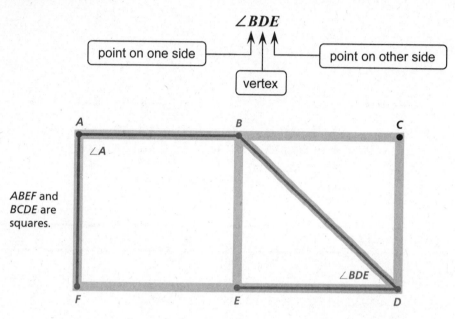

a. Name all of the right angles, acute angles, and obtuse angles.

b. Which pairs of angles do you think are *adjacent*? Explain.

Name_____ Date_____

3 ACTIVITY: Measuring Angles

Work with a partner.

a. How many angles are formed by the
   intersecting roads? Number the angles.

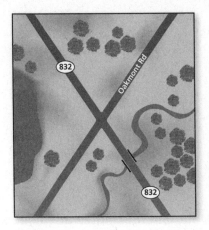

b. **CHOOSE TOOLS** Measure each angle
   formed by the intersecting roads. What
   do you notice?

What Is Your Answer?

4. **IN YOUR OWN WORDS** What can you conclude about the angles formed
   by two intersecting lines?

5. Draw two acute angles that are adjacent.

Name_____ Date _____

7.1 Practice
For use after Lesson 7.1

Name two pairs of adjacent angles and two pairs of vertical angles in the figure.

1.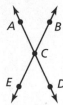

2.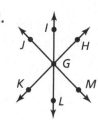

Tell whether the angles are *adjacent* or *vertical*. Then find the value of x.

3.

4.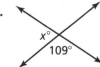

5. $(x + 42)°$ $(2x + 1)°$

6. $(x + 96)°$ $5x°$

7. A tree is leaning toward the ground. How many degrees does the tree have to fall before hitting the ground?

7.2 Complementary and Supplementary Angles
For use with Activity 7.2

Essential Question How can you classify two angles as complementary or supplementary?

1 ACTIVITY: Complementary and Supplementary Angles

Work with a partner.

a. The graph represents the measures of *complementary angles*. Use the graph to complete the table.

x		20°		30°	45°		75°	
y	80°		65°	60°		40°		

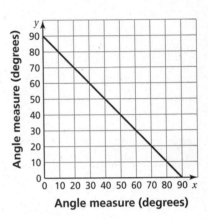

Angle measure (degrees)

b. How do you know when two angles are complementary? Explain.

c. The graph represents the measures of *supplementary angles*. Use the graph to complete the table.

x	20°		60°	90°		140°	
y		150°		90°	50°		30°

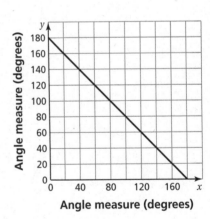

Angle measure (degrees)

d. How do you know when two angles are supplementary? Explain.

7.2 **Complementary and Supplementary Angles** (continued)

2 **ACTIVITY:** Exploring Rules About Angles

Work with a partner. Complete each sentence with *always*, *sometimes*, or *never*.

a. If *x* and *y* are complementary angles, then both *x* and *y* are _____ acute.

b. If *x* and *y* are supplementary angles, then *x* is _____ acute.

c. If *x* is a right angle, then *x* is _____ acute.

d. If *x* and *y* are complementary angles, then *x* and *y* are _____ adjacent.

e. If *x* and *y* are supplementary angles, then *x* and *y* are _____ vertical.

3 **ACTIVITY:** Classifying Pairs of Angles

Work with a partner. Tell whether the two angles shown on the clocks are *complementary*, *supplementary*, or *neither*. Explain your reasoning.

a.

b.

c.

d.

7.2 Complementary and Supplementary Angles (continued)

4 **ACTIVITY:** Identifying Angles

Work with a partner. Use a protractor and the figure shown.

a. Name four pairs of complementary angles
and four pairs of supplementary angles.

b. Name two pairs of vertical angles.

What Is Your Answer?

5. **IN YOUR OWN WORDS** How can you classify two angles as
complementary or supplementary? Give examples of each type.

Big Ideas Math Red Accelerated **149**
Record and Practice Journal

7.2 Practice
For use after Lesson 7.2

Tell whether the angles are *complementary*, *supplementary*, or *neither*.

1.
43°
47°

2.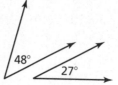
48°
27°

3.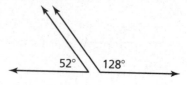
52° 128°

Tell whether the angles are *complementary* or *supplementary*. Then find the value of *x*.

4.
10$x°$
30°

5.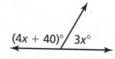
$(4x + 40)°$ 3$x°$

6. Find the value of x needed to hit the ball in the hole.

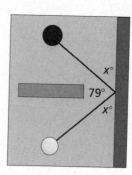
$x°$
79°
$x°$

Name_____ Date _____

7.3 Triangles
For use with Activity 7.3

Essential Question How can you construct triangles?

---

1 ACTIVITY: Constructing Triangles Using Side Lengths

Work with a partner. Cut different-colored straws to the lengths shown.
Then construct a triangle with the specified straws, if possible. Compare
your results with those of others in your class.

red   2 cm

blue   4 cm

green   6 cm

purple   7 cm

a. blue, green, purple   **b.** red, green, purple

c. red, blue, purple   **d.** red, blue, green

---

2 ACTIVITY: Using Technology to Draw Triangles (Side Lengths)

Work with a partner. Use geometry software
to draw a triangle with the two given side
lengths. What is the length of the third side
of your triangle? Compare your results with
those of others in your class.

   a. 4 units, 7 units

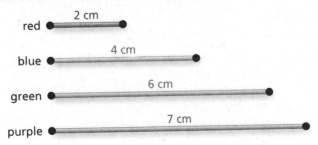

Begin by drawing the
side length of 4 units.

Then draw the side
length of 7 units.

7.3 Triangles (continued)

    b. 3 units, 5 units   **c.** 2 units, 8 units   **d.** 1 unit, 1 unit

3   **ACTIVITY:** Constructing Triangles Using Angle Measures

Work with a partner. Two angle measures of a triangle are given. Draw the triangle. What is the measure of the third angle? Compare your results with those of others in your class.

    a. 40°, 70°

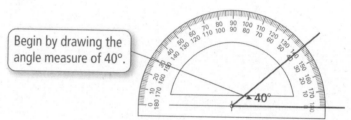

Begin by drawing the angle measure of 40°.

40°

    b. 60°, 75°   **c.** 90°, 30°   **d.** 100°, 40°

7.3 **Triangles** (continued)

4 **ACTIVITY:** Using Technology to Draw Triangles (Angle Measures)

Work with a partner. Use geometry software to draw a triangle with the two given angle measures. What is the measure of the third angle? Compare your results with those of others in your class.

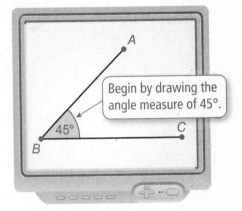

a. 45°, 55°

b. 50°, 40°

c. 110°, 35°

What Is Your Answer?

5. **IN YOUR OWN WORDS** How can you construct triangles?

6. **REASONING** Complete the table below for each set of side lengths in Activity 2. Write a rule that compares the sum of any two side lengths to the third side length.

Side Length			
Sum of Other Two Side Lengths			

7. **REASONING** Use a table to organize the angle measures of each triangle you formed in Activity 3. Include the sum of the angle measures. Then describe the pattern in the table and write a conclusion based on the pattern.

	∠1	∠2	∠3	∠1 + ∠2 + ∠3
a.				
b.				
c.				
d.				

Name_____ Date _____

Classify the triangle.

1.

2.

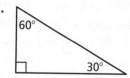

3.

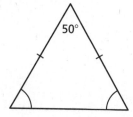

4.

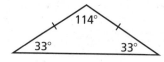

Draw a triangle with the given angle measures.

5. $28°, 42°, 110°$

6. $67°, 98°, 15°$

7. $31°, 59°, 90°$

8. What type of triangle must the hanger be to hang clothes evenly?

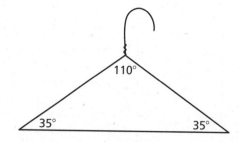

Extension 7.3 **Practice**
For use after Extension 7.3

Find the value of x. Then classify the triangle.

1.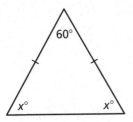

2.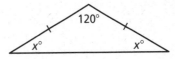

3.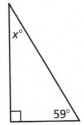

4.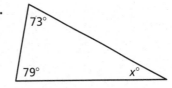

5. Find the value of x.

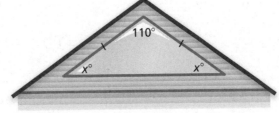

Extension 7.3 **Practice** (continued)

Tell whether a triangle can have the given angle measures. If not, change the first angle measure so that the angle measures form a triangle.

6. 25°, 64°, 91°

7. 55.5°, 94°, 31.5°

8. 85°, 64°, 30°

9. 33°, 140°, 12°

10. 99°, 53°, 28°

11. 79°, 54°, 47°

7.4 Quadrilaterals
For use with Activity 7.4

Essential Question How can you classify quadrilaterals?

Quad means *four* and *lateral* means *side*. So, quadrilateral means a polygon with *four sides*.

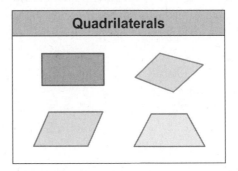

1 ACTIVITY: Using Descriptions to Form Quadrilaterals

Work with a partner. Use a geoboard to form a quadrilateral that fits the given description. Record your results on geoboard dot paper.

a. Form a quadrilateral with exactly one pair of parallel sides.

b. Form a quadrilateral with four congruent sides and four right angles.

c. Form a quadrilateral with four right angles that is *not* a square.

d. Form a quadrilateral with four congruent sides that is *not* a square.

e. Form a quadrilateral with two pairs of congruent adjacent sides and whose opposite sides are *not* congruent.

f. Form a quadrilateral with congruent and parallel opposite sides that is *not* a rectangle.

7.4 **Quadrilaterals** (continued)

---

2 **ACTIVITY:** Naming Quadrilaterals

Work with a partner. Match the names *square, rectangle, rhombus,*
parallelogram, trapezoid, **and** *kite* **with your 6 drawings in Activity 1.**

---

3 **ACTIVITY:** Forming Quadrilaterals

Work with a partner. Form each quadrilateral on your geoboard. Then
move *only one* **vertex to create the new type of quadrilateral. Record your**
results below.

a. Trapezoid Kite

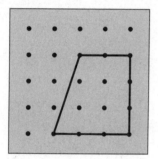 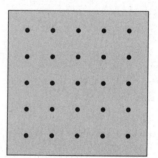

b. Kite Rhombus (*not* a square)

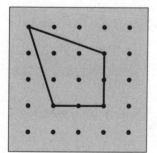 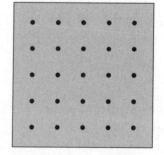

7.4 Quadrilaterals (continued)

---

4 **ACTIVITY:** Using Technology to Draw Quadrilaterals

Work with a partner. Use geometry software to draw a quadrilateral that fits the given description.

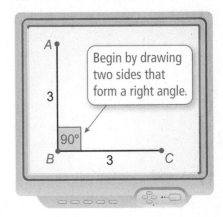

a. a square with a side length of 3 units

b. a rectangle with a width of 2 units and a length of 5 units

c. a parallelogram with side lengths of 6 units and 1 unit

d. a rhombus with a side length of 4 units

What Is Your Answer?

5. **REASONING** Measure the angles of each quadrilateral you formed in Activity 1. Record your results in a table. Include the sum of the angle measures. Then describe the pattern in the table and write a conclusion based on the pattern.

	∠1	∠2	∠3	∠4	∠1 + ∠2 + ∠3 + ∠4
a.					
b.					
c.					
d.					
e.					
f.					

6. **IN YOUR OWN WORDS** How can you classify quadrilaterals? Explain using properties of sides and angles.

7.4 **Practice**
For use after Lesson 7.4

Classify the quadrilateral.

1.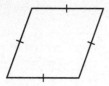

2.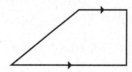

3.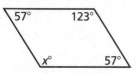

4.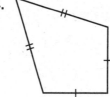

Find the value of x.

5.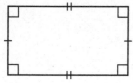

57°   123°

x°   57°

6.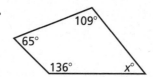

109°

65°

136°   x°

7. For a science fair, you are displaying your project on a trapezoidal piece of poster board. What is the measure of the missing angle?

132°

48°   48°

7.5 Scale Drawings
For use with Activity 7.5

Essential Question How can you enlarge or reduce a drawing proportionally?

> **1 ACTIVITY:** Comparing Measurements

Work with a partner. The diagram shows a food court at a shopping mall. Each centimeter in the diagram represents 40 meters.

a. Find the length and the width of the drawing of the food court.

length: _____ cm   width: _____ cm

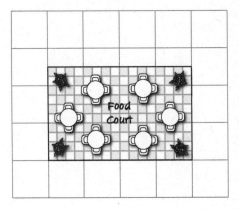

b. Find the actual length and width of the food court. Explain how you found your answers.

length: _____ m   width: _____ m

c. Find the ratios $\dfrac{\text{drawing length}}{\text{actual length}}$ and $\dfrac{\text{drawing width}}{\text{actual width}}$. What do you notice?

Name _____ Date _____

2 **ACTIVITY:** Recreating a Drawing

Work with a partner. Draw the food court in Activity 1 on the grid paper so that each centimeter represents 20 meters.

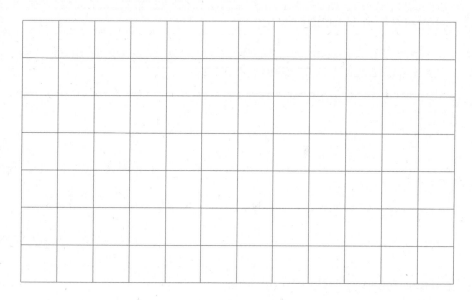

a. What happens to the size of the drawing?

b. Find the length and the width of your drawing. Compare these dimensions to the dimensions of the original drawing in Activity 1.

3 **ACTIVITY:** Comparing Measurements

Work with a partner. The diagram shows a sketch of a painting. Each unit in the sketch represents 8 inches.

a. Find the length and the width of the sketch.

length: _____ units   width: _____ units

b. Find the actual length and width of the painting. Explain how you found your answers.

length: _____ in.   width: _____ in.

7.5 **Scale Drawings** (continued)

c. Find the ratios $\dfrac{\text{sketch length}}{\text{actual length}}$ and $\dfrac{\text{sketch width}}{\text{actual width}}$. What do you notice?

4 **ACTIVITY:** Recreating a Drawing

Work with a partner. Let each unit in the grid paper represent 2 feet. Now sketch the painting in Activity 3 onto the grid paper.

a. What happens to the size of the sketch?

b. Find the length and the width of your sketch. Compare these dimensions to the dimensions of the original sketch in Activity 3.

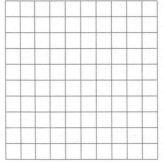

What Is Your Answer?

5. IN YOUR OWN WORDS How can you enlarge or reduce a drawing proportionally?

6. Complete the table for both the food court and the painting.

	Actual Object	Original Drawing	Your Drawing
Perimeter			
Area			

Compare the measurements in each table. What conclusions can you make?

7. RESEARCH Look at some maps in your school library or on the Internet. Make a list of the different scales used on the maps.

8. When you view a map on the Internet, how does the scale change when you zoom out? How does the scale change when you zoom in?

7.5 Practice
For use after Lesson 7.5

Find the missing dimension. Use the scale factor 1 : 8.

Item	Model	Actual
1. Statue	Height: 168 in.	Height _____ ft
2. Painting	Width: _____ cm	Width: 200 m
3. Alligator	Height: _____ in.	Height: 6.4 ft
4. Train	Length: 36.5 in.	Length: _____ ft

5. The diameter of the moon is 2160 miles. A model has a scale of 1 in. : 150 mi. What is the diameter of the model?

6. A map has a scale of 1 in. : 4 mi.

 a. You measure 3 inches between your house and the movie theater. How many miles is it from your house to the movie theater?

 b. It is 17 miles to the mall. How many inches is that on the map?

Name_____ Date_____

Identify the basic shapes in the figure.

1.

2.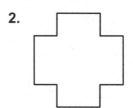

3.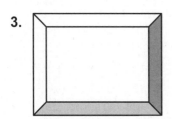

4.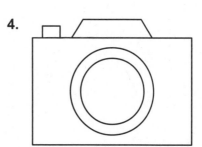

5. Identify the basic shapes that make up the top of your teacher's desk.

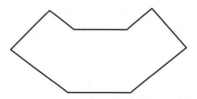

Chapter 8   Fair Game Review (continued)

Evaluate the expression.

6. 7^2 **7.** 11^2 **8.** $4(5)^2$

9. $7 \bullet 10^2$ **10.** $4(4 + 2)^2$ **11.** $5(6 + 3)^2$

12. $6(8 + 3)^2 + 2 \bullet 9$ **13.** $4(12)^2 - (6 + 4)$

14. A kilometer is 10^3 meters. You run a 5-kilometer race. How many meters do you run?

Name_____ Date _____

8.1 **Circles and Circumference**
For use with Activity 8.1

Essential Question How can you find the circumference of a circle?

Archimedes was a Greek mathematician, physicist, engineer, and astronomer.

Archimedes discovered that in any circle the ratio of circumference to diameter is always the same. Archimedes called this ratio pi, or π (a letter from the Greek alphabet).

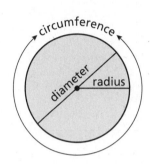

$$\pi = \frac{\text{circumference}}{\text{diameter}}$$

In Activities 1 and 2, you will use the same strategy Archimedes used to approximate π.

1 ACTIVITY: Approximating Pi

Work with a partner. Record your results in the first row of the table on the next page.

- Measure the perimeter of the large square in millimeters.

- Measure the diameter of the circle in millimeters.

- Measure the perimeter of the small square in millimeters.

- Calculate the ratios of the two perimeters to the diameter.

- The average of these two ratios is an approximation of π.

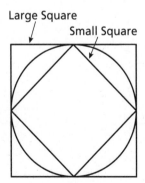

8.1   **Circles and Circumference** (continued)

Sides	Large Perimeter	Diameter of Circle	Small Perimeter	Large Perimeter / Diameter	Small Perimeter / Diameter	Average of Ratios
4						
6						
8						
10						

2   **ACTIVITY:** Approximating Pi

Continue your approximation of pi. Complete the table above using a hexagon (6 sides), an octagon (8 sides), and a decagon (10 sides).

a. Large Hexagon

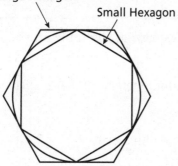

Small Hexagon

b. Large Octagon

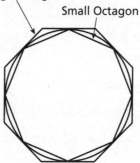

Small Octagon

c. Large Decagon

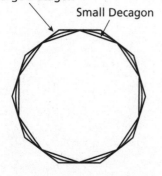

Small Decagon

8.1 Circles and Circumference (continued)

d. From the table, what can you conclude about the value of π? Explain your reasoning.

e. Archimedes calculated the value of π using polygons with 96 sides. Do you think his calculations were more or less accurate than yours?

What Is Your Answer?

3. IN YOUR OWN WORDS Now that you know an approximation for pi, explain how you can use it to find the circumference of a circle. Write a formula for the circumference C of a circle whose diameter is d.

4. CONSTRUCTION Use a compass to draw three circles. Use your formula from Question 3 to find the circumference of each circle.

Name _____ Date _____

8.1 Practice
For use after Lesson 8.1

1. Find the diameter of the circle.

9 in.

2. Find the radius of the circle.

12 in.

Find the circumference of the circle. Use 3.14 or $\frac{22}{7}$ for π.

3.

20 cm

4.

14 in.

5.

8 ft

Find the perimeter of the semicircular region.

6.

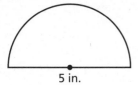

5 in.

7.

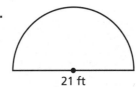

21 ft

8. A simple impact crater on the moon has a diameter of 15 kilometers. A complex impact crater has a radius of 30 kilometers. How much greater is the circumference of the complex impact crater than the simple impact crater?

Name_____ Date _____

Essential Question How can you find the perimeter of a composite figure?

1 ACTIVITY: Finding a Pattern

Work with a partner. Describe the pattern of the perimeters. Use your pattern to find the perimeter of the tenth figure in the sequence. (Each small square has a perimeter of 4.)

a.

b.

c.

Name _____ Date _____

2 **ACTIVITY:** Combining Figures

Work with a partner.

a. A rancher is constructing a rectangular corral and a trapezoidal corral, as shown. How much fencing does the rancher need to construct both corrals?

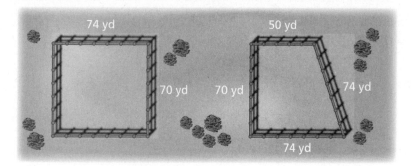

b. Another rancher is constructing one corral by combining the two corrals above, as shown. Does this rancher need more or less fencing? Explain your reasoning.

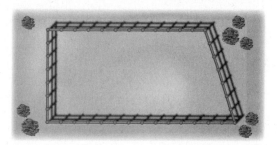

c. How can the rancher in part (b) combine the two corrals to use even less fencing?

3 **ACTIVITY:** Submitting a Bid

Work with a partner. You want to bid on a tiling contract. You will be supplying and installing the tile that borders the swimming pool shown on the next page. In the figure, each grid square represents 1 square foot.

- **Your cost for the tile is $4 per linear foot.**

- **It takes about 15 minutes to prepare, install, and clean each foot of tile.**

a. How many tiles do you need for the border?

8.2 **Perimeters of Composite Figures** (continued)

b. Write a bid for how much you will charge to supply and install the tile. Include what you want to charge as an hourly wage. Estimate what you think your profit will be.

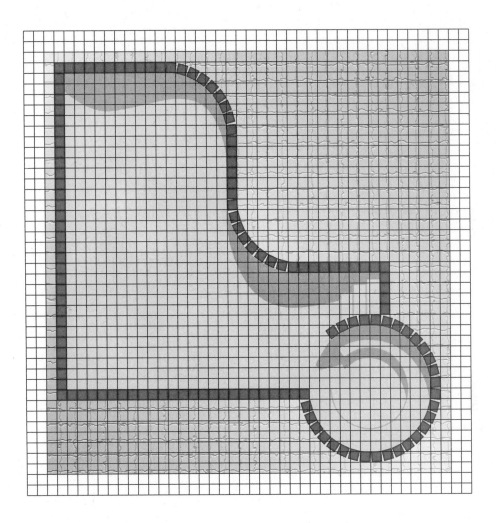

What Is Your Answer?

4. **IN YOUR OWN WORDS** How can you find the perimeter of a composite figure? Use a semicircle, a triangle, and a parallelogram to draw a composite figure. Label the dimensions. Find the perimeter of the figure.

8.2 Practice
For use after Lesson 8.2

Estimate the perimeter of the figure.

1.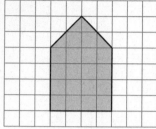

2.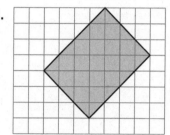

Find the perimeter of the figure.

3.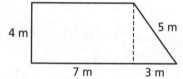

4 m   5 m
7 m   3 m

4.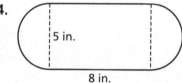

5 in.
8 in.

5. You are having a swimming pool installed.

   a. Find the perimeter of the swimming pool.

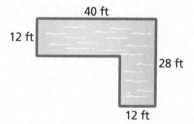

40 ft
12 ft
28 ft
12 ft

   b. Tiling costs $15 per yard. How much will it cost to put tiles along the edge of the pool?

8.3 Areas of Circles
For use with Activity 8.3

Essential Question How can you find the area of a circle?

> **1 ACTIVITY:** Estimating the Area of a Circle

Work with a partner. Each square in the grid is 1 unit by 1 unit.

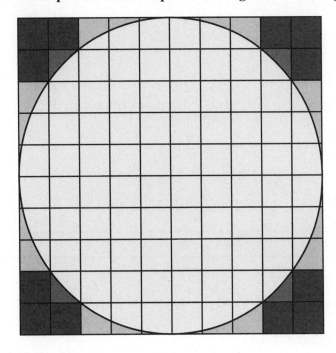

a. Find the area of the large 10-by-10 square.

b. Complete the table.

Region			
Area (square units)			

c. Use your results to estimate the area of the circle. Explain your reasoning.

8.3 **Areas of Circles** (continued)

d. Fill in the blanks. Explain your reasoning.

Area of large square = _____ • 5^2 square units

Area of circle ≈ _____ • 5^2 square units

e. What dimension of the circle does 5 represent? What can you conclude?

2 **ACTIVITY:** Approximating the Area of a Circle

Work with a partner.

a. Draw a circle. Label the radius as r.*

b. Divide the circle into 24 equal sections.

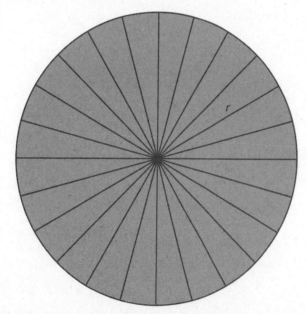

*Cut-outs are available in the back of the Record and Practice Journal.

8.3 Areas of Circles (continued)

c. Cut the sections apart. Then arrange them to approximate a parallelogram.

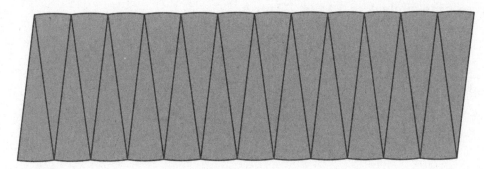

d. What is the approximate height and base of the parallelogram?

e. Find the area of the parallelogram. What can you conclude?

What Is Your Answer?

3. IN YOUR OWN WORDS How can you find the area of a circle?

4. Write a formula for the area of a circle with radius r. Find an object that is circular. Use your formula to find the area.

Name_____ Date _____

Find the area of the circle. Use 3.14 or $\frac{22}{7}$ for π.

1.

6 cm

2.

28 in.

Find the area of the semicircle.

3.
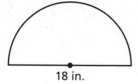
18 in.

4.
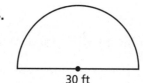
30 ft

5. An FM radio station signal travels in a 40-mile radius. An AM radio station signal travels in a 4-mile radius. How much more area does the FM station cover than the AM station?

8.4 Areas of Composite Figures
For use with Activity 8.4

Essential Question How can you find the area of a composite figure?

---

1 ACTIVITY: Estimating Area

Work with a partner.

a. Choose a state. On grid paper, draw a larger outline of the state.

b. Use your drawing to estimate the area (in square miles) of the state.

c. Which state areas are easy to find? Which are difficult? Why?

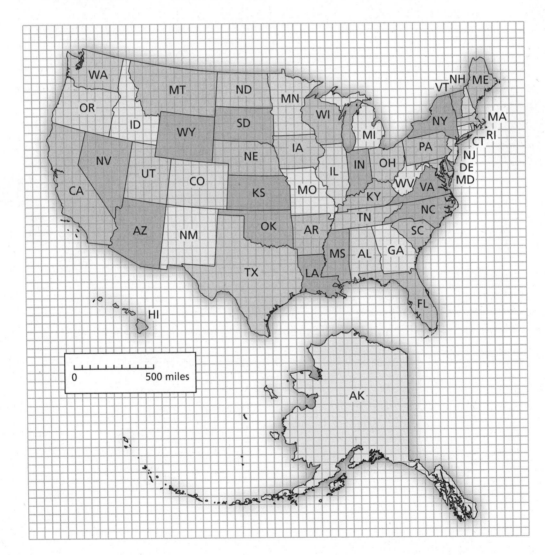

8.4 **Areas of Composite Figures** (continued)

2 **ACTIVITY:** Estimating Areas

Work with a partner. The completed puzzle has an area of 150 square centimeters.*

    a. Estimate the area of each puzzle piece.

    b. Check your work by adding the six areas. Why is this a check?

3 **ACTIVITY:** Filling a Square with Circles

Work with a partner. Which pattern fills more of the square with circles? Explain.

    a.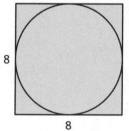

    b.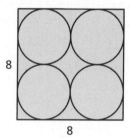

*Cut-outs are available in the back of the Record and Practice Journal.

8.4 **Areas of Composite Figures** (continued)

c.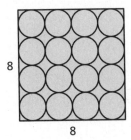

8
8

d.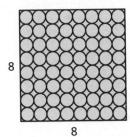

8
8

What Is Your Answer?

4. **IN YOUR OWN WORDS** How can you find the area of a composite figure?

5. Summarize the area formulas for all the basic figures you have studied. Draw a single composite figure that has each type of basic figure. Label the dimensions and find the total area.

Name _____ Date _____

Find the area of the figure.

1.

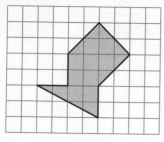

2.

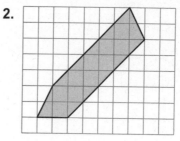

Find the area of the figure.

3.

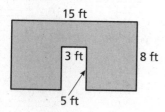

15 ft

3 ft   8 ft

5 ft

4.

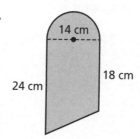

14 cm

24 cm   18 cm

5. The diagram shows the shape of the green of a miniature golf hole. What is the area of the green?

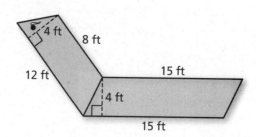

4 ft   8 ft

12 ft

15 ft

4 ft

15 ft

Name_____ Date _____

Find the area of the square or rectangle.

1.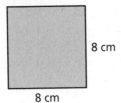

8 cm

8 cm

2.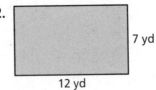

7 yd

12 yd

3.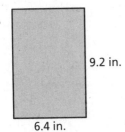

9.2 in.

6.4 in.

4.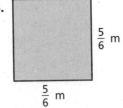

$\frac{5}{6}$ m

$\frac{5}{6}$ m

5.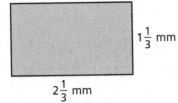

$1\frac{1}{3}$ mm

$2\frac{1}{3}$ mm

6.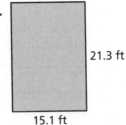

21.3 ft

15.1 ft

7. An artist buys a square canvas with a side length of 2.5 feet. What is the area of the canvas?

Chapter 9 **Fair Game Review** (continued)

Find the area of the triangle.

8.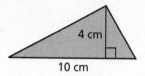
4 cm
10 cm

9.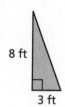
8 ft
3 ft

10.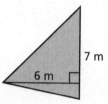
7 m
6 m

11.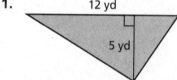
12 yd
5 yd

12.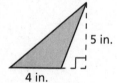
5 in.
4 in.

13.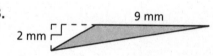
9 mm
2 mm

14. A spirit banner for a pep rally has the shape of a triangle. The base of the banner is 8 feet and the height is 6 feet. Find the area of the banner.

9.1 Surface Areas of Prisms
For use with Activity 9.1

Essential Question How can you find the surface area of a prism?

---

1 ACTIVITY: Surface Area of a Rectangular Prism

Work with a partner. Use the net for a rectangular prism. Label each side as
h, *w*, or *ℓ*. **Then write a formula for the surface area of a rectangular prism.**

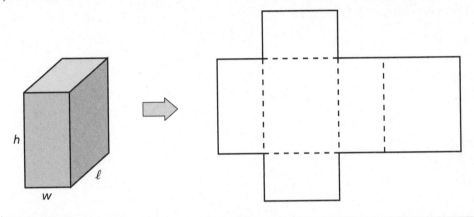

---

2 ACTIVITY: Surface Area of a Triangular Prism

Work with a partner.

a. Find the surface area of the solid shown by the net. Use a cut-out of the net.* Fold it to form a solid. Identify the solid.

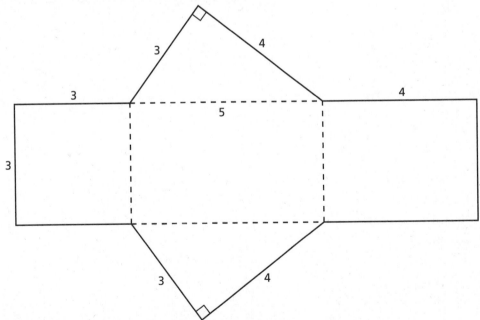

b. Which of the surfaces of the solid are bases? Why?

*Cut-outs are available in the back of the Record and Practice Journal.

Name _____ Date _____

3 **ACTIVITY:** Forming Rectangular Prisms

Work with a partner.

- Use **24 one-inch cubes** to form a rectangular prism that has the given dimensions.

- Draw each prism.

- Find the surface area of each prism.

   a. $4 \times 3 \times 2$ **b.** $1 \times 1 \times 24$

   c. $1 \times 2 \times 12$ **d.** $1 \times 3 \times 8$

   e. $1 \times 4 \times 6$ **f.** $2 \times 2 \times 6$

   g. $2 \times 4 \times 3$

9.1 Surface Areas of Prisms (continued)

What Is Your Answer?

4. Use your formula from Activity 1 to verify your results in Activity 3.

5. IN YOUR OWN WORDS How can you find the surface area of a prism?

6. REASONING When comparing ice blocks with the same volume, the ice with the greater surface area will melt faster. Which will melt faster, the bigger block or the three smaller blocks? Explain your reasoning.

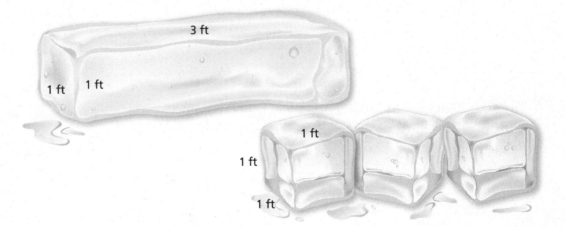

Big Ideas Math Red Accelerated   **187**
Record and Practice Journal

Name_____ Date _____

Find the surface area of the prism.

1.

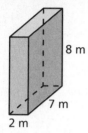

8 m
7 m
2 m

2.

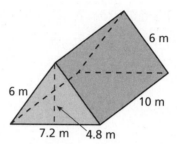

6 m
6 m
10 m
7.2 m   4.8 m

3.

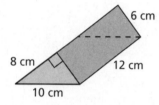

6 cm
8 cm   12 cm
10 cm

4.

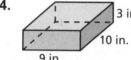

3 in.
10 in.
9 in.

5. You buy a ring box as a birthday gift that is in the shape of a triangular prism. What is the least amount of wrapping paper needed to wrap the box?

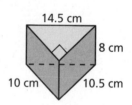

14.5 cm
8 cm
10 cm   10.5 cm

Name_____ Date_____

Essential Question How can you find the surface area of a pyramid?

Even though many well-known pyramids have square bases, the base of a pyramid can be any polygon.

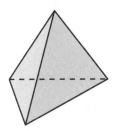

Triangular Base

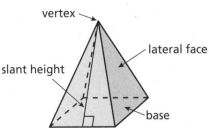
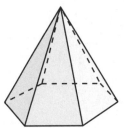

vertex
lateral face
slant height
base

Square Base

Hexagonal Base

1 **ACTIVITY:** Making a Scale Model

Work with a partner. Each pyramid has a square base.

- **Draw a net for a scale model of one of the pyramids. Describe your scale.**

- **Cut out the net and fold it to form a pyramid.**

- **Find the lateral surface area of the real-life pyramid.**

a. Cheops Pyramid in Egypt
Side = 230 m, Slant height ≈ 186 m

b. Muttart Conservatory in Edmonton
Side = 26 m, Slant height ≈ 27 m

c. Louvre Pyramid in Paris
Side = 35 m, Slant height ≈ 28 m

d. Pyramid of Caius Cestius in Rome
Side = 22 m, Slant height ≈ 29 m

9.2 **Surface Areas of Pyramids** (continued)

2 **ACTIVITY:** Estimation

Work with a partner. There are many different types of gemstone cuts. Here is one called a brilliant cut.

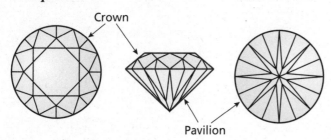

Top View   *Side View*   *Bottom View*

Crown

Pavilion

The size and shape of the pavilion can be approximated by an octagonal pyramid.

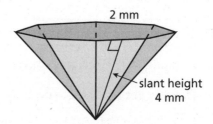

2 mm

slant height
4 mm

a. What does *octagonal* mean?

b. Draw a net for the pyramid.

c. Find the lateral surface area of the pyramid.

9.2 Surface Areas of Pyramids (continued)

3 **ACTIVITY:** Comparing Surface Areas

**Work with a partner. Both pyramids have the same
side lengths of the base and the same slant heights.**

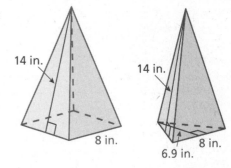

a. **REASONING** Without calculating, which
pyramid has the greater surface area? Explain.

b. Verify your answer to part (a) by finding
the surface area of each pyramid.

What Is Your Answer?

4. **IN YOUR OWN WORDS** How can you find the surface area of a pyramid?
Draw a diagram with your explanation.

9.2 Practice
For use after Lesson 9.2

Find the surface area of the regular pyramid.

1.

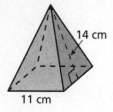

14 cm

11 cm

2.

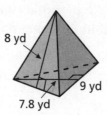

8 yd

9 yd

7.8 yd

3.

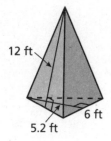

12 ft

6 ft

5.2 ft

4.

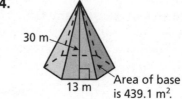

30 m

13 m

Area of base is 439.1 m².

5. The surface area of a triangular pyramid is 305 square inches. The area of the base is 35 square inches. Each face has a base of 9 inches. What is the slant height?

Name_____ Date _____

Essential Question How can you find the surface area of a cylinder?

A *cylinder* is a solid that has two parallel, identical circular bases.

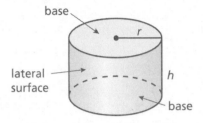

---

1 ACTIVITY: Finding Area

Work with a partner. Use a cardboard cylinder.

- **Talk about how you can find the area of the outside of the roll.**

- **Estimate the area using the methods you discussed.**

- **Use the roll and the scissors to find the actual area of the cardboard.**

- **Compare the actual area to your estimates.**

---

2 ACTIVITY: Finding Surface Area

Work with a partner.

- **Make a net for the can. Name the shapes in the net.**

9.3 **Surface Areas of Cylinders** (continued)

- **Find the surface area of the can**

- **How are the dimensions of the rectangle related to the dimensions of the can?**

3 **ACTIVITY:** Estimation

Work with a partner. From memory, estimate the dimensions of the real-life item in inches. Then use the dimensions to estimate the surface area of the item in square inches.

a.

b.

9.3 Surface Areas of Cylinders (continued)

c.

d.

What Is Your Answer?

4. **IN YOUR OWN WORDS** How can you find the surface area of a cylinder?
   Give an example with your description. Include a drawing of the cylinder.

5. To eight decimal places, $\pi \approx 3.14159265$. Which of the following is
   closest to π?

   a. 3.14   **b.** $\dfrac{22}{7}$ **c.** $\dfrac{355}{113}$

"To approximate $\pi \approx 3.141593$,
I simply remember 1, 1, 3, 3, 5, 5."

"Then I compute $\frac{355}{113} \approx 3.141593$."

Name _____ Date _____

Find the surface area of the cylinder. Round your answer to the nearest tenth.

1.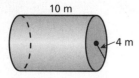
10 m
4 m

2.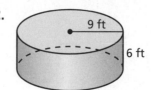
9 ft
6 ft

Find the lateral surface area of the cylinder. Round your answer to the nearest tenth.

3.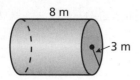
8 m
3 m

4.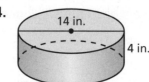
14 in.
4 in.

5. How much paper is used in the label for the can of cat food? Round your answer to the nearest whole number.

30 mm
24 mm

Name_____ Date_____

9.4 Volumes of Prisms
For use with Activity 9.4

Essential Question How can you find the volume of a prism?

---

1 **ACTIVITY:** Pearls in a Treasure Chest

Work with a partner. A treasure chest is filled with
valuable pearls. Each pearl is about 1 centimeter in
diameter and is worth about $80.

Use the diagrams below to describe two ways that
you can estimate the number of pearls in the
treasure chest.

a.
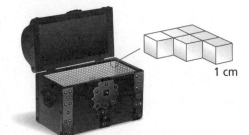
1 cm

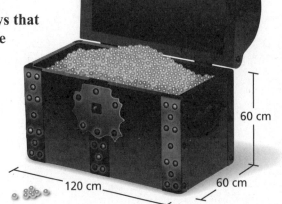
60 cm
120 cm
60 cm

b.

c. Use the method in part (a) to estimate the value of the pearls in the chest.

9.4 Volumes of Prisms (continued)

2 ACTIVITY: Finding a Formula for Volume

Work with a partner. You know that the formula for the volume of a rectangular prism is $V = \ell wh$.

a. Write a formula that gives the volume in terms of the area of the base B and the height h.

b. Use both formulas to find the volume of each prism. Do both formulas give you the same volume?

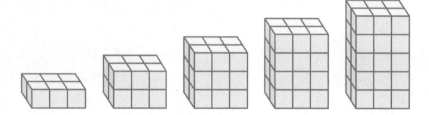

3 ACTIVITY: Finding a Formula for Volume

Work with a partner. Use the concept in Activity 2 to find a formula that gives the volume of any prism.

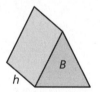

Triangular Prism

Rectangular Prism

Pentagonal Prism

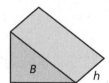

Triangular Prism

Hexagonal Prism

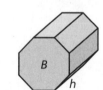

Octagonal Prism

Name_____ Date_____

4 **ACTIVITY:** Using a Formula

Work with a partner. A ream of paper has 500 sheets.

   a. Does a single sheet of paper have a volume? Why or why not?

   b. If so, explain how you can find the volume of a single piece of paper.

What Is Your Answer?

   5. IN YOUR OWN WORDS How can you find the volume of a prism?

   6. STRUCTURE Draw a prism that has a trapezoid as its base. Use your formula to find the volume of the prism.

9.4 Practice

For use after Lesson 9.4

Find the volume of the prism.

1.

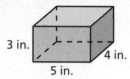

3 in.
4 in.
5 in.

2.

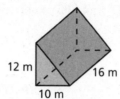

12 m
16 m
10 m

3.

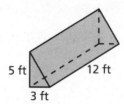

5 ft
12 ft
3 ft

4.

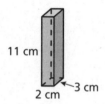

11 cm
3 cm
2 cm

5. $B = 60$ ft^2

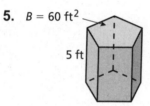

5 ft

6. $B = 80$ m^2

11 m

7. Each box is shaped like a rectangular prism.
Which has more storage space? Explain.

Box 1

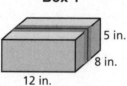

5 in.
8 in.
12 in.

Box 2

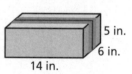

5 in.
6 in.
14 in.

9.5 Volumes of Pyramids
For use with Activity 9.5

Essential Question How can you find the volume of a pyramid?

---

1 ACTIVITY: Finding a Formula Experimentally

Work with a partner.

- **Draw the two nets on cardboard and cut them out.***

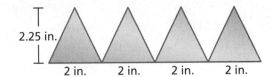

2.25 in.

2 in.   2 in.   2 in.   2 in.

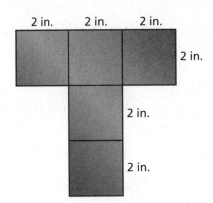

2 in.   2 in.   2 in.

2 in.

2 in.

2 in.

- **Fold and tape the nets to form an open square box and an open pyramid.**

- **Both figures should have the same size square base and the same height.**

- **Fill the pyramid with pebbles. Then pour the pebbles into the box. Repeat this until the box is full. How many pyramids does it take to fill the box?**

- **Use your result to find a formula for the volume of a pyramid.**

---

2 ACTIVITY: Comparing Volumes

Work with a partner. You are an archaeologist studying two ancient pyramids. What factors would affect how long it took to build each pyramid? Given similar conditions, which pyramid took longer to build? Explain your reasoning.

The Sun Pyramid in Mexico
Height: 246 ft
Base: 738 ft by 738 ft

Cheops Pyramid in Egypt
Height: about 480 ft
Base: about 755 ft by 755 ft

*Cut-outs are available in the back of the Record and Practice Journal.

9.5 Volumes of Pyramids (continued)

3 ACTIVITY: Finding and Using a Pattern

Work with a partner.

- **Find the volumes of the pyramids.**

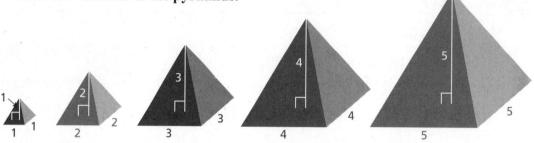

- **Organize your results in a table.**

Pyramid	Volume (cubic units)
1	
2	
3	
4	
5	

- **Describe the pattern.**

- **Use your pattern to find the volume of a pyramid with a side length and a height of 20.**

9.5 Volumes of Pyramids (continued)

4 **ACTIVITY:** Breaking a Prism into Pyramids

Work with a partner. The rectangular prism can be cut to form three pyramids. Show that the sum of the volumes of the three pyramids is equal to the volume of the prism.

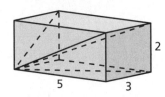

a.    b. 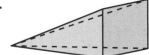   c.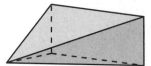

What Is Your Answer?

5. **IN YOUR OWN WORDS** How can you find the volume of a pyramid?

6. **STRUCTURE** Write a general formula for the volume of a pyramid.

9.5 **Practice**
For use after Lesson 9.5

Find the volume of the pyramid.

1.

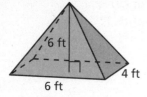

6 ft

6 ft

4 ft

2.

10 yd

9 yd

8 yd

3.

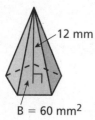

12 mm

B = 60 mm²

4.

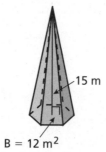

15 m

B = 12 m²

5. You create a simple tent in the shape of a pyramid. What is the volume of the tent?

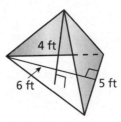

4 ft

6 ft

5 ft

6. You work at a restaurant that has 20 tables. Each table has a set of salt and pepper shakers on it that are in the shape of square pyramids. How much salt do you need to fill all the salt shakers?

3 in.

2 in.

2 in.

Extension 9.5 **Practice**
For use after Extension 9.5

Describe the intersection of the plane and the solid.

1.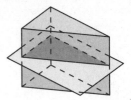

2.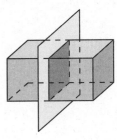

3.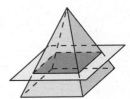

4.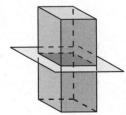

Describe the shape that is formed by the cut made in the food shown.

5.

6.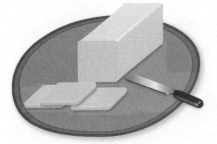

Extension 9.5 Practice (continued)

Describe the intersection of the plane and the solid.

7.

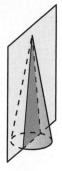

8.

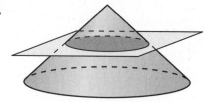

9.

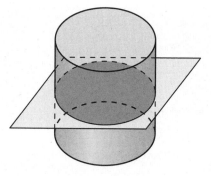

10.

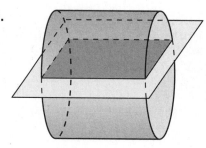

Describe the shape that is formed by the cut made in the food shown.

11.

12.

Name_____ Date_____

Write the ratio in simplest form.

1. bats to baseballs

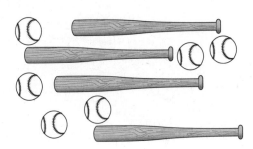

2. bows to gift boxes

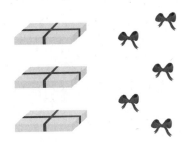

3. hammers to screwdrivers

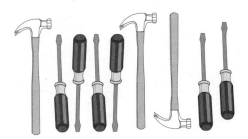

4. apples to bananas

5. There are 100 students in the sixth grade. There are 15 sixth-grade teachers. What is the ratio of teachers to students?

Chapter 10 Fair Game Review (continued)

Write the ratio in simplest form.

6. golf balls to total number of balls

7. rulers to total pieces of equipment

8. apples to total number of fruit

9. small fish to total number of fish

10. There are 24 flute players and 18 trumpet players in the band. Write the ratio of trumpet players to total number of trumpet players and flute players.

Name_____ Date _____

10.1 Outcomes and Events
For use with Activity 10.1

Essential Question In an experiment, how can you determine the number of possible results?

An *experiment* is an investigation or a procedure that has varying results. Flipping a coin, rolling a number cube, and spinning a spinner are all examples of experiments.

1 ACTIVITY: Conducting Experiments

Work with a partner.

a. You flip a dime.

There are _____ possible results.

Out of 20 flips, you think you will flip heads _____ times.

Flip a dime 20 times. Tally your results in a table. How close was your guess?

Flip	1	2	3	4	5	6	7	8	9	10	11	12	13	14	15	16	17	18	19	20
Result																				

b. You spin the spinner shown.

There are _____ possible results.

Out of 20 spins, you think you will spin orange _____ times.

Spin the spinner 20 times. Tally your results in a table. How close was your guess?

Spin	1	2	3	4	5	6	7	8	9	10	11	12	13	14	15	16	17	18	19	20
Result																				

c. You spin the spinner shown.

There are _____ possible results.

Out of 20 spins, you think you will spin a 4 _____ times.

Spin the spinner 20 times. Tally your results in a table. How close was your guess?

Spin	1	2	3	4	5	6	7	8	9	10	11	12	13	14	15	16	17	18	19	20
Result																				

10.1 Outcomes and Events (continued)

2 **ACTIVITY:** Comparing Different Results

Work with a partner. Use the spinner in Activity 1(c).

a. Do you have a better chance of spinning an even number or a multiple of 4? Explain your reasoning.

b. Do you have a better chance of spinning an even number or an odd number? Explain your reasoning.

3 **ACTIVITY:** Rock Paper Scissors

Work with a partner.

a. Play Rock Paper Scissors 30 times. Tally your results in the table.

		Player A		
		Rock	Paper	Scissors
Player B	Rock			
	Paper			
	Scissors			

Rock *breaks* scissors.
Paper *covers* rock.
Scissors *cut* paper.

Name_____ Date _____

10.1 Outcomes and Events (continued)

b. How many possible results are there?

c. Of the possible results, in how many ways can Player A win? Player B win? the players tie?

d. Does one of the players have a better chance of winning than the other player? Explain your reasoning.

What Is Your Answer?

4. IN YOUR OWN WORDS In an experiment, how can you determine the number of possible results?

Name_____ Date _____

10.1 Practice
For use after Lesson 10.1

A bag is filled with 4 red marbles, 3 blue marbles, 3 yellow marbles, and 2 green marbles. You randomly choose one marble from the bag. (a) Find the number of ways the event can occur. (b) Find the favorable outcomes of the event.

1. Choosing red

2. Choosing green

3. Choosing yellow

4. Choosing *not* blue

5. In order to figure out who will go first in a game, your friend asks you to pick a number between 1 and 25.

    a. What are the possible outcomes?

    b. What are the favorable outcomes of choosing an even number?

    c. What are the favorable outcomes of choosing a number less than 20?

10.2 Probability
For use with Activity 10.2

Essential Question How can you describe the likelihood of an event?

1 ACTIVITY: Black-and-White Spinner Game

Work with a partner. You work for a game company. You need to create a game that uses the spinner below.

a. Write rules for a game that uses the spinner. Then play it.

b. After playing the game, do you want to revise the rules? Explain.

c. **CHOOSE TOOLS** Using the center of the spinner as the vertex, measure the angle of each pie-shaped section. Is each section the same size? How do you think this affects the likelihood of spinning a given number?

d. Your friend is about to spin the spinner and wants to know how likely it is to spin a 3. How would you describe the likelihood of this event to your friend?

10.2 Probability (continued)

2 **ACTIVITY:** Changing the Spinner

Work with a partner. For each spinner, do the following.

- Measure the angle of each pie-shaped section.

- Tell whether you are more likely to spin a particular number. Explain your reasoning.

- Tell whether your rules from Activity 1 make sense for these spinners. Explain your reasoning.

a.

b.

10.2 Probability (continued)

3 ACTIVITY: Is This Game Fair?

Work with a partner. Apply the following rules to each spinner in Activities 1 and 2. Is the game fair? Why or why not? If not, who has the better chance of winning?

- Take turns spinning the spinner.

- If you spin an odd number, Player 1 wins.

- If you spin an even number, Player 2 wins.

What Is Your Answer?

4. **IN YOUR OWN WORDS** How can you describe the likelihood of an event?

5. Describe the likelihood of spinning an 8 in Activity 1.

6. Describe a career in which it is important to know the likelihood of an event.

10.2 Practice
For use after Lesson 10.2

Describe the likelihood of the event given its probability.

1. There is a 30% chance of snow tomorrow.

2. You solve a brain teaser 0.75 of the time.

You randomly choose one hat from 3 green hats, 4 black hats, 2 white hats, 2 red hats, and 1 blue hat. Find the probability of the event.

3. Choosing a red hat

4. Choosing a black hat

5. *Not* choosing a white hat

6. Choosing a blue hat

7. *Not* choosing a black hat

8. *Not* choosing a green hat

9. The probability that you draw a mechanical pencil from a group of 25 mechanical and wooden pencils is $\frac{3}{5}$. How many are mechanical pencils?

10.3 Experimental and Theoretical Probability
For use with Activity 10.3

Essential Question How can you use relative frequencies to find probabilities?

When you conduct an experiment, the **relative frequency** of an event is the fraction or percent of the time that the event occurs.

$$\text{relative frequency} = \frac{\text{number of times the event occurs}}{\text{total number of times you conduct the experiment}}$$

---

1 ACTIVITY: Finding Relative Frequencies

Work with a partner.

a. Flip a quarter 20 times and record your results. Then complete the table. Are the relative frequencies the same as the probability of flipping heads or tails? Explain.

	Flipping Heads	Flipping Tails
Relative Frequency		

b. Compare your results with those of other students in your class. Are the relative frequencies the same? If not, why do you think they differ?

c. Combine all of the results in your class. Then complete the table again. Did the relative frequencies change? What do you notice? Explain.

d. Suppose everyone in your school conducts this experiment and you combine the results. How do you think the relative frequencies will change?

10.3 **Experimental and Theoretical Probability** (continued)

2 **ACTIVITY:** Using Relative Frequencies

Work with a partner. You have a bag of colored
chips. You randomly select a chip from the bag
and replace it. The table shows the number of
times you select each color.

Red	Blue	Green	Yellow
24	12	15	9

a. There are 20 chips in the bag. Can you use the table to find the exact number
of each color in the bag? Explain.

b. You randomly select a chip from the bag and replace it. You do this 50 times,
then 100 times, and you calculate the relative frequencies after each experiment.
Which experiment do you think gives a better approximation of the exact number
of each color in the bag? Explain.

3 **ACTIVITY:** Conducting an Experiment

Work with a partner. You toss a thumbtack
onto a table. There are two ways the thumbtack
can land.

a. Your friend says that because there are
two outcomes, the probability of the

thumbtack landing point up must be $\frac{1}{2}$.

Do you think this conclusion is true?
Explain.

Point up   On its side

b. Toss a thumbtack onto a table 50 times and record your results. In a *uniform
probability model*, each outcome is equally likely to occur. Do you think this
experiment represents a uniform probability model? Explain.

Use the relative frequencies to complete the following.

P(point up) = _____ P(on its side) = _____

10.3 **Experimental and Theoretical Probability** (continued)

What Is Your Answer?

4. **IN YOUR OWN WORDS** How can you use relative frequencies to find probabilities? Give an example.

5. Your friend rolls a number cube 500 times. How many times do you think your friend will roll an odd number? Explain your reasoning.

6. In Activity 2, your friend says, "There are no orange-colored chips in the bag." Do you think this conclusion is true? Explain.

7. Give an example of an experiment that represents a uniform probability model.

8. Tell whether you can use each spinner to represent a uniform probability model. Explain your reasoning.

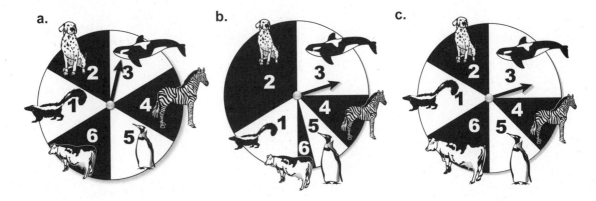

a.   b.   c.

Name _____ Date _____

Use the bar graph to find the experimental probability of the event.

1. Drawing red

2. Drawing orange

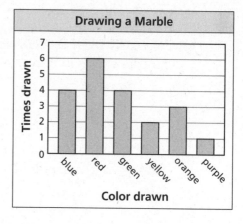

3. Drawing *not* yellow

4. Drawing a color with more than 4 letters in its name

5. There are 25 students' names in a hat. You choose 5 names. Three are boys' names and two are girls' names. How many of the 25 names would you expect to be boys' names?

Use a number cube to determine the theoretical probability of the event.

6. Rolling a 2

7. Rolling a 5

8. Rolling an even number

9. Rolling a number greater than 1

10.4 Compound Events
For use with Activity 10.4

Essential Question How can you find the number of possible outcomes of one or more events?

1 ACTIVITY: Comparing Combination Locks

Work with a partner. You are buying a combination lock. You have three choices.

a. This lock has 3 wheels. Each wheel is numbered from 0 to 9.

The least three-digit combination possible is _____.

The greatest three-digit combination possible is _____.

How many possible combinations are there?

b. Use the lock in part (a).

There are _____ possible outcomes for the first wheel.

There are _____ possible outcomes for the second wheel.

There are _____ possible outcomes for the third wheel.

How can you use multiplication to determine the number of possible combinations?

c. This lock is numbered from 0 to 39. Each combination uses three numbers in a right, left, right pattern. How many possible combinations are there?

d. This lock has 4 wheels.

Wheel 1: 0–9   **Wheel 2:** A–J

Wheel 3: K–T   **Wheel 4:** 0–9

How many possible combinations are there?

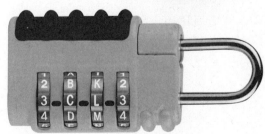

10.4 **Compound Events** (continued)

    e. For which lock is it most difficult to guess the combination? Why?

---

2 **ACTIVITY:** Comparing Password Security

Work with a partner. Which password requirement is most secure? Explain your reasoning. Include the number of different passwords that are possible for each requirement.

    a. The password must have four digits.

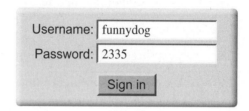

    b. The password must have five digits.

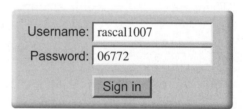

    c. The password must have six letters.

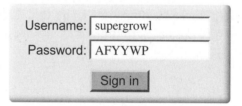

    d. The password must have eight digits or letters.

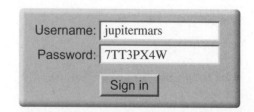

Name_____ Date_____

What Is Your Answer?

3. **IN YOUR OWN WORDS** How can you find the number of possible outcomes of one or more events?

4. **SECURITY** A hacker uses a software program to guess the passwords in Activity 2. The program checks 600 passwords per minute. What is the greatest amount of time it will take the program to guess each of the four types of passwords?

   a. four digits

   b. five digits

   c. six letters

   d. eight digits or letters

10.4 Practice
For use after Lesson 10.4

1. Use a tree diagram to find the total number of possible outcomes.

Bed Sheets	
Size	Twin, Twin XL, Full, Queen, King
Style	Solid, Patterned

Use the Fundamental Counting Principle to find the total number of possible outcomes.

2.

Photos	
Size	Wallet, 4 by 6, 5 by 7, 8 by 10, 11 by 14, 16 by 20
Finish	Matte, Glossy
Edits	Red eye, Black and white, Crop

3.

Laptops	
Hard Drive	250 GB, 320 GB, 500 GB
Style	HD, LCD
Color	Black, White, Red, Blue, Pink, Green, Purple

You spin the spinner and flip a coin. Find the probability of the events.

4. Spinning a 2 and flipping tails

5. Spinning a 7 and flipping heads

6. *Not* spinning a 4 and flipping tails

10.5 Independent and Dependent Events
For use with Activity 10.5

Essential Question What is the difference between dependent and independent events?

1 ACTIVITY: Drawing Marbles from a Bag (With Replacement)

Work with a partner. You have three marbles in a bag. There are two green marbles and one purple marble. Randomly draw a marble from the bag. Then put the marble back in the bag and draw a second marble.

a. Complete the tree diagram. Let G = Green and P = Purple. Find the probability that both marbles are green.

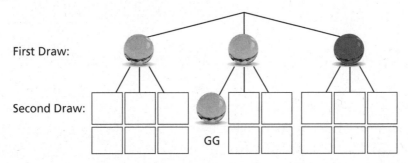

First Draw:

Second Draw:

GG

b. Does the probability of getting a green marble on the second draw *depend* on the color of the first marble? Explain.

2 ACTIVITY: Drawing Marbles from a Bag (Without Replacement)

Work with a partner. Using the same marbles from Activity 1, randomly draw two marbles from the bag.

a. Complete the tree diagram. Let G = Green and P = Purple. Find the probability that both marbles are green.

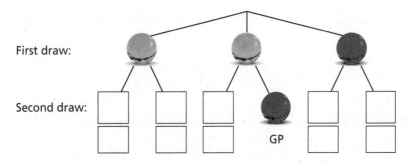

First draw:

Second draw:

GP

Is this event more likely than the event in Activity 1? Explain.

b. Does the probability of getting a green marble on the second draw *depend* on the color of the first marble? Explain.

Name_____ Date _____

3 **ACTIVITY:** Conducting an Experiment

Work with a partner. Conduct two experiments using two green marbles (G) and one purple marble (P).

a. In the first experiment, randomly draw one marble from the bag. Put it back. Draw a second marble. Repeat this 36 times. Record each result. Make a bar graph of your results.

GG	
GP	
PP	

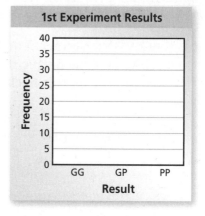

b. In the second experiment, randomly draw two marbles from the bag 36 times. Record each result. Make a bar graph of your results.

GG	
GP	
PP	

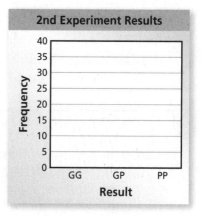

c. For each experiment, estimate the probability of drawing two green marbles.

d. Which experiment do you think represents *dependent events*? Which represents *independent events*? Explain your reasoning.

10.5 Independent and Dependent Events (continued)

What Is Your Answer?

4. **IN YOUR OWN WORDS** What is the difference between *dependent* and *independent* events? Describe a real-life example of each.

In Questions 5–7, tell whether the events are *independent* or *dependent*. Explain your reasoning.

5. You roll a 5 on a number cube and spin blue on a spinner.

6. Your teacher chooses one student to lead a group, and then chooses another student to lead another group.

7. You spin red on one spinner and green on another spinner.

8. In Activities 1 and 2, what is the probability of drawing a green marble on the first draw? on the second draw? How do you think you can use these two probabilities to find the probability of drawing two green marbles?

10.5 Practice
For use after Lesson 10.5

You roll a number cube twice. Find the probability of the events.

1. Rolling a 3 twice

2. Rolling an even number and a 5

3. Rolling an odd number and a 2 or a 4

4. Rolling a number less than 6 and a 3 or a 1

You randomly choose a letter from a hat with the letters A through J. Without replacing the first letter, you choose a second letter. Find the probability of the events.

5. Choosing an H and then a D

6. Choosing a consonant and then an E or an I

7. Choosing a vowel and then an F

8. Choosing a vowel and then a consonant

9. You have 3 clasp bracelets, 4 watches, and 5 stretch bracelets. You randomly choose two from your jewelry box. What is the probability that you will choose 2 watches?

You flip a coin, and then roll a number cube twice. Find the probability of the event.

10. Flipping heads, rolling a 5, and rolling a 2

11. Flipping tails, rolling an odd number, and rolling a 4

12. Flipping tails, rolling a 6 or a 1, and rolling a 3

13. Flipping heads, *not* rolling a 2, and rolling an even number

Practice

For use after Extension 10.5

1. You write a four-question survey. Each question has a *yes* or *no* answer.
   You have your friend answer the survey.

   a. Design a simulation that you can use to model the answers.

   b. Use your simulation to find the experimental probability that your friend
   answers *yes* to all four questions.

Big Ideas Math Red Accelerated   **229**
Record and Practice Journal

Name _____ Date _____

2. There is a 70% chance of snow today and tomorrow.

    a. Design and use a simulation that generates 50 randomly generated numbers.

    b. Find the experimental probability that it snows one of those days.

10.6 Samples and Populations
For use with Activity 10.6

Essential Question How can you determine whether a sample accurately represents a population?

A **population** is an entire group of people or objects. A **sample** is a part of the population. You can use a sample to make an inference, or conclusion, about a population.

Identify a population.   **Select a sample.**   **Interpret the data in the sample.**   **Make an inference about the population.**

Population → Sample → Interpretation → Inference

---

1 **ACTIVITY:** Identifying Populations and Samples

Work with a partner. Identify the population and the sample.

a.

The students in a school   The students in a math class

b.

The grizzly bears with GPS collars in a park   The grizzly bears in a park

c.

150 Quarters   All quarters in circulation

d.

All books in a library   10 fiction books in a library

10.6 Samples and Populations (continued)

2 ACTIVITY: Identifying Random Samples

Work with a partner. When a sample is selected at random, each member of the population is equally likely to be selected. You want to know the favorite extracurricular activity of students at your school. Determine whether each method will result in a random sample. Explain your reasoning.

a. You ask members of the school band.

b. You publish a survey in the school newspaper.

c. You ask every eighth student who enters the school in the morning.

d. You ask students in your class.

3 ACTIVITY: Identifying Representative Samples

Work with a partner. A new power plant is being built outside a town. In each situation below and on the next page, residents of the town are asked how they feel about the new power plant. Determine whether each conclusion is valid. Explain your reasoning.

a. A local radio show takes calls from 500 residents. The table shows the results. The radio station concludes that most of the residents of the town oppose the new power plant.

New Power Plant	
For	70
Against	425
Don't know	5

10.6 **Samples and Populations** (continued)

b. A news reporter randomly surveys 2 residents outside a supermarket. The graph shows the results. The reporter concludes that the residents of the town are evenly divided on the new power plant.

New Power Plant

For 50%   Against 50%

c. You randomly survey 250 residents at a shopping mall. The table shows the results. You conclude that there are about twice as many residents of the town against the new power plant than for the new power plant.

New Power Plant	
For	32%
Against	62%
Don't know	6%

What Is Your Answer?

4. IN YOUR OWN WORDS How can you determine whether a sample accurately represents a population?

5. RESEARCH Choose a topic that you would like to ask people's opinions about, and then write a survey question. How would you choose people to survey so that your sample is random? How many people would you survey? Conduct your survey and display your results. Would you change any part of your survey to make it more accurate? Explain.

6. Does increasing the size of a sample necessarily make the sample representative of a population? Give an example to support your explanation.

10.6 Practice
For use after Lesson 10.6

Determine whether the sample is *biased* or *unbiased*. Explain.

1. You want to estimate the number of students in your school who want a football stadium to be built. You survey the first 20 students who attend a Friday night football game.

2. You want to estimate the number of students in your school who drive their own cars to school. You survey every 8th person who enters the cafeteria for lunch.

Determine whether the conclusion is valid. Explain.

3. You want to determine the number of city residents who want to have 38th Street repaved. You randomly survey 15 residents who live on 38th Street. Twelve want the street to be repaved and three do not. So, you conclude that 80% of city residents want the street to be repaved.

4. You want to determine how many students consider math to be their favorite school subject. You randomly survey 75 students. Thirty-three students consider math to be their favorite subject and forty-two do not. So, you conclude that 40% of students at your school consider math to be their favorite subject.

Extension 10.6 — Generating Multiple Samples
For use with Extension 10.6

You have already used unbiased samples to make inferences about a population. In some cases, making an inference about a population from only one sample is not as precise as using multiple samples.

1 ACTIVITY: Using Multiple Random Samples

Work with a partner. You and a group of friends want to know how many students in your school listen to pop music. There are 840 students in your school. Each person in the group randomly surveys 20 students.

Step 1: The table shows your results. Make an inference about the number of students in your school who prefer pop music.

Favorite Type of Music			
Country	Pop	Rock	Rap
4	10	5	1

Step 2: The table shows Kevin's results. Use these results to make another inference about the number of students in your school who prefer pop music.

Favorite Type of Music			
Country	Pop	Rock	Rap
2	13	4	1

Compare the results of Steps 1 and 2.

Step 3: The table shows the results of three other friends. Use these results to make three more inferences about the number of students in your school who prefer pop music.

	Favorite Type of Music			
	Country	Pop	Rock	Rap
Steve	3	8	7	2
Laura	5	10	4	1
Ming	5	9	3	3

Extension 10.6 **Generating Multiple Samples** (continued)

Step 4: Describe the variation of the five inferences. Which one would you use to describe the number of students in your school who prefer pop music? Explain your reasoning.

Step 5: Show how you can use all five samples to make an inference.

Practice

1. Work with a partner. Mark 24 packing peanuts with either a red or a black marker. Put the peanuts into a paper bag. Trade bags with other students in the class.

   a. Generate a sample by choosing a peanut from your bag six times, replacing the peanut each time. Record the number of times you choose each color. Repeat this process to generate four more samples. Organize the results in a table.

   b. Use each sample to make an inference about the number of red peanuts in the bag. Then describe the variation of the five inferences. Make inferences about the numbers of red and black peanuts in the bag based on all the samples.

   c. Take the peanuts out of the bag. How do your inferences compare to the population? Do you think you can make a more accurate prediction? If so, explain how.

Extension 10.6 Generating Multiple Samples (continued)

2 ACTIVITY: Using Measures from Multiple Random Samples

Work with a partner. You want to know the mean number of hours students with part-time jobs work each week. You go to 8 different schools. At each school, you randomly survey 10 students with part-time jobs. Your results are shown at the right.

Hours Worked Each Week
1: 6, 8, 6, 6, 7, 4, 10, 8, 7, 8
2: 10, 4, 4, 6, 8, 6, 7, 12, 8, 8
3: 10, 9, 8, 6, 5, 8, 6, 6, 9, 10
4: 4, 8, 4, 4, 5, 4, 4, 6, 5, 6
5: 6, 8, 8, 6, 12, 4, 10, 8, 6, 12
6: 10, 10, 8, 9, 16, 8, 7, 12, 16, 14
7: 4, 5, 6, 6, 4, 5, 6, 6, 4, 4
8: 16, 20, 8, 12, 10, 8, 8, 14, 16, 8

Step 1: Find the mean of each sample.

Step 2: Make a box-and-whisker plot of the sample means.

Step 3: Use the box-and-whisker plot to estimate the actual mean number of hours students with part-time jobs work each week. How does your estimate compare to the mean of the entire data set?

3 ACTIVITY: Using a Simulation

Work with a partner. Another way to generate multiple samples of data is to use a simulation. Suppose 70% of all seventh graders watch reality shows on television.

Step 1: Design a simulation involving 50 packing peanuts by marking 70% of the peanuts with a certain color. Put the peanuts into a paper bag.

Step 2: Simulate choosing a sample of 30 students by choosing peanuts from the bag, replacing the peanut each time. Record the results. Repeat this process to generate eight more samples. How much variation do you expect among the samples? Explain.

**Extension
10.6** **Generating Multiple Samples** (continued)

Step 3: Display your results.

Practice

2. You want to know whether student-athletes prefer water or sports drinks during games. You go to 10 different schools. At each school, you randomly survey 10 student-athletes. The percents of student-athletes who prefer water are shown.

     60%   70%   60%   50%   80%   70%   30%   70%   80%   40%

   a. Make a box-and-whisker plot of the data.

   b. Use the box-and-whisker plot to estimate the actual percent of student-athletes who prefer water. How does your estimate compare to the mean of the data?

3. Repeat Activity 2 using the medians of the samples.

4. In Activity 3, how do the percents in your samples compare to the actual percent of seventh graders who watch reality shows on television?

5. **REASONING** Why is it better to make inferences about a population based on multiple samples instead of only one sample? What additional information do you gain by taking multiple random samples? Explain.

10.7 Comparing Populations
For use with Activity 10.7

Essential Question How can you compare data sets that represent two populations?

---

1 **ACTIVITY:** Comparing Two Data Distributions

Work with a partner. You want to compare the shoe sizes of male students in two classes. You collect the data shown in the table.

Male Students in Eighth-Grade Class														
7	9	8	$7\frac{1}{2}$	$8\frac{1}{2}$	10	6	$6\frac{1}{2}$	8	8	$8\frac{1}{2}$	9	11	$7\frac{1}{2}$	$8\frac{1}{2}$

Male Students in Sixth-Grade Class														
6	$5\frac{1}{2}$	6	$6\frac{1}{2}$	$7\frac{1}{2}$	$8\frac{1}{2}$	7	$5\frac{1}{2}$	5	$5\frac{1}{2}$	$6\frac{1}{2}$	7	$4\frac{1}{2}$	6	6

a. How can you display both data sets so that you can visually compare the measures of center and of variation? Make the data display you chose.

b. Describe the shape of each distribution.

c. Complete the table.

	Male Students in Eighth Grade Class	Male Students in Sixth Grade Class
Mean		
Median		
Mode		
Range		
Interquartile Range (IQR)		
Mean Absolute Deviation (MAD)		

10.7 **Comparing Populations** (continued)

d. Compare the measures of center for the data sets.

e. Compare the measures of variation for the data sets. Does one data set show more variation than the other? Explain.

f. Do the distributions overlap? How can you tell using the data display you chose in part (a)?

g. The double box-and-whisker plot below shows the shoe sizes of the members of two girls basketball teams. Can you conclude that at least one girl from each team has the same shoe size? Can you conclude that at least one girl from the Bobcats has a larger shoe size than one of the girls from the Tigers? Explain your reasoning.

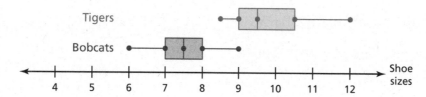

2 ACTIVITY: Comparing Two Data Distributions

Work with a partner. Compare the shapes of the distributions. Do the two data sets overlap? Explain. If so, use measures of center and the least and the greatest values to describe the overlap between the two data sets.

a.

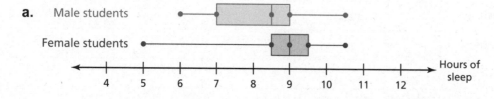

10.7 **Comparing Populations** (continued)

b. **Heights (inches)**

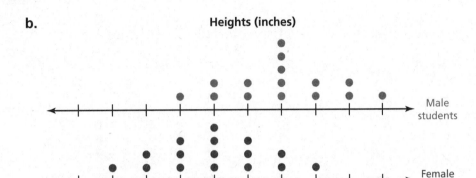

Male students

Female students

56 57 58 59 60 61 62 63 64 65

c. **Ages of People in Two Exercise Classes**

10:00 A.M. Class   **8:00 P.M. Class**

	1	8 9
	2	1 2 2 7 9 9
	3	0 3 4 5 7
9 7 3 2 2 2	4	0
7 5 4 3 1	5	
7 0 0	6	
0	7	

Key: 1 | 8 = 18

What Is Your Answer?

3. IN YOUR OWN WORDS How can you compare data sets that represent two populations?

10.7 **Practice**
For use after Lesson 10.7

1. The dot plots show the quiz scores for two classes taught by the same teacher.

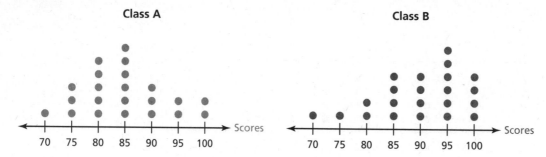

a. Compare the populations using measures of center and variation.

b. Express the difference in the measures of center as a multiple of the measure of variation.

2. The double box-and-whisker plot shows the number of song downloads a month by two seventh grade classes.

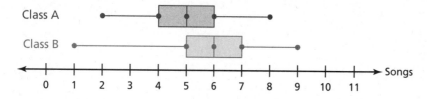

a. Compare the populations using measures of center and variation.

b. Express the difference in the measures of center as a multiple of the measure of variation.

Chapter 11 — Fair Game Review

Reflect the point in (a) the *x*-axis and (b) the *y*-axis.

1. $(1, 1)$

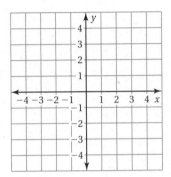

2. $(-2, -4)$

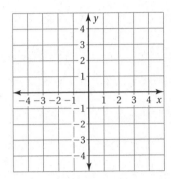

3. $(-3, 3)$

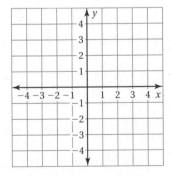

4. $(4, -3)$

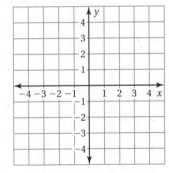

5. $(-1, 2)$

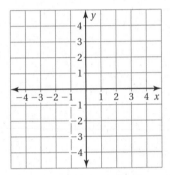

6. $(3, 2)$

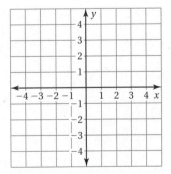

Chapter 11 **Fair Game Review** (continued)

Draw the polygon with the given vertices in a coordinate plane.

7. $A(2, 2), B(2, 7), C(6, 7), D(6, 2)$

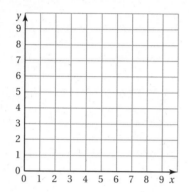

8. $E(3, 8), F(3, 1), G(6, 1), H(6, 8)$

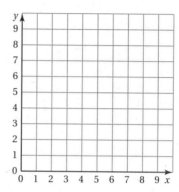

9. $I(7, 6), J(5, 2), K(2, 4)$

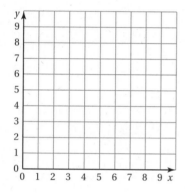

10. $L(1, 5), M(1, 2), N(8, 2)$

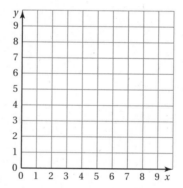

11. $O(3, 7), P(6, 7), Q(9, 3), R(1, 3)$

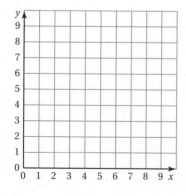

12. $S(9, 9), T(7, 1), U(2, 4), V(4, 7)$

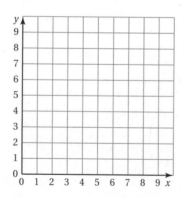

11.1 Congruent Figures
For use with Activity 11.1

Essential Question How can you identify congruent triangles?

Two figures are congruent when they have the same size and the same shape.

1 ACTIVITY: Identifying Congruent Triangles

Work with a partner.

- **Which of the geoboard triangles below are congruent to the geoboard triangle at the right?**

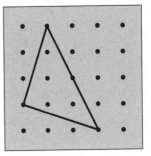

a.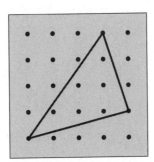

b.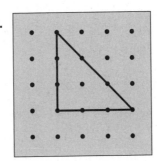

c.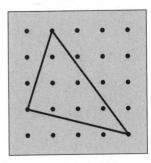

d.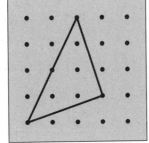

e.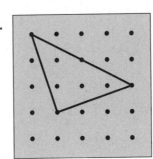

f.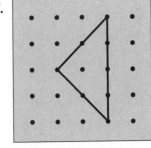

11.1 Congruent Figures (continued)

- Form each triangle on a geoboard.

- Measure each side with a ruler. Record your results in the table.

	Side 1	Side 2	Side 3
Given Triangle			
a.			
b.			
c.			
d.			
e.			
f.			

- Write a conclusion about the side lengths of triangles that are congruent.

11.1 **Congruent Figures** (continued)

2 **ACTIVITY:** Forming Congruent Triangles

Work with a partner.

   a. Form the given triangle in Activity 1 on your geoboard. Record the triangle on geoboard dot paper.

   b. Move each vertex of the triangle one peg to the right. Is the new triangle congruent to the original triangle? How can you tell?

   c. On a 5-by-5 geoboard, make as many different triangles as possible, each of which is congruent to the given triangle in Activity 1. Record each triangle on geoboard dot paper.

What Is Your Answer?

   3. **IN YOUR OWN WORDS** How can you identify congruent triangles? Use the conclusion you wrote in Activity 1 as part of your answer.

   4. Can you form a triangle on your geoboard whose side lengths are 3, 4, and 5 units? If so, draw such a triangle on geoboard dot paper.

11.1 Practice

For use after Lesson 11.1

The figures are congruent. Name the corresponding angles and the corresponding sides.

1.

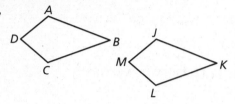

2.

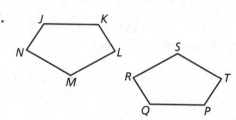

Tell whether the two figures are congruent. Explain your reasoning.

3.

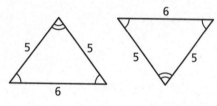

4.

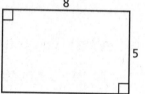 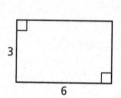

5. The tops of the desks are identical.

   a. What is the length of side *NP*?

   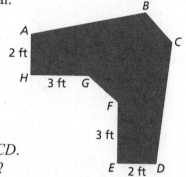 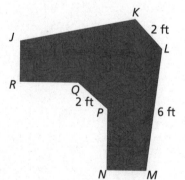

   b. Side *AB* is congruent to side *CD*. What is the length of side *AB*?

11.2 Translations

For use with Activity 11.2

Essential Question How can you arrange tiles to make a tessellation?

---

1 **ACTIVITY:** Describing Tessellations

Work with a partner. Can you make the tessellation by translating single tiles that are all of the same shape and design? If so, show how.

   a. Sample:

   Tile Pattern   **Single Tiles**

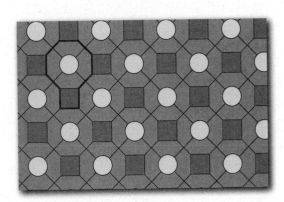   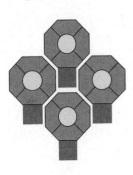

   b.   c.

11.2 **Translations** (continued)

2 **ACTIVITY:** Tessellations and Basic Shapes

Work with a partner.

   a. Which pattern blocks can you use to make a tessellation? For each one that works, draw the tessellation.

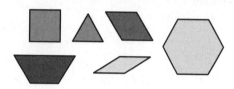

   b. Can you make the tessellation by translating? Or do you have to rotate or flip the pattern blocks?

3 **ACTIVITY:** Designing Tessellations

Work with a partner. Design your own tessellation. Use one of the basic shapes from Activity 2.

Sample:

    Step 1: Start with a square.   **Step 2:** Cut a design out of one side.   **Step 3:** Tape it to the other side to make your pattern.

    Step 4: Translate the pattern to make your tessellation.

    Step 5: Color the tessellation.

11.2 **Translations** (continued)

4 **ACTIVITY:** Translating in the Coordinate Plane

Work with a partner.

a. Draw a rectangle in a coordinate plane. Find the dimensions of the rectangle.

b. Move each vertex 3 units right and 4 units up. Draw the new figure. List the vertices.

c. Compare the dimensions and the angle measures of the new figure to those of the original rectangle.

d. Are the opposite sides of the new figure parallel? Explain.

e. Can you conclude that the two figures are congruent? Explain.

f. Compare your results with those of other students in your class. Do you think the results are true for any type of figure?

What Is Your Answer?

5. IN YOUR OWN WORDS How can you arrange tiles to make a tessellation? Give an example.

6. PRECISION Explain why any parallelogram can be translated to make a tessellation.

Name _____ Date _____

11.2 **Practice**
For use after Lesson 11.2

Tell whether the shaded figure is a translation of the nonshaded figure.

1.

2.

3.

4. Translate the figure 4 units left and 1 unit down. What are the coordinates of the image?

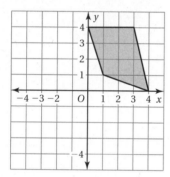

5. Translate the triangle 5 units right and 4 units up. What are the coordinates of the image?

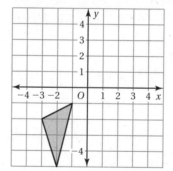

6. Describe the translation from the shaded figure to the nonshaded figure.

Name_____ Date_____

11.3 Reflections
For use with Activity 11.3

Essential Question How can you use reflections to classify a frieze pattern?

Frieze

A *frieze* is a horizontal band that runs at the top of a building. A frieze is often decorated with a design that repeats.

- All frieze patterns are translations of themselves.
- Some frieze patterns are reflections of themselves.

---

1 ACTIVITY: Frieze Patterns and Reflections

Work with a partner. Consider the frieze pattern shown. *

a. Is the frieze pattern a reflection of itself when folded horizontally? Explain.

b. Is the frieze pattern a reflection of itself when folded vertically? Explain.

*Cut-outs are available in the back of the Record and Practice Journal.

11.3 **Reflections** (continued)

---

2 **ACTIVITY:** Frieze Patterns and Reflections

Work with a partner. Is the frieze pattern a reflection of itself when folded
horizontally, *vertically*, or *neither*?

a.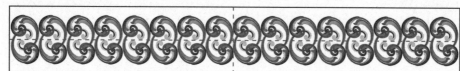

b.

---

3 **ACTIVITY:** Reflecting in the Coordinate Plane

Work with a partner.

a. Draw a rectangle in Quadrant I of a coordinate
plane. Find the dimensions of the rectangle.

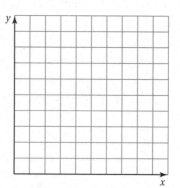

b. Copy the axes and the rectangle onto a piece of
transparent paper.

Flip the transparent paper once so that the rectangle
is in Quadrant IV. Then align the origin and the axes
with the coordinate plane.

Draw the new figure in the coordinate plane.
List the vertices.

11.3 **Reflections** (continued)

c. Compare the dimensions and the angle measures of the new figure to those of the original rectangle.

d. Are the opposite sides of the new figure still parallel? Explain.

e. Can you conclude that the two figures are congruent? Explain.

f. Flip the transparent paper so that the original rectangle is in Quadrant II. Draw the new figure in the coordinate plane. List the vertices. Then repeat parts (c)–(e).

g. Compare your results with those of other students in your class. Do you think the results are true for any type of figure?

What Is Your Answer?

4. **IN YOUR OWN WORDS** How can you use reflections to classify a frieze pattern?

Name _____ Date _____

Tell whether the shaded figure is a reflection of the nonshaded figure.

1. 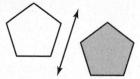   2. 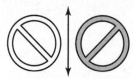   3.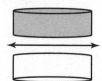

Draw the figure and its reflection in the *x*-axis. Identify the coordinates of the image.

4. $A(1, 2)$, $B(3, 2)$, $C(1, 4)$

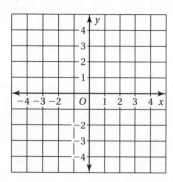

5. $W(3, 1)$, $X(3, 4)$, $Y(1, 4)$, $Z(1, 1)$

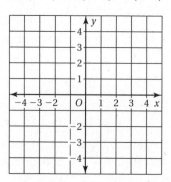

Draw the figure and its reflection in the *y*-axis. Identify the coordinates of the image.

6. $J(3, 4)$, $K(3, 0)$, $L(2, 4)$

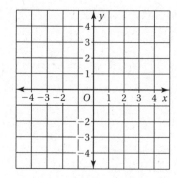

7. $M(2, 2)$, $N(2, 3)$, $P(3, 3)$, $Q(4, 1)$

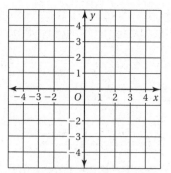

8. In a pinball game, when you perfectly reflect the ball off of the wall, will the ball hit the bonus target?

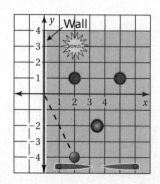

11.4 Rotations
For use with Activity 11.4

Essential Question What are the three basic ways to move an object in a plane?

1 ACTIVITY: Three Basic Ways to Move Things

There are three basic ways to move objects on a flat surface.

_____ the object. _____ the object. _____ the object.

Work with a partner.

a. What type of triangle is the shaded triangle? Is it congruent to the other triangles? Explain.

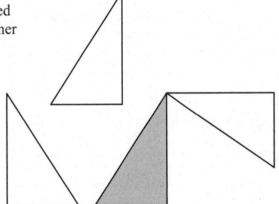

b. Decide how you can move the shaded triangle to obtain each of the other triangles.

c. Is each move a *translation*, a *reflection*, or a *rotation*?

11.4 **Rotations** (continued)

---

2 **ACTIVITY:** Rotating in the Coordinate Plane

Work with a partner.

    a. Draw a rectangle in Quadrant II of a coordinate plane. Find the dimensions of the rectangle.

    b. Copy the axes and the rectangle onto a piece of transparent paper.

    Align the origin and the vertices of the rectangle on the transparent paper with the coordinate plane. Turn the transparent paper so that the rectangle is in Quadrant I and the axes align.

    Draw the new figure in the coordinate plane. List the vertices.

    c. Compare the dimensions and the angle measures of the new figure to those of the original rectangle.

    d. Are the opposite sides of the new figure still parallel? Explain.

    e. Can you conclude that the two figures are congruent? Explain.

    f. Turn the transparent paper so that the original rectangle is in Quadrant IV. Draw the new figure in the coordinate plane. List the vertices. Then repeat parts (c)–(e).

11.4 **Rotations** (continued)

g. Compare your results with those of other students in your class. Do you think the results are true for any type of figure?

What Is Your Answer?

3. **IN YOUR OWN WORDS** What are the three basic ways to move an object in a plane? Draw an example of each.

4. **PRECISION** Use the results of Activity 2(b).

   a. Draw four angles using the conditions below.

   • The origin is the vertex of each angle.

   • One side of each angle passes through a vertex of the original rectangle.

   • The other side of each angle passes through the corresponding vertex of the rotated rectangle.

   b. Measure each angle in part (a). For each angle, measure the distances between the origin and the vertices of the rectangles. What do you notice?

   c. How can the results of part (b) help you rotate a figure?

5. **PRECISION** Repeat the procedure in Question 4 using the results of Activity 2(f).

Name _____ Date _____

Tell whether the shaded figure is a rotation of the nonshaded figure about the origin. If so, give the angle and the direction of rotation.

1.
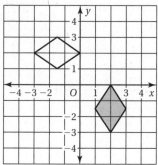

2.
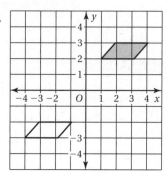

The vertices of a triangle are $A(1, 1)$, $B(3, 1)$, **and** $C(3, 4)$. **Rotate the triangle as described. Find the coordinates of the image.**

3. $90°$ clockwise about the origin

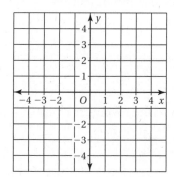

4. $270°$ counterclockwise about vertex A

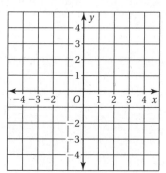

5. A triangle is rotated $180°$ about the origin. Its image is reflected in the x-axis. The vertices of the final triangle are $(-4, -4)$, $(-2, -4)$, and $(-3, -1)$. What are the vertices of the original triangle?

11.5 **Similar Figures**
For use with Activity 11.5

Essential Question How can you use proportions to help make decisions in art, design, and magazine layouts?

Original Photograph

In a computer art program, when you click and drag on a side of a photograph, you distort it.

But when you click and drag on a corner of the photograph, the dimensions remain proportional to the original.

Distorted

Distorted

Proportional

1 **ACTIVITY:** Reducing Photographs

Work with a partner. You are trying to reduce the photograph to the indicated size for a nature magazine. Can you reduce the photograph to the indicated size without distorting or cropping? Explain your reasoning.

a.

5 in.

6 in.

4 in.

5 in.

b.

6 in.

8 in.

3 in.

4 in.

11.5 Similar Figures (continued)

2 ACTIVITY: Creating Designs

Work with a partner.

a. Tell whether the dimensions of the new designs are proportional to the dimensions of the original design. Explain your reasoning.

Original

8   8

7

Design 1

7   7

6

Design 2

$6\frac{6}{7}$ $6\frac{6}{7}$

6

b. Draw two designs whose dimensions are proportional to the given design. Make one bigger and one smaller. Label the sides of the designs with their lengths.

5

4

8   10

6

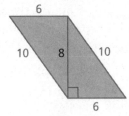

6

10   8   10

6

11.5 **Similar Figures** (continued)

What Is Your Answer?

3. **IN YOUR OWN WORDS** How can you use proportions to help make decisions in art, design, and magazine layouts? Give two examples.

4. **a.** Use a computer art program to draw two rectangles whose dimensions are proportional to each other.

   b. Print the two rectangles on the same piece of paper.

   c. Use a centimeter ruler to measure the length and the width of each rectangle. Record your measurements here.

"I love this statue. It seems similar to a big statue I saw in New York."

   d. Find the following ratios. What can you conclude?

   Length of larger   Width of larger
   ―――――――――   ――――――――
   Length of smaller   Width of smaller

Name_____ Date _____

Tell whether the two figures are similar. Explain your reasoning.

1.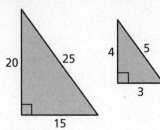

2.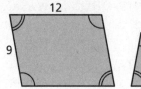

3. In your classroom, a dry erase board is 8 feet long and 4 feet wide. Your teacher makes individual dry erase boards for you to use at your desk that are 11.5 inches long and 9.5 inches wide. Are the boards similar?

4. You have a 4 x 6 photo of you and your friend.

   a. You order a 5 x 7 print of the photo. Is the new photo similar to the original?

   b. You enlarge the original photo to three times its size on your computer. Is the new photo similar to the original?

Name_____ Date_____

11.6 Perimeters and Areas of Similar Figures
For use with Activity 11.6

Essential Question How do changes in dimensions of similar geometric figures affect the perimeters and the areas of the figures?

---

1 ACTIVITY: Creating Similar Figures

Work with a partner. Use pattern blocks to make a figure whose dimensions are 2, 3, and 4 times greater than those of the original figure.*

a. Square

b. Rectangle

---

2 ACTIVITY: Finding Patterns for Perimeters

Work with a partner. Complete the table for the perimeter *P* of each figure in Activity 1. Describe the pattern.

Figure	Original Side Lengths	Double Side Lengths	Triple Side Lengths	Quadruple Side Lengths
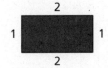	P = _____			
	P = _____			

*Cut-outs are available in the back of the Record and Practice Journal.

11.6 **Perimeters and Areas of Similar Figures** (continued)

---

3 **ACTIVITY:** Finding Patterns for Areas

Work with a partner. Complete the table for the area A of each figure in Activity 1. Describe a pattern.

Figure	Original Side Lengths	Double Side Lengths	Triple Side Lengths	Quadruple Side Lengths
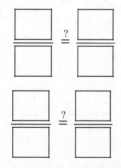	$A = $ _____			
	$A = $ _____			

---

4 **ACTIVITY:** Drawing and Labeling Similar Figures

Work with a partner.

a. Find another rectangle that is similar and has one side from $(-1, -6)$ to $(5, -6)$. Label the vertices.

Check that the two rectangles are similar by showing that the ratios of corresponding sides are equal.

$$\frac{\text{Shaded Length}}{\text{Unshaded Length}} \overset{?}{=} \frac{\text{Shaded Width}}{\text{Unshaded Width}}$$

$$\frac{\text{change in } y}{\text{change in } y} \overset{?}{=} \frac{\text{change in } x}{\text{change in } x}$$

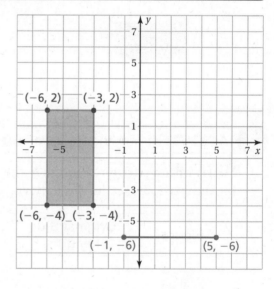

$$\frac{\boxed{}}{\boxed{}} \overset{?}{=} \frac{\boxed{}}{\boxed{}}$$

$$\frac{\boxed{}}{\boxed{}} \overset{?}{=} \frac{\boxed{}}{\boxed{}}$$

The ratios are _____. So, the rectangles are _____.

11.6 **Perimeters and Areas of Similar Figures** (continued)

b. Compare the perimeters and the areas of the figures. Are the results the same as your results from Activities 2 and 3? Explain.

c. There are three other rectangles that are similar to the shaded rectangle and have the given side.

- Draw each one. Label the vertices of each.

- Show that each is similar to the original shaded rectangle.

What Is Your Answer?

5. **IN YOUR OWN WORDS** How do changes in dimensions of similar geometric figures affect the perimeters and the areas of the figures?

6. What information do you need to know to find the dimensions of a figure that is similar to another figure? Give examples to support your explanation.

Name _____ Date _____

The two figures are similar. Find the ratios (shaded to nonshaded) of the perimeters and of the areas.

1.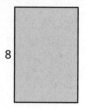
   8   3

2.
   6   10

The polygons are similar. Find x.

3.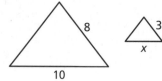
   8   3   x   10

4.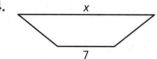
   x   7   12   5

5. You buy two picture frames that are similar. The ratio of the corresponding side lengths is 4 : 5. What is the ratio of the areas?

11.7 Dilations
For use with Activity 11.7

Essential Question How can you enlarge or reduce a figure in the coordinate plane?

1 ACTIVITY: Comparing Triangles in a Coordinate Plane

Work with a partner. Write the coordinates of the vertices of the shaded triangle. Then write the coordinates of the vertices of the nonshaded triangle.

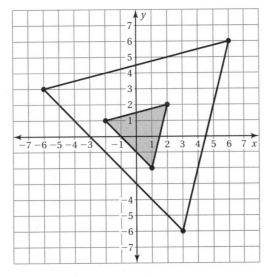

a. How are the two sets of coordinates related?

b. How are the two triangles related? Explain your reasoning.

c. Draw a dashed triangle whose coordinates are twice the values of the corresponding coordinates of the shaded triangle. How are the dashed and shaded triangles related? Explain your reasoning.

11.7 **Dilations** (continued)

    d. How are the coordinates of the nonshaded and dashed triangles related? How are the two triangles related? Explain your reasoning.

---

2 **ACTIVITY:** Drawing Triangles in a Coordinate Plane

Work with a partner.

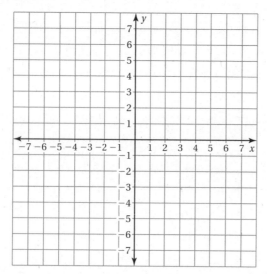

    a. Draw the triangle whose vertices are $(0, 2), (-2, 2),$ and $(1, -2)$.

    b. Multiply each coordinate of the vertices by 2 to obtain three new vertices. Draw the triangle given by the three new vertices. How are the two triangles related?

    c. Repeat part (b) by multiplying by 3 instead of 2.

11.7 Dilations (continued)

3 ACTIVITY: Summarizing Transformations

Work with a partner. Make a table that summarizes the relationships between the original figure and its image for the four types of transformations you studied in this chapter.

What Is Your Answer?

4. **IN YOUR OWN WORDS** How can you enlarge or reduce a figure in the coordinate plane?

5. Describe how knowing how to enlarge or reduce figures in a technical drawing is important in a career such as drafting.

Name _____ Date _____

Tell whether the shaded figure is a dilation of the nonshaded figure.

1.

2.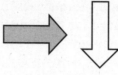

3.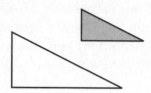

The vertices of a figure are given. Draw the figure and its image after a dilation with the given scale factor. Identify the type of dilation.

4. $A(-2, 2), B(1, 2), C(1, -1); k = 3$

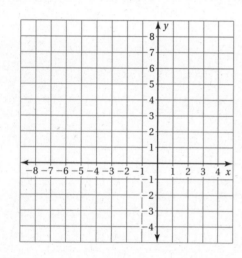

5. $D(4, 2), E(4, 8), F(8, 8), G(8, 2); k = \dfrac{1}{2}$

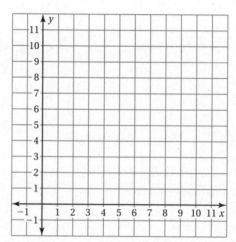

6. A rectangle is dilated using a scale factor of 6. The image is then dilated using a scale factor of $\dfrac{1}{3}$. What scale factor could you use to dilate the original rectangle to get the final rectangle? Explain.

Chapter 12 Fair Game Review

Tell whether the angles are *adjacent* or *vertical*. Then find the value of *x*.

1.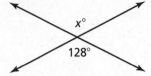
   $x°$
   $128°$

2.
   $x°$
   $35°$

3.
   $75°$
   $(2x + 1)°$

4.
   $4x°$
   $2x°$

5. The tree is tilted 14°. Find the value of *x*.

$14°$
$x°$

Chapter 12 **Fair Game Review** (continued)

Tell whether the angles are *complementary* or *supplementary*. Then find the value of *x*.

6.

7.

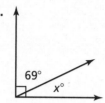

8.

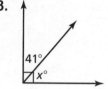

9.

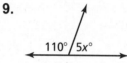

10. A tributary joins a river at an angle. Find the value of *x*.

12.1 Parallel Lines and Transversals
For use with Activity 12.1

Essential Question How can you describe angles formed by parallel lines and transversals?

---

1 ACTIVITY: A Property of Parallel Lines

Work with a partner.

- **Discuss what it means for two lines to be parallel. Decide on a strategy for drawing two parallel lines. Then draw the two parallel lines.**

- **Draw a third line that intersects the two parallel lines. This line is called a *transversal*.**

a. How many angles are formed by the parallel lines and the transversal? Label the angles.

b. Which of these angles have equal measures? Explain your reasoning.

12.1 **Parallel Lines and Transversals** (continued)

2 ACTIVITY: Creating Parallel Lines

Work with a partner.

a. If you were building the house in the photograph, how could you make sure that the studs are parallel to each other?

b. Identify sets of parallel lines and transversals in the photograph.

3 ACTIVITY: Using Technology to Draw Parallel Lines and a Transversal

Work with a partner. Use geometry software to draw two parallel lines intersected by a transversal.

a. Find all of the angle measures.

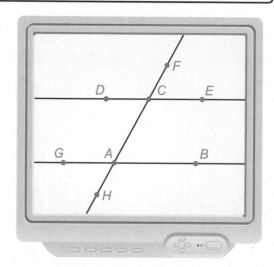

12.1 **Parallel Lines and Transversals** (continued)

b. Adjust the figure by moving the parallel lines or the transversal to a different position. Describe how the angle measures and relationships change.

What Is Your Answer?

4. IN YOUR OWN WORDS How can you describe angles formed by parallel lines and transversals? Give an example.

5. Use geometry software to draw a transversal that is perpendicular to two parallel lines. What do you notice about the angles formed by the parallel lines and the transversal?

12.1 Practice
For use after Lesson 12.1

Use the figure to find the measures of the numbered angles.

1.

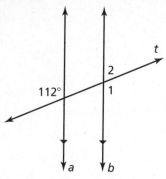

2.

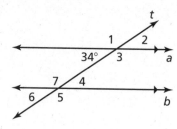

Complete the statement. Explain your reasoning.

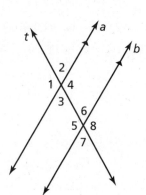

3. If the measure of $\angle 1 = 150°$, then the measure of $\angle 6 = $ _____.

4. If the measure of $\angle 3 = 42°$, then the measure of $\angle 5 = $ _____.

5. If the measure of $\angle 6 = 28°$, then the measure of $\angle 3 = $ _____.

6. You paint a border around the top of the walls in your room. What angle does x need to be to repeat the pattern?

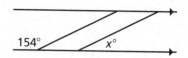

12.2 Angles of Triangles
For use with Activity 12.2

Essential Question How can you describe the relationships among the angles of a triangle?

1 ACTIVITY: Exploring the Interior Angles of a Triangle

Work with a partner.

a. Draw a triangle. Label the interior angles A, B, and C.

b. Carefully cut out the triangle. Tear off the three corners of the triangle.

c. Arrange angles A and B so that they share a vertex and are adjacent.

d. How can you place the third angle to determine the sum of the measures of the interior angles? What is the sum?

e. Compare your results with others in your class.

f. **STRUCTURE** How does your result in part (d) compare to your conclusion in Lesson 7.3, Activity Question 7?

12.2 Angles of Triangles (continued)

2 ACTIVITY: Exploring the Interior Angles of a Triangle

Work with a partner.

   a. Describe the figure.

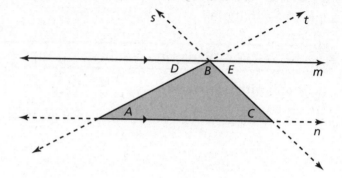

   b. LOGIC Use what you know about parallel lines and transversals to justify your result in part (d) of Activity 1.

3 ACTIVITY: Exploring an Exterior Angle of a Triangle

Work with a partner.

   a. Draw a triangle. Label the interior angles *A*, *B*, and *C*.

   b. Carefully cut out the triangle.

   c. Place the triangle on a piece of paper and extend one side to form *exterior angle D*, as shown.

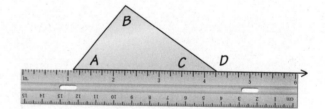

   d. Tear off the corners that are not adjacent to the exterior angle. Arrange them to fill the exterior angle, as shown. What does this tell you about the measure of exterior angle *D*?

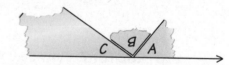

12.2 **Angles of Triangles** (continued)

4 **ACTIVITY:** Measuring the Exterior Angles of a Triangle

Work with a partner.

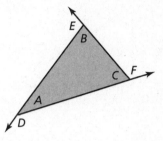

a. Draw a triangle and label the interior and exterior angles as shown.

b. Use a protractor to measure all six angles of your triangle. Complete the table to organize your results. What does the table tell you about the measure of an exterior angle of a triangle?

Exterior Angle	$D = $ _____ °	$E = $ _____ °	$F = $ _____ °
Interior Angle	$B = $ _____ °	$A = $ _____ °	$A = $ _____ °
Interior Angle	$C = $ _____ °	$C = $ _____ °	$B = $ _____ °

What Is Your Answer?

5. **REPEATED REASONING** Draw three triangles that have different shapes. Repeat parts (b)–(d) from Activity 1 for each triangle. Do you get the same results? Explain.

6. **IN YOUR OWN WORDS** How can you describe the relationships among angles of a triangle?

12.2 Practice
For use after Lesson 12.2

Find the measures of the interior angles.

1.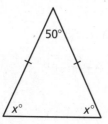

2.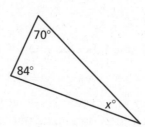

3.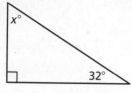

4.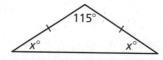

Find the measure of the exterior angle.

5.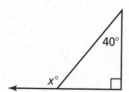

6.

7. Find the value of x on the clothes hanger.

12.3 Angles of Polygons
For use with Activity 12.3

Essential Question How can you find the sum of the interior angle measures and the sum of the exterior angle measures of a polygon?

---

1 ACTIVITY: Exploring the Interior Angles of a Polygon

Work with a partner. In parts (a)–(e), identify each polygon and the number of sides *n*. Then find the sum of the interior angle measures of the polygon.

a. Polygon: _____   Number of sides: $n =$ _____

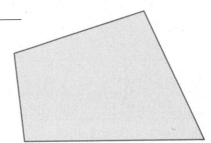

Draw a line segment on the figure that divides it into two triangles. Is there more than one way to do this? Explain.

What is the sum of the interior angle measures of each triangle?

What is the sum of the interior angle measures of the figure?

b.

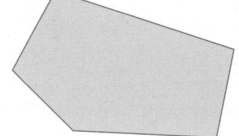

c.

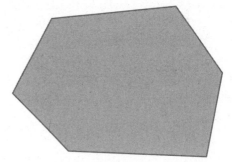

d.

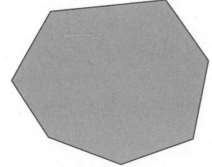

e.

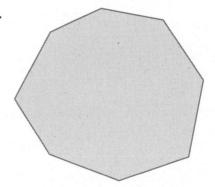

12.3 Angles of Polygons (continued)

f. REPEATED REASONING Use your results to complete the table. Then find the sum of the interior angle measures of a polygon with 12 sides.

Number of Sides, n	3	4	5	6	7	8
Number of Triangles						
Angle Sum, S						

2 ACTIVITY: Exploring the Exterior Angles of a Polygon

Work with a partner.

a. Draw a convex pentagon. Extend the sides to form the exterior angles. Label one exterior angle at each vertex A, B, C, D, and E, as shown.

b. Cut out the exterior angles. How can you join the vertices to determine the sum of the angle measures? What do you notice?

c. **REPEATED REASONING** Repeat the procedure in parts (a) and (b) for each figure below.

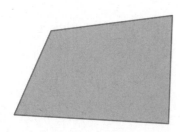 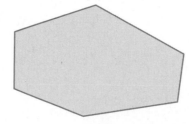

What can you conclude about the sum of the measures of the exterior angles of a convex polygon? Explain.

12.3   Angles of Polygons (continued)

What Is Your Answer?

3. **STRUCTURE** Use your results from Activity 1 to write an expression that represents the sum of the interior angle measures of a polygon.

4. **IN YOUR OWN WORDS** How can you find the sum of the interior angle measures and the sum of the exterior angle measures of a polygon?

Name_____ Date _____

Find the sum of the interior angle measures of the polygon.

1.

2.

3.

Find the measures of the interior angles.

4.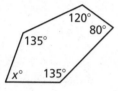

5.

Find the measure of each interior angle of the regular polygon.

6.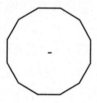

7.

8. In pottery class, you are making a pot that is shaped as a regular hexagon. What is the measure of each angle in the regular hexagon?

12.4 Using Similar Triangles
For use with Activity 12.4

Essential Question How can you use angles to tell whether triangles are similar?

---

1 **ACTIVITY:** Constructing Similar Triangles

Work with a partner.

- **Use a straightedge to draw a line segment that is 4 centimeters long.**

- **Then use the line segment and a protractor to draw a triangle that has a 60° and a 40° angle as shown. Label the triangle *ABC*.**

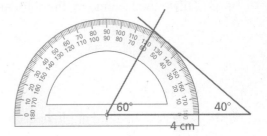

a. Explain how to draw a larger triangle that has the same two angle measures. Label the triangle *JKL*.

b. Explain how to draw a smaller triangle that has the same two angle measures. Label the triangle *PQR*.

c. Are all of the triangles similar? Explain.

12.4 **Using Similar Triangles** (continued)

---

2 **ACTIVITY:** Using Technology to Explore Triangles

Work with a partner. Use geometry software to draw the triangle shown.

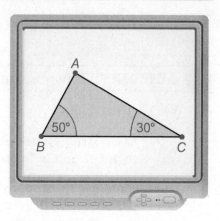

a. Dilate the triangle by the following scale factors.

$$2 \qquad \frac{1}{2} \qquad \frac{1}{4} \qquad 2.5$$

b. Measure the third angle in each triangle. What do you notice?

c. **REASONING** When two angles in one triangle are congruent to two angles in another triangle, can you conclude that the triangles are similar? Explain.

---

3 **ACTIVITY:** Indirect Measurement

Work with a partner.

a. Use the fact that two rays from the Sun are parallel to explain why $\triangle ABC$ and $\triangle DEF$ are similar.

12.4 **Using Similar Triangles** (continued)

b. Explain how to use similar triangles to find the height of the flagpole.

What Is Your Answer?

4. **IN YOUR OWN WORDS** How can you use angles to tell whether triangles are similar?

5. **PROJECT** Work with a partner or in a small group.

   a. Explain why the process in Activity 3 is called "indirect" measurement.

   b. **CHOOSE TOOLS** Use indirect measurement to measure the height of something outside your school (a tree, a building, a flagpole). Before going outside, decide what materials you need to take with you.

   c. **MODELING** Draw a diagram of the indirect measurement process you used. In the diagram, label the lengths that you actually measured and also the lengths that you calculated.

6. **PRECISION** Look back at Exercise 17 in Section 11.5. Explain how you can show that the two triangles are similar.

12.4 **Practice**
For use after Lesson 12.4

Tell whether the triangles are similar. Explain.

1.

2.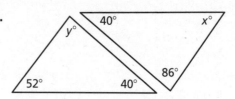

3.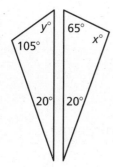

4.

5. You can use similar triangles to find the height of a tree. Triangle *ABC* is similar to triangle *DEC*. What is the height of the tree?

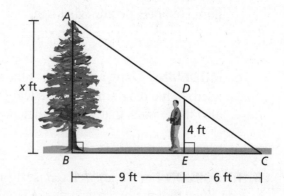

Chapter 13 Fair Game Review

Evaluate the expression when $x = \dfrac{1}{2}$ **and** $y = -5$.

1. $-2xy$

2. $4x^2 - 3y$

3. $\dfrac{10y}{12x + 4}$

4. $11x - 8(x - y)$

Evaluate the expression when $a = -9$ **and** $b = -4$.

5. $3ab$

6. $a^2 - 2(b + 12)$

7. $\dfrac{4b^2}{3b - 7}$

8. $7b^2 + 5(ab - 6)$

9. You go to the movies with five friends. You and one of your friends each buy a ticket and a bag of popcorn. The rest of your friends buy just one ticket each. The expression $4x + 2(x + y)$ represents the situation. Evaluate the expression when tickets cost $7.25 and a bag of popcorn costs $3.25.

Chapter 13 **Fair Game Review** (continued)

Use the graph to answer the question.

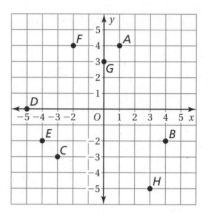

10. Write the ordered pair that corresponds to Point *D*.

11. Write the ordered pair that corresponds to Point *H*.

12. Which point is located at $(-2, 4)$?

13. Which point is located at $(0, 3)$?

14. Which point(s) are located in Quadrant IV?

15. Which point(s) are located in Quadrant III?

Plot the point.

16. $(3, -1)$

17. $(0, 2)$

18. $(-5, -4)$

19. $(-1, 0)$

20. $(-2, 3)$

13.1 **Graphing Linear Equations**
For use with Activity 13.1

Essential Question How can you recognize a linear equation? How can you draw its graph?

---

1 **ACTIVITY:** Graphing a Linear Equation

Work with a partner.

a. Use the equation $y = \frac{1}{2}x + 1$

to complete the table. (Choose any two x-values and find the y-values).

	Solution Points	
x		
$y = \frac{1}{2}x + 1$		

b. Write the two ordered pairs given by the table. These are called *solution points* of the equation.

c. **PRECISION** Plot the two solution points. Draw a line *exactly* through the two points.

d. Find a different point on the line. Check that this point is a solution point of the equation $y = \frac{1}{2}x + 1$.

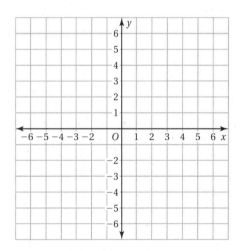

e. **LOGIC** Do you think it is true that *any* point on the line is a solution point of the equation $y = \frac{1}{2}x + 1$? Explain.

13.1 **Graphing Linear Equations** (continued)

f. Choose five additional *x*-values for the table. (Choose positive and negative *x*-values.) Plot the five corresponding solution points on the previous page. Does each point lie on the line?

	Solution Points				
x					
$y = \dfrac{1}{2}x + 1$					

g. **LOGIC** Do you think it is true that *any* solution point of the equation $y = \dfrac{1}{2}x + 1$ is a point on the line? Explain.

h. Why do you think $y = ax + b$ is called a *linear equation*?

2 **ACTIVITY:** Using a Graphing Calculator

Use a graphing calculator to graph $y = 2x + 5$.

a. Enter the equation $y = 2x + 5$ into your calculator.

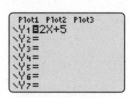

b. Check the settings of the *viewing window*. The boundaries of the graph are set by the minimum and maximum *x*- and *y*-values. The numbers of units between the tick marks are set by the *x*- and *y*-scales.

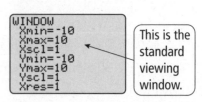

This is the standard viewing window.

Name_____ Date_____

   c. Graph $y = 2x + 5$ on your calculator.

   d. Change the settings of the viewing
      window to match those shown.
      Compare the two graphs.

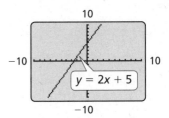

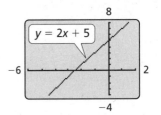

What Is Your Answer?

  3. **IN YOUR OWN WORDS** How can you recognize a linear equation? How
     can you draw its graph? Write an equation that is linear. Write an equation
     that is *not* linear.

  4. Use a graphing calculator to graph $y = 5x - 12$ in the standard viewing
     window.

    a. Can you tell where the line crosses the *x*-axis? Can you tell where
       the line crosses the *y*-axis?

    b. How can you adjust the viewing window so that you can determine
       where the line crosses the *x*- and *y*-axes?

  5. **CHOOSE TOOLS** You want to graph $y = 2.5x - 3.8$. Would you graph
     it by hand or by using a graphing calculator? Why?

13.1 Practice
For use after Lesson 13.1

Graph the linear equation. Use a graphing calculator to check your graph, if possible.

1. $y = 4$

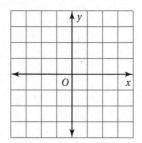

2. $y = -\dfrac{1}{3}x$

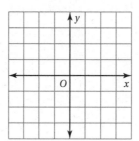

Solve for y. Then graph the equation. Use a graphing calculator to check your graph.

3. $y + 2x = 3$

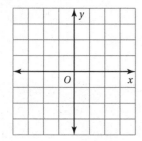

4. $2y - 3x = 1$

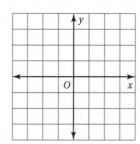

5. The equation $y = 2x + 4$ represents the cost y (in dollars) of renting a movie after x days of late charges.

a. Graph the equation.

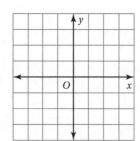

b. Use the graph to determine how much it costs after 3 days of late charges.

13.2 Slope of a Line
For use with Activity 13.2

Essential Question How can the slope of a line be used to describe the line?

Slope is the rate of change between any two points on a line. It is the measure of the *steepness* of the line.

To find the slope of a line, find the ratio of the change in y (vertical change) to the change in x (horizontal change).

$$\text{slope} = \frac{\text{change in } y}{\text{change in } x}$$

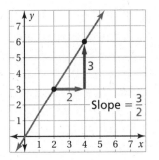

Slope $= \dfrac{3}{2}$

---

1 ACTIVITY: Finding the Slope of a Line

Work with a partner. Find the slope of each line using two methods.

    Method 1: Use the two black points.

    Method 2: Use the two gray points.

Do you get the same slope using each method? Why do you think this happens?

a.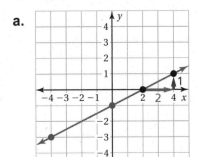

b.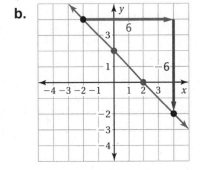

c.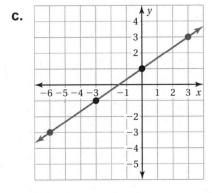

d.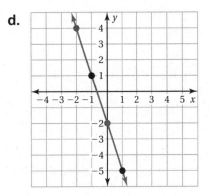

13.2 **Slope of a Line** (continued)

2 **ACTIVITY:** Using Similar Triangles

Work with a partner. Use the figure shown.

a. $\triangle ABC$ is a right triangle formed by drawing a horizontal line segment from point A and a vertical line segment from point B. Use this method to draw another right triangle, $\triangle DEF$.

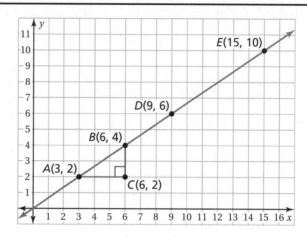

b. What can you conclude about $\triangle ABC$ and $\triangle DEF$? Justify your conclusion.

c. For each triangle, find the ratio of the length of the vertical side to the length of the horizontal side. What do these ratios represent?

d. What can you conclude about the slope between any two points on the line?

3 **ACTIVITY:** Drawing Lines with Given Slopes

Work with a partner.

a. Draw two lines with slope $\dfrac{3}{4}$. One line passes through $(-4, 1)$, and the other line passes through $(4, 0)$. What do you notice about the two lines?

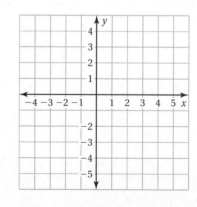

13.2 Slope of a Line (continued)

b. Draw two lines with slope $-\dfrac{4}{3}$. One line passes through $(2, 1)$, and the other line passes through $(-1, -1)$. What do you notice about the two lines?

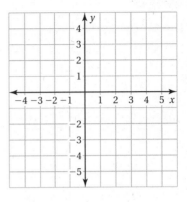

c. **CONJECTURE** Make a conjecture about two different nonvertical lines in the same plane that have the same slope.

d. Graph one line from part (a) and one line from part (b) in the same coordinate plane. Describe the angle formed by the two lines. What do you notice about the product of the slopes of the two lines?

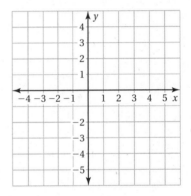

e. **REPEATED REASONING** Repeat part (d) for the two lines you did *not* choose. Based on your results, make a conjecture about two lines in the same plane whose slopes have a product of -1.

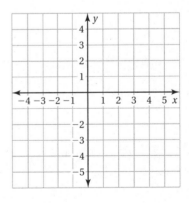

What Is Your Answer?

4. **IN YOUR OWN WORDS** How can you use the slope of a line to describe the line?

Name _____ Date _____

13.2 Practice
For use after Lesson 13.2

Find the slope of the line.

1.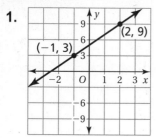

2.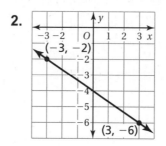

3.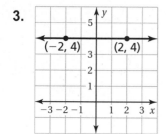

4.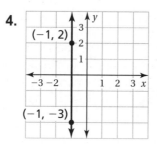

5. Which set of stairs is more difficult to climb? Explain.

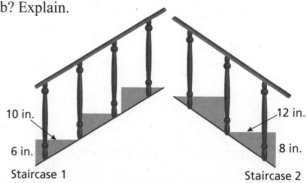

Extension 13.2 **Practice**
For use after Extension 13.2

Which lines are parallel? How do you know?

1.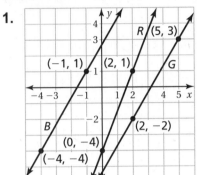

2.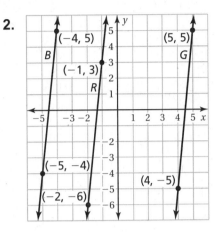

Are the given lines parallel? Explain your reasoning.

3. $y = 2, y = -4$

4. $x = 3, y = -3$

5. Is the quadrilateral a parallelogram? Justify your answer.

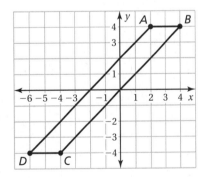

Extension 13.2 **Practice** (continued)

Which lines are perpendicular? How do you know?

6.

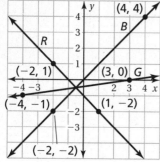

7.

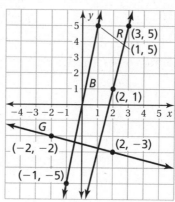

Are the given lines perpendicular? Explain your reasoning.

8. $x = 0, y = 3$

9. $y = 2, y = -\dfrac{1}{2}$

10. Is the parallelogram a rectangle? Justify your answer.

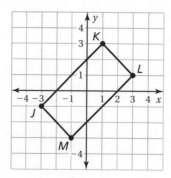

13.3 Graphing Proportional Relationships
For use with Activity 13.3

Essential Question How can you describe the graph of the equation $y = mx$?

---

1 **ACTIVITY:** Identifying Proportional Relationships

Work with a partner. Tell whether x and y are in a proportional relationship. Explain your reasoning.

a.   Money

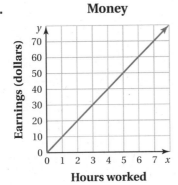

b.   Helicopter

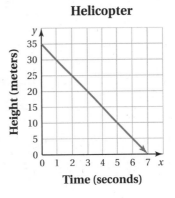

c.   Tickets

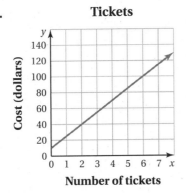

d.   Pizzas

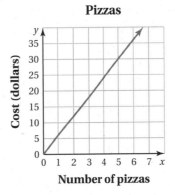

e.

Laps, x	1	2	3	4
Time (seconds), y	90	200	325	480

f.

Cups of Sugar, x	$\frac{1}{2}$	1	$1\frac{1}{2}$	2
Cups of Flour, y	1	2	3	4

13.3 Graphing Proportional Relationships (continued)

2 ACTIVITY: Analyzing Proportional Relationships

Work with a partner. Use only the proportional relationships in Activity 1 to do the following.

- **Find the slope of the line.**
- **Find the value of y for the ordered pair $(1, y)$.**

What do you notice? What does the value of y represent?

3 ACTIVITY: Deriving an Equation

Work with a partner. Let (x, y) represent any point on the graph of a proportional relationship.

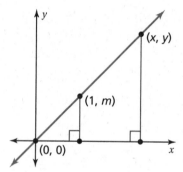

a. Explain why the two triangles are similar.

b. Because the triangles are similar, the corresponding side lengths are proportional. Use the vertical and horizontal side lengths to complete the steps below.

$$\frac{\boxed{}}{\boxed{}} = \frac{m}{1} \qquad \text{Ratios of side lengths}$$

$$\frac{\boxed{}}{\boxed{}} = m \qquad \text{Simplify.}$$

$$\boxed{} = m \cdot \boxed{} \qquad \text{Multiplication Property of Equality}$$

What does the final equation represent?

13.3 Graphing Proportional Relationships (continued)

   c. Use your result in part (b) to write an equation that represents each proportional relationship in Activity 1.

What Is Your Answer?

   4. IN YOUR OWN WORDS How can you describe the graph of the equation $y = mx$? How does the value of m affect the graph of the equation?

   5. Give a real-life example of two quantities that are in a proportional relationship. Write an equation that represents the relationship and sketch its graph.

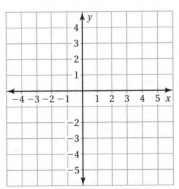

Name _____ Date _____

1. The amount p (in dollars) that you earn by working h hours is represented by the equation $p = 9h$. Graph the equation and interpret the slope.

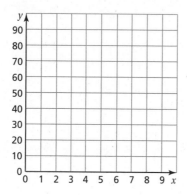

2. The cost c (in dollars) to rent a bicycle is proportional to the number h of hours that you rent the bicycle. It costs $20 to rent the bicycle for 4 hours.

   a. Write an equation that represents the situation.

   b. Interpret the slope.

   c. How much does it cost to rent the bicycle for 6 hours?

Name_____ Date _____

13.4 Graphing Linear Equations in Slope-Intercept Form
For use with Activity 13.4

Essential Question How can you describe the graph of the equation
$y = mx + b$?

1 ACTIVITY: Analyzing Graphs of Lines

Work with a partner.

- Graph each equation.
- Find the slope of each line.
- Find the point where each line crosses the y-axis.
- Complete the table.

Equation	Slope of Graph	Point of Intersection with y-axis
a. $y = -\dfrac{1}{2}x + 1$		
b. $y = -x + 2$		
c. $y = -x - 2$		
d. $y = \dfrac{1}{2}x + 1$		
e. $y = x + 2$		
f. $y = x - 2$		
g. $y = \dfrac{1}{2}x - 1$		
h. $y = -\dfrac{1}{2}x - 1$		
i. $y = 3x + 2$		

13.4 **Graphing Linear Equations in Slope-Intercept Form** (continued)

Equation	Slope of Graph	Point of Intersection with *y*-axis
j. $y = 3x - 2$		

k. Do you notice any relationship between the slope of the graph and its equation? Between the point of intersection with the *y*-axis and its equation? Compare the results with those of other students in your class.

2 **ACTIVITY:** Deriving an Equation

Work with a partner.

a. Look at the graph of each equation in Activity 1. Do any of the graphs represent a proportional relationship? Explain.

b. For a nonproportional linear relationship, the graph crosses the *y*-axis at some point $(0, b)$, where *b* does not equal 0.

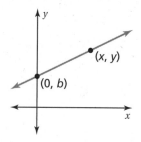

Let (x, y) represent any other point on the graph. You can use the formula for slope to write the equation for a nonproportional linear relationship.

Use the graph to complete the steps.

$$\frac{y_2 - y_1}{x_2 - x_1} = m$$ **Slope formula**

$$\frac{y - \boxed{}}{x - \boxed{}} = m$$ **Substitute values.**

$$\frac{\boxed{}}{\boxed{}} = m$$ **Simplify.**

 $\bullet \; \boxed{} = m \bullet \boxed{}$ **Multiplication Property of Equality**

$y - \boxed{} = m \bullet \boxed{}$ **Simplify.**

$y = m\boxed{} + \boxed{}$ **Addition Property of Equality**

13.4 Graphing Linear Equations in Slope-Intercept Form (continued)

c. What do m and b represent in the equation?

What Is Your Answer?

3. **IN YOUR OWN WORDS** How can you describe the graph of the equation $y = mx + b$?

   a. How does the value of m affect the graph of the equation?

   b. How does the value of b affect the graph of the equation?

   c. Check your answers to parts (a) and (b) with three equations that are not in Activity 1.

4. **LOGIC** Why do you think $y = mx + b$ is called the *slope-intercept form* of the equation of a line? Use drawings or diagrams to support your answer.

Name _____ Date _____

Find the slope and *y*-intercept of the graph of the linear equation.

1. $y = -3x + 9$

2. $y = 4 - \dfrac{2}{5}x$

3. $6 + y = 8x$

Graph the linear equation. Identify the *x*-intercept. Use a graphing calculator to check your answer.

4. $y = \dfrac{2}{3}x + 6$

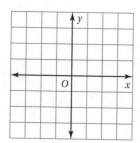

5. $y - 10 = -5x$

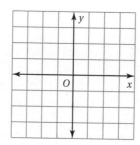

6. The equation $y = -90x + 1440$ represents the time (in minutes) left after *x* games of a tournament.

   a. Graph the equation.

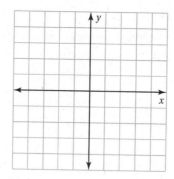

   b. Interpret the *x*-intercept and slope.

13.5 Graphing Linear Equations in Standard Form
For use with Activity 13.5

Essential Question How can you describe the graph of the equation $ax + by = c$?

---

1 **ACTIVITY:** Using a Table to Plot Points

Work with a partner. You sold a total of $16 worth of tickets to a school concert. You lost track of how many of each type of ticket you sold.

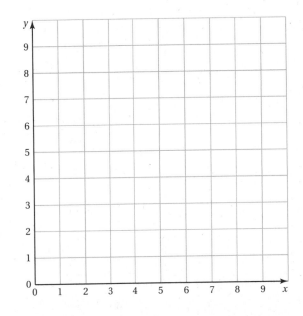

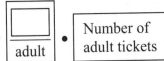 • Number of adult tickets + • Number of student tickets =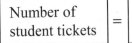

a. Let x represent the number of adult tickets.
Let y represent the number of student tickets.
Write an equation that relates x and y.

b. Complete the table showing the different combinations of tickets you might have sold.

Number of Adult Tickets, x					
Number of Student Tickets, y					

c. Plot the points from the table. Describe the pattern formed by the points.

d. If you remember how many adult tickets you sold, can you determine how many student tickets you sold? Explain your reasoning.

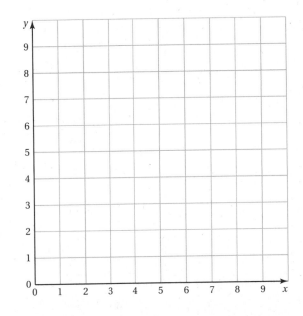

Big Ideas Math Red Accelerated **311**
Record and Practice Journal

13.5 **Graphing Linear Equations in Standard Form** (continued)

2 **ACTIVITY:** Rewriting an Equation

Work with a partner. You sold a total of $16 worth of cheese. You forgot how many pounds of each type of cheese you sold.

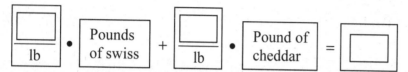

a. Let x represent the number of pounds of swiss cheese. Let y represent the number of pounds of cheddar cheese. Write an equation that relates x and y.

b. Rewrite the equation in slope-intercept form. Then graph the equation.

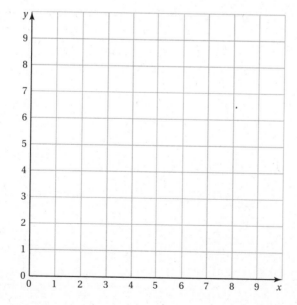

13.5 **Graphing Linear Equations in Standard Form** (continued)

c. You sold 2 pounds of cheddar cheese. How many pounds of swiss cheese did you sell?

d. Does the value $x = 2.5$ make sense in the context of the problem? Explain.

What Is Your Answer?

3. **IN YOUR OWN WORDS** How can you describe the graph of the equation $ax + by = c$?

4. Activities 1 and 2 show two different methods for graphing $ax + by = c$. Describe the two methods. Which method do you prefer? Explain.

5. Write a real-life problem that is similar to those shown in Activities 1 and 2.

6. Why do you think it might be easier to graph $x + y = 10$ without rewriting it in slope-intercept form and then graphing?

13.5 Practice
For use after Lesson 13.5

Write the linear equation in slope-intercept form.

1. $2x - y = 7$

2. $\frac{1}{4}x + y = -\frac{2}{7}$

3. $3x - 5y = -20$

Graph the linear equation using intercepts. Use a graphing calculator to check your graph.

4. $2x - 3y = 12$

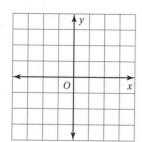

5. $x + 9y = -27$

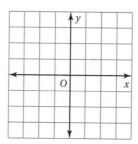

6. You go shopping and buy x shirts for \$12 and y jeans for \$28. The total spent is \$84.

   a. Write an equation in standard form that models how much money you spent.

   b. Graph the equation and interpret the intercepts.

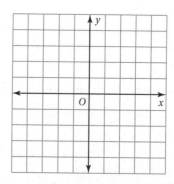

13.6 Writing Equations in Slope-Intercept Form
For use with Activity 13.6

Essential Question How can you write an equation of a line when you are given the slope and *y*-intercept of the line?

---

1 ACTIVITY: Writing Equations of Lines

Work with a partner.

- Find the slope of each line.

- Find the *y*-intercept of each line.

- Write an equation for each line.

- What do the three lines have in common?

a.
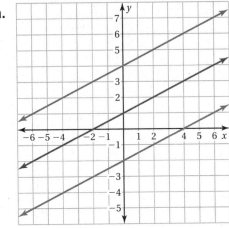

b.
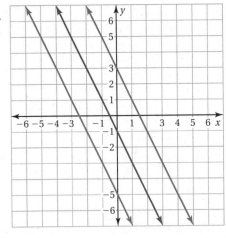

c.
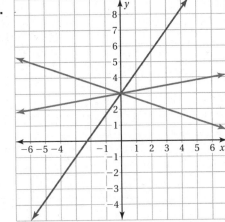

d.
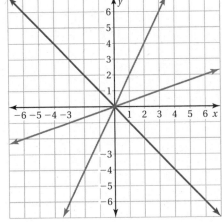

13.6 **Writing Equations in Slope-Intercept Form** (continued)

2 **ACTIVITY:** Describing a Parallelogram

Work with a partner.

- Find the area of each parallelogram.

- Write an equation that represents each side of each parallelogram.

a. 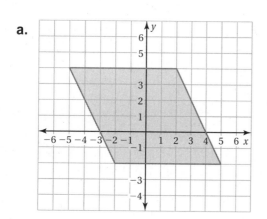 **b.**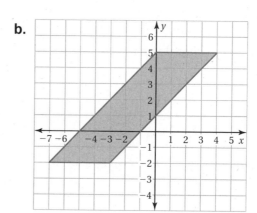

3 **ACTIVITY:** Interpreting the Slope and the *y*-Intercept

Work with a partner. The graph shows a trip taken by a car, where *t* is the time (in hours) and *y* is the distance (in miles) from Phoenix.

a. Find the *y*-intercept of the graph. What does it represent?

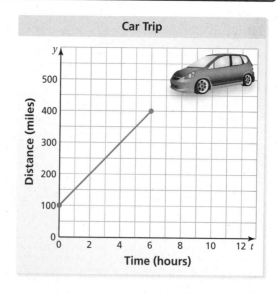

13.6 **Writing Equations in Slope-Intercept Form** (continued)

b. Find the slope of the graph. What does it represent?

c. How long did the trip last?

d. How far from Phoenix was the car at the end of the trip?

e. Write an equation that represents the graph.

What Is Your Answer?

4. IN YOUR OWN WORDS How can you write an equation of a line when you are given the slope and the y-intercept of the line? Give an example that is different from those in Activities 1, 2, and 3.

5. Two sides of a parallelogram are represented by the equations $y = 2x + 1$ and $y = -x + 3$. Give two equations that can represent the other two sides.

Name_____ Date _____

Write an equation of the line in slope-intercept form.

1.

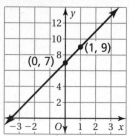

2.

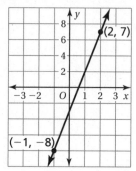

3.

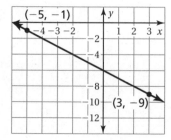

4.

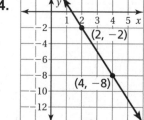

Write an equation of the line that passes through the points.

5. $(3, 8), (-2, 8)$

6. $(4, 3), (6, -3)$

7. $(-1, 0), (-5, 0)$

8. You organize a garage sale. You have $30 at the beginning of the sale. You earn an average of $20 per hour. Write an equation that represents the amount of money y you have after x hours.

13.7 Writing Equations in Point-Slope Form
For use with Activity 13.7

Essential Question   How can you write an equation of a line when you are given the slope and a point on the line?

---

1 **ACTIVITY:** Writing Equations of Lines

Work with a partner.

- Sketch the line that has the given slope and passes through the given point.

- Find the *y*-intercept of the line.

- Write an equation of the line.

a. $m = -2$

b. $m = \dfrac{1}{3}$

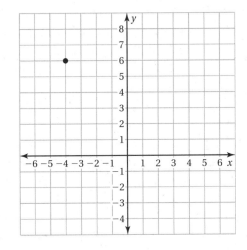

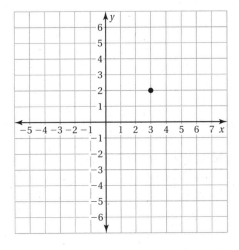

c. $m = -\dfrac{2}{3}$

d. $m = \dfrac{5}{2}$

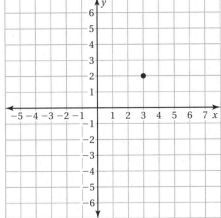

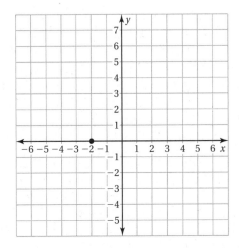

13.7 Writing Equations in Point-Slope Form (continued)

2 ACTIVITY: Deriving an Equation

Work with a partner.

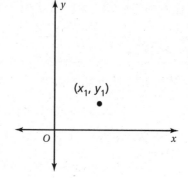

a. Draw a nonvertical line that passes through the point (x_1, y_1).

b. Plot another point on your line. Label this point as (x, y). This point represents any other point on the line.

c. Label the rise and run of the line through the points (x_1, y_1) and (x, y).

d. The rise can be written as $y - y_1$. The run can be written as $x - x_1$. Explain why this is true.

e. Write an equation for the slope m of the line using the expressions from part (d).

f. Multiply each side of the equation by the expression in the denominator. Write your result. What does this result represent?

Name_____ Date_____

3 **ACTIVITY:** Writing an Equation

Work with a partner.

For 4 months, you saved $25 a month. You
now have $175 in your savings account.

- Draw a graph that shows the balance
  in your account after t months.

- Use your result from Activity 2 to
  write an equation that represents
  the balance A after t months.

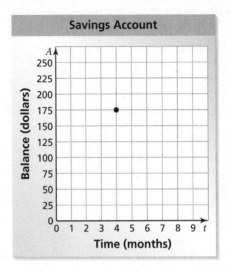

What Is Your Answer?

4. Redo Activity 1 using the equation you found in Activity 2. Compare
the results. What do you notice?

5. Why do you think $y - y_1 = m(x - x_1)$ is called the *point-slope form* of
the equation of a line? Why do you think this is important?

6. **IN YOUR OWN WORDS** How can you write an equation of a line when
you are given the slope and a point on the line? Give an example that is
different from those in Activity 1.

13.7 Practice
For use after Lesson 13.7

Write in point-slope form an equation of the line that passes through the given point that has the given slope.

1. $m = -3; (-4, 6)$

2. $m = -\dfrac{4}{3}; (3, -1)$

Write in slope-intercept form an equation of the line that passes through the given points.

3. $(-3, 0), (-2, 3)$

4. $(-6, 10), (6, -10)$

5. The total cost for bowling includes the fee for shoe rental plus a fee per game. The cost of each game increases the price by $4. After 3 games, the total cost with shoe rental is $14.

   a. Write an equation to represent the total cost y to rent shoes and bowl x games.

   b. How much is shoe rental? How is this represented in the equation?

Name_____ Date_____

Chapter 14 Fair Game Review

Complete the number sentence with <, >, or =.

1. 3.4 _____ 3.45

2. −6.01 _____ −6.1

3. 3.50 _____ 3.5

4. −0.84 _____ −0.91

Find three decimals that make the number sentence true.

5. −5.2 ≥ _____

6. 2.65 > _____

7. −3.18 ≤ _____

8. 0.03 < _____

9. The table shows the times of a 100-meter dash. Order the runners from first place to fifth place.

Runner	Time (seconds)
A	12.60
B	12.55
C	12.49
D	12.63
E	12.495

Chapter 14 **Fair Game Review** (continued)

Evaluate the expression.

10. $10^2 - 48 \div 6 + 25 \bullet 3$

11. $8\left(\dfrac{16}{4}\right) + 2^2 - 11 \bullet 3$

12. $\left(\dfrac{6}{3} + 4\right)^2 \div 4 \bullet 7$

13. $5(9 - 4)^2 - 3^2$

14. $5^2 - 2^2 \bullet 4^2 - 12$

15. $\left(\dfrac{50}{5^2}\right)^2 \div 4$

16. The table shows the numbers of students in 4 classes. The teachers are combining the classes and dividing the students in half to form two groups for a project. Write an expression to represent this situation. How many students are in each group?

Class	Students
1	24
2	32
3	30
4	28

14.1 Finding Square Roots
For use with Activity 14.1

Essential Question How can you find the dimensions of a square or a circle when you are given its area?

When you multiply a number by itself, you square the number.

> Symbol for squaring is the exponent 2. → $4^2 = 4 \cdot 4$
> $= 16$

4 squared is 16.

To "undo" this, take the *square root* of the number.

> Symbol for square root is a *radical sign*, $\sqrt{\ }$. → $\sqrt{16} = \sqrt{4^2} = 4$

The square root of 16 is 4.

---

1 ACTIVITY: Finding Square Roots

Work with a partner. Use a square root symbol to write the side length of the square. Then find the square root. Check your answer by multiplying.

a. **Sample:** $s = \sqrt{121} =$ **Check:**

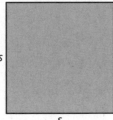

Area = 121 ft²

s

s

The length of each side of the square is _____.

b.   Area = 81 yd²

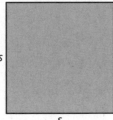

s

s

c.   Area = 324 cm²

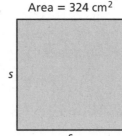

s

s

d.   Area = 361 mi²

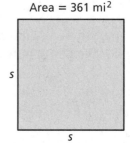

s

s

14.1 **Finding Square Roots** (continued)

e. Area = 225 mi²

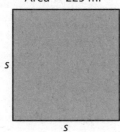

s   s

f. Area = 2.89 in.²

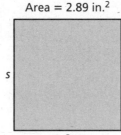

s   s

g. Area = $\frac{4}{9}$ ft²

s

---

2 **ACTIVITY:** Using Square Roots

Work with a partner. Find the radius of each circle.

a.

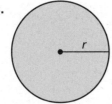

Area = 36π in.²

b.

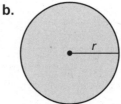

Area = π yd²

c.

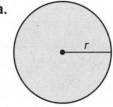

Area = 0.25π ft²

d.

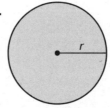

Area = $\frac{9}{16}$π m²

---

3 **ACTIVITY:** The Period of a Pendulum

Work with a partner.

The period of a pendulum is the time (in seconds) it takes the pendulum to swing back *and* forth.

The period T is represented by $T = 1.1\sqrt{L}$, where L is the length of the pendulum (in feet).

Complete the table. Then graph the ordered pairs on the next page. Is the equation linear?

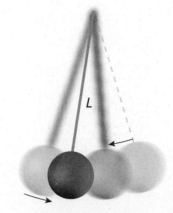

L

14.1 **Finding Square Roots** (continued)

L	1.00	1.96	3.24	4.00	4.84	6.25	7.29	7.84	9.00
T									

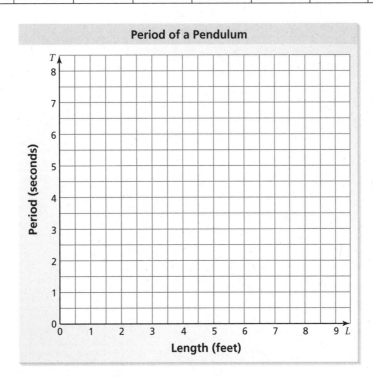

What Is Your Answer?

4. **IN YOUR OWN WORDS** How can you find the dimensions of a square or circle when you are given its area? Give an example of each. How can you check your answers?

14.1 Practice
For use after Lesson 14.1

Find the two square roots of the number.

1. 16
2. 100
3. 196

Find the square root(s).

4. $\sqrt{169}$
5. $\sqrt{\dfrac{4}{225}}$
6. $-\sqrt{12.25}$

Evaluate the expression.

7. $2\sqrt{36} + 9$
8. $8 - 11\sqrt{\dfrac{25}{121}}$
9. $3\left(\sqrt{\dfrac{125}{5}} - 8\right)$

10. A trampoline has an area of 49π square feet. What is the diameter of the trampoline?

14.2 Finding Cube Roots
For use with Activity 14.2

Essential Question How is the cube root of a number different from the square root of a number?

When you multiply a number by itself twice, you cube the number.

> Symbol for cubing is the exponent 3.

$4^3 = 4 \cdot 4 \cdot 4$
  $= 64$

4 cubed is 64.

To "undo" this, take the *cube root* of the number.

> Symbol for cube root is $\sqrt[3]{\ }$.

$\sqrt[3]{64} = \sqrt[3]{4^3} = 4$

The cube root of 64 is 4.

---

1 ACTIVITY: Finding Cube Roots

Work with a partner. Use a cube root symbol to write the edge length of the cube. Then find the cube root. Check your answer by multiplying.

a. Sample: $s = \sqrt[3]{343} = \sqrt[3]{7^3} = 7$ inches

Volume = 343 in.³

Check
$7 \cdot 7 \cdot 7 = 49 \cdot 7$
$\qquad\qquad = 343$ ✓

The edge length of the cube is 7 inches.

b. Volume = 27 ft³

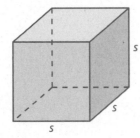

c. Volume = 125 m³

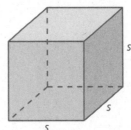

14.2 **Finding Cube Roots** (continued)

d. Volume = 0.001 cm³

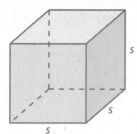

s

s

s

e. Volume = $\frac{1}{8}$ yd³

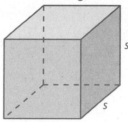

s

s

s

2 **ACTIVITY:** Use Prime Factorizations to Find Cube Roots

Work with a partner. Write the prime factorization of each number. Then use the prime factorization to find the cube root of the number.

a. 216

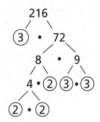

$$216 = 3 \cdot 2 \cdot 3 \cdot 3 \cdot 2 \cdot 2 \qquad \text{Prime factorization}$$

$$= \left(3 \cdot \boxed{}\right) \cdot \left(3 \cdot \boxed{}\right) \cdot \left(3 \cdot \boxed{}\right) \qquad \begin{array}{l}\text{Commutative Property}\\\text{of Multiplication}\end{array}$$

$$= \boxed{} \cdot \boxed{} \cdot \boxed{} \qquad \text{Simplify.}$$

The cube root of 216 is _____.

b. 1000

c. 3375

14.2 **Finding Cube Roots** (continued)

    d. STRUCTURE Does this procedure work for every number? Explain why or why not.

What Is Your Answer?

3. Complete each statement using *positive* or *negative*.

    a. A positive number times a positive number is a _____ number.

    b. A negative number times a negative number is a _____ number.

    c. A positive number multiplied by itself twice is a _____ number.

    d. A negative number multiplied by itself twice is a _____ number.

4. REASONING Can a negative number have a cube root? Give an example to support your explanation.

5. IN YOUR OWN WORDS How is the cube root of a number different from the square root of a number?

6. Give an example of a number whose square root and cube root are equal.

7. A cube has a volume of 13,824 cubic meters. Use a calculator to find the edge length.

14.2 **Practice**
For use after Lesson 14.2

Find the cube root.

1. $\sqrt[3]{27}$

2. $\sqrt[3]{8}$

3. $\sqrt[3]{-64}$

4. $\sqrt[3]{-\dfrac{125}{216}}$

Evaluate the expression.

5. $10 - \left(\sqrt[3]{12}\right)^3$

6. $2\sqrt[3]{512} + 10$

7. The volume of a cube is 1000 cubic inches. What is the edge length of the cube?

Name_____ Date_____

14.3 The Pythagorean Theorem
For use with Activity 14.3

Essential Question How are the lengths of the sides of a right triangle related?

Pythagoras was a Greek mathematician and philosopher who discovered one of the most famous rules in mathematics. In mathematics, a rule is called a **theorem**. So, the rule that Pythagoras discovered is called the Pythagorean Theorem.

Pythagoras
(c. 570–c. 490 B.C.)

1   ACTIVITY: Discovering the Pythagorean Theorem

Work with a partner.

a. On grid paper, draw any right triangle. Label the lengths of the two shorter sides a and b.

b. Label the length of the longest side c.

c. Draw squares along each of the three sides. Label the areas of the three squares a^2, b^2, and c^2.

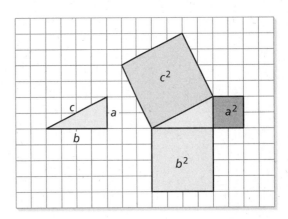

d. Cut out the three squares. Make eight copies of the right triangle and cut them out. Arrange the figures to form two identical larger squares.

e. **MODELING** The Pythagorean Theorem describes the relationship among a^2, b^2, and c^2. Use your result from part (d) to write an equation that describes this relationship.

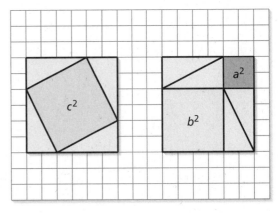

14.3 **The Pythagorean Theorem** (continued)

2 **ACTIVITY:** Using the Pythagorean Theorem in Two Dimensions

Work with a partner. Use a ruler to measure the longest side of each right triangle. Verify the result of Activity 1 for each right triangle.

a.

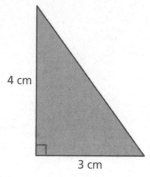

4 cm

3 cm

b.

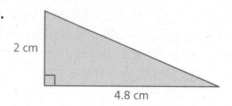

2 cm

4.8 cm

c.

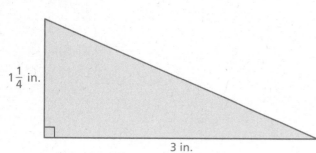

$1\frac{1}{4}$ in.

3 in.

d.

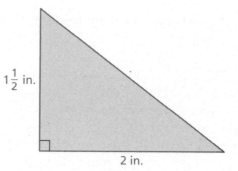

$1\frac{1}{2}$ in.

2 in.

14.3 **The Pythagorean Theorem** (continued)

3 **ACTIVITY:** Using the Pythagorean Theorem in Three Dimensions

Work with a partner. A guy wire attached 24 feet above ground level on a telephone pole provides support for the pole.

a. **PROBLEM SOLVING** Describe a procedure that you could use to find the length of the guy wire without directly measuring the wire.

guy wire

b. Find the length of the wire when it meets the ground 10 feet from the base of the pole.

What Is Your Answer?

4. **IN YOUR OWN WORDS** How are the lengths of the sides of a right triangle related? Give an example using whole numbers.

14.3 Practice
For use after Lesson 14.3

Find the missing length of the triangle.

1.

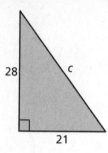

28   c

21

2.

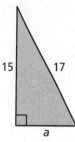

15   17

a

3.

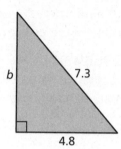

b   7.3

4.8

Find the missing length of the figure.

4.

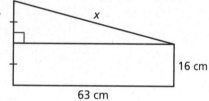

x

16 cm

63 cm

5.

x   13 m

35 m   5 m

6. In wood shop, you make a bookend that is in the shape of a right triangle. What is the base *b* of the bookend?

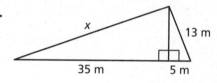

8 in.   10 in.

b

14.4 Approximating Square Roots
For use with Activity 14.4

Essential Question How can you find decimal approximations of square roots that are not rational?

---

1 ACTIVITY: Approximating Square Roots

Work with a partner. Archimedes was a Greek mathematician, physicist, engineer, inventor, and astronomer. He tried to find a rational number whose square is 3. Two that he tried were $\dfrac{265}{153}$ and $\dfrac{1351}{780}$.

a. Are either of these numbers equal to $\sqrt{3}$? Explain.

b. Use a calculator to approximate $\sqrt{3}$. Write the number on a piece of paper. Enter it into the calculator and square it. Then subtract 3. Do you get 0? What does this mean?

c. The value of $\sqrt{3}$ is between which two integers?

d. Tell whether the value of $\sqrt{3}$ is between the given numbers. Explain your reasoning.

| 1.7 and 1.8 | 1.72 and 1.73 | 1.731 and 1.732 |

---

2 ACTIVITY: Approximating Square Roots Geometrically

Work with a partner. Refer to the square on the number line below.

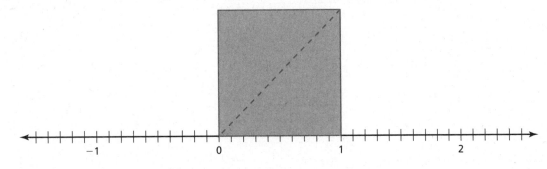

a. What is the length of the diagonal of the square?

b. Copy the square and its diagonal onto a piece of transparent paper. Rotate it about zero on the number line so that the diagonal aligns with the number line. Use the number line to estimate the length of the diagonal.

14.4 **Approximating Square Roots** (continued)

   c. **STRUCTURE** How do you think your answers in parts (a) and (b) are
   related?

---

3 **ACTIVITY:** Approximating Square Roots Geometrically

Work with a partner.

   a. Use grid paper and the given scale to draw a horizontal line segment 1 unit in
   length. Draw your segment near the bottom of the grid. Label this segment *AC*.

   b. Draw a vertical line segment 2 units in length. Draw your segment near the left
   edge of the grid. Label this segment *DC*.

   c. Set the point of a compass on *A*.   **d.** Use the Pythagorean Theorem to
   Set the compass to 2 units. Swing   find the length of segment *BC*.
   the compass to intersect segment
   DC. Label this intersection as *B*.

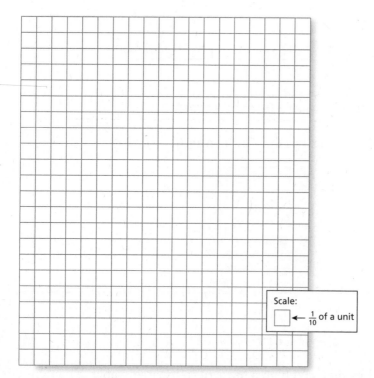

Scale:

☐ ← $\frac{1}{10}$ of a unit

   e. Use the grid paper to approximate $\sqrt{3}$ to the nearest tenth.

14.4 Approximating Square Roots (continued)

4. Compare your approximation in Activity 3 with your results from Activity 1.

What Is Your Answer?

5. Repeat Activity 3 for a triangle in which segment *AC* is 2 units and segment *BA* is 3 units. Use the Pythagorean Theorem to find the length of segment *BC*. Use the grid paper to approximate $\sqrt{5}$ to the nearest tenth.

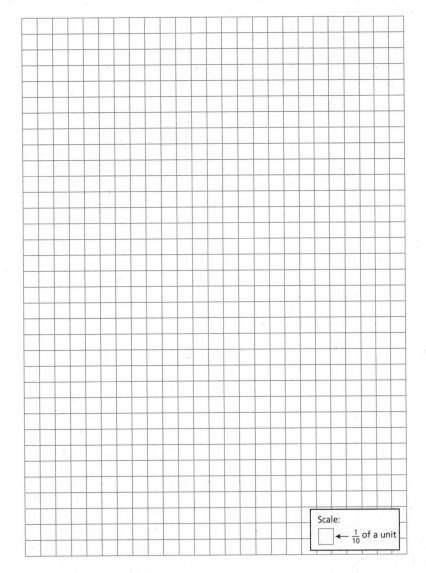

Scale:

□ ← $\frac{1}{10}$ of a unit

6. **IN YOUR OWN WORDS** How can you find decimal approximations of square roots that are not rational?

14.4 Practice

For use after Lesson 14.4

Classify the real number.

1. $\sqrt{14}$

2. $-\dfrac{3}{7}$

3. $\dfrac{153}{3}$

Estimate the square root to the nearest (a) integer and (b) tenth.

4. $\sqrt{8}$

5. $\sqrt{60}$

6. $-\sqrt{\dfrac{172}{25}}$

Which number is greater? Explain.

7. $\sqrt{88}$, 12

8. $-\sqrt{18}$, -6

9. 14.5, $\sqrt{220}$

10. The velocity in meters per second of a ball that is dropped from a window at a height of 10.5 meters is represented by the equation $v = \sqrt{2(9.8)(10.5)}$. Estimate the velocity of the ball. Round your answer to the nearest tenth.

Name_____ Date _____

Write the decimal as a fraction or a mixed number.

1. $0.\overline{3}$

2. $-0.\overline{2}$

3. $1.\overline{7}$

4. $-2.\overline{6}$

5. $0.4\overline{6}$

6. $-1.8\overline{3}$

**Extension
14.4** **Practice** (continued)

7. $-0.7\overline{3}$

8. $0.\overline{18}$

9. $-3.\overline{24}$

10. $1.\overline{09}$

11. The length of a pencil is $1.5\overline{6}$ inches. Represent the length of the pencil as a mixed number.

14.5 Using the Pythagorean Theorem
For use with Activity 14.5

Essential Question In what other ways can you use the Pythagorean Theorem?

The *converse* of a statement switches the hypothesis and the conclusion.

Statement:
If p, then q.

Converse of the statement:
If q, then p.

1 ACTIVITY: Analyzing Converses of Statements

Work with a partner. Write the converse of the true statement. Determine whether the converse is *true* or *false*. If it is true, justify your reasoning. If it is false, give a counterexample.

a. If $a = b$, then $a^2 = b^2$.

Converse:_____

b. If $a = b$, then $a^3 = b^3$.

Converse:_____

c. If one figure is a translation of another figure, then the figures are congruent.

Converse:_____

d. If two triangles are similar, then the triangles have the same angle measures.

Converse:_____

Is the converse of a true statement always true? always false? Explain.

14.5 **Using the Pythagorean Theorem** (continued)

2 **ACTIVITY:** The Converse of the Pythagorean Theorem

Work with a partner. The converse of the Pythagorean Theorem states: "If the equation $a^2 + b^2 = c^2$ is true for the side lengths of a triangle, then the triangle is a right triangle."

a. Do you think the converse of the Pythagorean Theorem is *true* or *false*? How could you use deductive reasoning to support your answer?

b. Consider $\triangle DEF$ with side lengths a, b, and c, such that $a^2 + b^2 = c^2$. Also consider $\triangle JKL$ with leg lengths a and b, where $\angle K = 90°$.

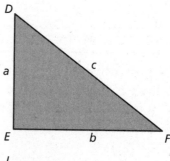

- What does the Pythagorean Theorem tell you about $\triangle JKL$?

- What does this tell you about c and x?

- What does this tell you about $\triangle DEF$ and $\triangle JKL$?

- What does this tell you about $\angle E$?

- What can you conclude?

14.5 Using the Pythagorean Theorem (continued)

3 **ACTIVITY:** Developing the Distance Formula

Work with a partner. Follow the steps below to write a formula that you can use to find the distance between and two points in a coordinate plane.

Step 1: Choose two points in the coordinate plane that do not lie on the same horizontal or vertical line. Label the points (x_1, y_1) and (x_2, y_2).

Step 2: Draw a line segment connecting the points. This will be the hypotenuse of a right triangle.

Step 3: Draw horizontal and vertical line segments from the points to form the legs of the right triangle.

Step 4: Use the x-coordinates to write an expression for the length of the horizontal leg.

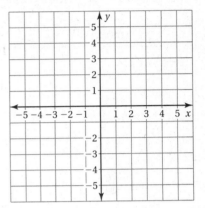

Step 5: Use the y-coordinates to write an expression for the length of the vertical leg.

Step 6: Substitute the expressions for the lengths of the legs into the Pythagorean Theorem.

Step 7: Solve the equation in Step 6 for the hypotenuse c.

What does the length of the hypotenuse tell you about the two points?

What Is Your Answer?

4. **IN YOUR OWN WORDS** In what other ways can you use the Pythagorean Theorem?

5. What kind of real-life problems do you think the converse of the Pythagorean Theorem can help you solve?

14.5 Practice
For use after Lesson 14.5

Tell whether the triangle with the given side lengths is a right triangle.

1.

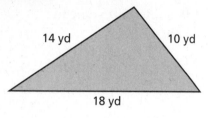

14 yd   10 yd

18 yd

2.

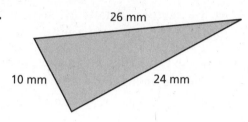

26 mm

10 mm   24 mm

3. 4 m, 4.2 m, 5.8 m

4. 31 in., 35 in., 16 in.

Find the distance between the two points.

5. $(2, 1), (-3, 6)$

6. $(-6, -4), (2, 2)$

7. $(1, -7), (4, -5)$

8. $(-9, 3), (-5, -8)$

9. The cross-section of a wheelchair ramp is shown. Does the ramp form a right triangle?

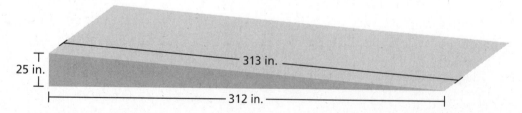

25 in.

313 in.

312 in.

Name_____ Date_____

Find the area of the figure.

1.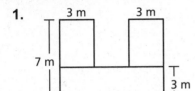

2.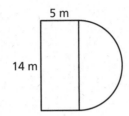

3.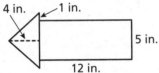

4.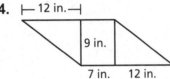

5.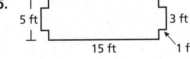

6.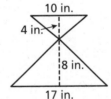

7. You are carpeting 2 rooms of your house. The carpet costs $1.48 per square foot. How much does it cost to carpet the rooms?

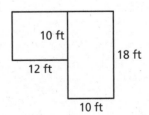

Chapter 15 **Fair Game Review** (continued)

Find the area of the circle.

8.

20 in.

9.

6 m

10.

12 cm

11.

14 ft

12.

25 yd

13.

15 mm

14. Find the area of the shaded region.

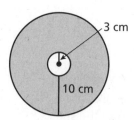

3 cm

10 cm

15.1 Volumes of Cylinders
For use with Activity 15.1

Essential Question   How can you find the volume of a cylinder?

1   **ACTIVITY:** Finding a Formula Experimentally

Work with a partner.

a.   Find the area of the face of a coin.

b.   Find the volume of a stack of a dozen coins.

c.   Write a formula for the volume of a cylinder.

 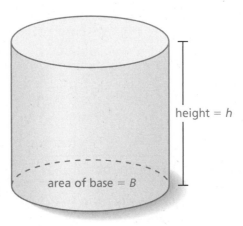

height = h

area of base = B

15.1 Volumes of Cylinders (continued)

2 **ACTIVITY:** Making a Business Plan

Work with a partner. You are planning to make and sell three different sizes of cylindrical candles. You buy 1 cubic foot of candle wax for $20 to make 8 candles of each size.

    a. Design the candles. What are the dimensions of each size of candle?

    b. You want to make a profit of $100. Decide on a price for each size of candle.

    c. Did you set the prices so that they are proportional to the volume of each size of candle? Why or why not?

3 **ACTIVITY:** Science Experiment

Work with a partner. Use the diagram to describe how you can find the volume of a small object.

15.1 Volumes of Cylinders (continued)

4 **ACTIVITY:** Comparing Cylinders

Work with a partner.

a. Just by looking at the two
cylinders, which one do you
think has the greater volume?
Explain your reasoning.

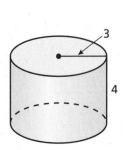
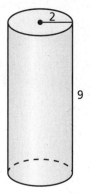

b. Find the volume of each cylinder. Was your prediction in part (a) correct?
Explain your reasoning.

What Is Your Answer?

5. **IN YOUR OWN WORDS** How can you find the volume of a cylinder?

6. Compare your formula for the volume of a cylinder with the formula for
the volume of a prism. How are they the same?

Name _____ Date _____

Find the volume of the cylinder. Round your answer to the nearest tenth.

1.

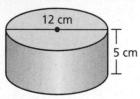

12 cm

5 cm

2. 4 in.

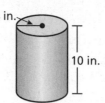

10 in.

Find the missing dimension of the cylinder. Round your answer to the nearest whole number.

3. Volume = 84 in.^{3}

6 in.

h

4. Volume = 650 cm^3

8 cm

h

5. To make orange juice, the directions call for a can of orange juice concentrate to be mixed with three cans of water. What is the volume of orange juice that you make?

3 in.

Orange Juice

5 in.

15.2 Volumes of Cones
For use with Activity 15.2

Essential Question How can you find the volume of a cone?

You already know how the volume of a pyramid relates to the volume of a prism. In this activity, you will discover how the volume of a cone relates to the volume of a cylinder.

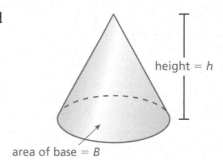

height = h

area of base = B

---

1 ACTIVITY: Finding a Formula Experimentally

Work with a partner. Use a paper cup that is shaped like a cone.

- Estimate the height of the cup.

- Trace the top of the cup on a piece of paper. Find the diameter of the circle.

- Use these measurements to draw a net for a cylinder with the same base and height as the paper cup.

- Cut out the net. Then fold and tape it to form an open cylinder.

- Fill the paper cup with rice. Then pour the rice into the cylinder. Repeat this until the cylinder is full. How many cones does it take to fill the cylinder?

- Use your result to write a formula for the volume of a cone.

15.2 **Volumes of Cones** (continued)

2 **ACTIVITY:** Summarizing Volume Formulas

Work with a partner. You can remember the volume formulas for prisms, cylinders, pyramids, and cones with just two concepts.

Volumes of Prisms and Cylinders

Volume = | Area of base | × | _____ |

Volumes of Pyramids and Cones

Volume = | _____ | Volume of prism or cylinder with same base and height |

Make a list of all the formulas you need to remember to find the area of a base. Talk about strategies for remembering these formulas.

3 **ACTIVITY:** Volumes of Oblique Solids

Work with a partner. Think of a stack of paper. When you adjust the stack so that the sides are oblique (slanted), do you change the volume of the stack? If the volume of the stack does not change, then the formulas for volumes of right solids also apply to oblique solids.

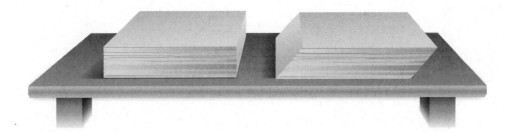

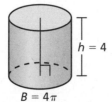

$B = 4\pi$

Right Cylinder

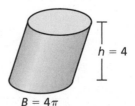

$h = 4$

$B = 4\pi$

Oblique Cylinder

15.2 **Volumes of Cones** (continued)

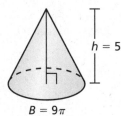

$h = 5$

$B = 9\pi$

Right Cone

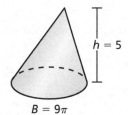

$h = 5$

$B = 9\pi$

Oblique Cone

What Is Your Answer?

4. IN YOUR OWN WORDS How can you find the volume of a cone?

5. Describe the intersection of the plane and the cone. Then explain how to find the volume of each section of the solid.

a.

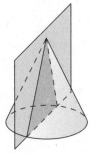

b.

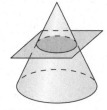

Name _____ Date _____

Find the volume of the cone. Round your answer to the nearest tenth.

1.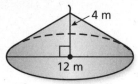
   4 m
   12 m

2.
   11 ft
   3 ft

3.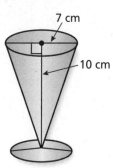
   7 cm
   10 cm

Find the missing dimension of the cone. Round your answer to the nearest tenth.

4. Volume $= 300\pi$ mm^3

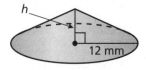
   h
   12 mm

5. Volume $= 78.5$ cm^3

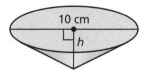
   10 cm
   h

6. What is the volume of the catch and click cone?

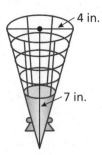
   4 in.
   7 in.

15.3 Volumes of Spheres
For use with Activity 15.3

Essential Question How can you find the volume of a sphere?

A **sphere** is the set of all points in space that are the same distance from a point called the *center*. The *radius r* is the distance from the center to any point on the sphere.

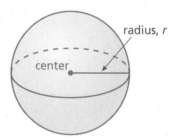

A sphere is different from the other solids you have studied so far because it does not have a base. To discover the volume of a sphere, you can use an activity similar to the one in the previous section.

---

1 **ACTIVITY: Exploring the Volume of a Sphere**

Work with a partner. Use a plastic ball similar to the one shown.

- Estimate the diameter and the radius of the ball.

- Use these measurements to draw a net for a cylinder with a diameter and a height equal to the diameter of the ball. How is the height *h* of the cylinder related to the radius *r* of the ball? Explain.

- Cut out the net. Then fold and tape it to form an open cylinder. Make two marks on the cylinder that divide it into thirds, as shown.

- Cover the ball with aluminum foil or tape. Leave one hole open. Fill the ball with rice. Then pour the rice into the cylinder. What fraction of the cylinder is filled with rice?

15.3 Volume of Spheres (continued)

2 ACTIVITY: Deriving the Formula for the Volume of a Sphere

Work with a partner. Use the results from Activity 1 and the formula for the volume of a cylinder to complete the steps.

$V = \pi r^2 h$ Write formula for volume of a cylinder.

$= \dfrac{\boxed{}}{\boxed{}}\ \pi r^2 h$ Multiply by $\dfrac{\boxed{}}{\boxed{}}$ because the volume of a sphere is $\dfrac{\boxed{}}{\boxed{}}$

of the volume of the cylinder.

$= \dfrac{\boxed{}}{\boxed{}}\ \pi r^2 \boxed{}$ Substitute $\boxed{}$ for h.

$= \dfrac{\boxed{}}{\boxed{}}\ \pi \boxed{}$ Simplify.

3 ACTIVITY: Deriving the Formula for the Volume of a Sphere

Work with a partner. Imagine filling the inside of a sphere with *n* small pyramids. The vertex of each pyramid is at the center of the sphere and the height of each pyramid is approximately equal to *r*, as shown. Complete the steps. $\left(\text{The surface area of a sphere is equal to } 4\pi r^2.\right)$

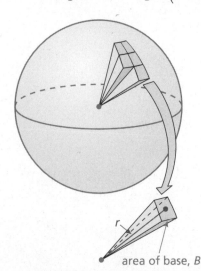
r
area of base, B

$V = \dfrac{1}{3} Bh$ Write formula for volume of a pyramid.

$= n\dfrac{1}{3} B\,\boxed{}$ Multiply by the number of small pyramids *n* and substitute $\boxed{}$ for *h*.

$= \dfrac{1}{3}\left(4\pi r^2\right)\boxed{}$ $4\pi r^2 \approx n \cdot \boxed{}$.

Show how this result is equal to the result in Activity 2.

15.3 **Volume of Spheres** (continued)

What Is Your Answer?

4. IN YOUR OWN WORDS How can you find the volume of a sphere?

5. Describe the intersection of the plane and the sphere. Then explain how to find the volume of each section of the solid.

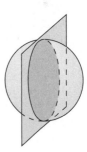

15.3 Practice
For use after Lesson 15.3

Find the volume of the sphere. Round your answer to the nearest tenth.

1.

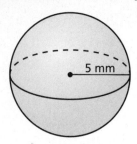

5 mm

2.

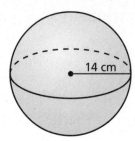

14 cm

3.

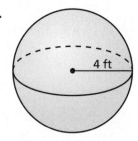

4 ft

4.

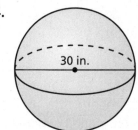

30 in.

5. Find the volume of the exercise ball. Round your answer to the nearest tenth.

55 cm

Name_____ Date_____

15.4 Surface Areas and Volumes of Similar Solids
For use with Activity 15.4

Essential Question When the dimensions of a solid increase by a factor of k, how does the surface area change? How does the volume change?

1 ACTIVITY: Comparing Surface Areas and Volumes

Work with a partner. Complete the table. Describe the pattern. Are the dimensions proportional? Explain your reasoning.

a.

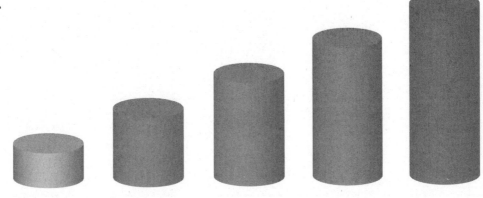

Radius	1	1	1	1	1
Height	1	2	3	4	5
Surface Area					
Volume					

15.4 Surface Areas and Volumes of Similar Solids (continued)

b.

Radius	1	2	3	4	5
Height	1	2	3	4	5
Surface Area					
Volume					

2 ACTIVITY: Comparing Surface Areas and Volumes

Work with a partner. Complete the table. Describe the pattern. Are the dimensions proportional? Explain.

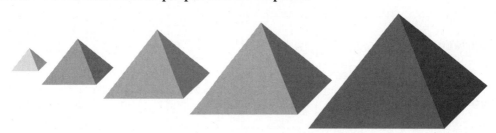

Base Side	6	12	18	24	30
Height	4	8	12	16	20
Slant Height	5	10	15	20	25
Surface Area					
Volume					

15.4 Surface Areas and Volumes of Similar Solids (continued)

What Is Your Answer?

3. **IN YOUR OWN WORDS** When the dimensions of a solid increase by a factor of k, how does the surface area change?

4. **IN YOUR OWN WORDS** When the dimensions of a solid increase by a factor of k, how does the volume change?

5. **REPEATED REASONING** All the dimensions of a prism increase by a factor of 5.

   a. How many times greater is the surface area? Explain.

   | 5 | 10 | 25 | 125 |

   b. How many times greater is the volume? Explain.

   | 5 | 10 | 25 | 125 |

15.4 Practice
For use after Lesson 15.4

Determine whether the solids are similar.

1.

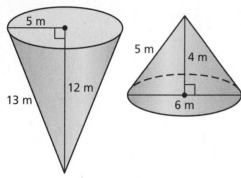

2.

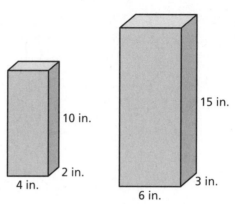

The solids are similar. Find the missing dimension(s).

3.

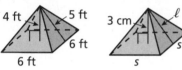

4.

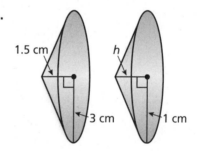

The solids are similar. Find the surface area *S* or volume *V* of the shaded solid.

5.

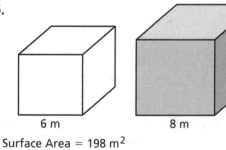

Surface Area = 198 m²

6.

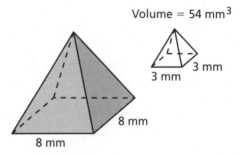

Volume = 54 mm³

Name_____ Date_____

 Chapter 16 **Fair Game Review**

Evaluate the expression.

1. $2 + 1 \bullet 4^2 - 12 \div 3$

2. $8^2 \div 16 \bullet 2 - 5$

3. $7(9 - 3) + 6^2 \bullet 10 - 8$

4. $3 \bullet 5 - 10 + 9(2 + 1)^2$

5. $8(6 + 5) - (9^2 + 3) \div 7$

6. $5[3(12 - 8)] - 6 \bullet 8 + 2^2$

7. $4 + 4 + 5 \times 2 \times 5 + (3 + 3 + 3) \times 6 \times 6 + 2 + 2$

    a. Evaluate the expression.

    b. Rewrite the expression using what you know about order of operations. Then evaluate.

Chapter 16 **Fair Game Review** (continued)

Find the product or quotient.

8. $3.92 \cdot 0.6$

9. $0.78 \cdot 0.13$

10. $\begin{array}{r} 5.004 \\ \times \ \ 1.2 \\ \hline \end{array}$

11. $6.3 \div 0.7$

12. $2.25 \div 1.5$

13. $0.003\overline{)8.1}$

14. Grapes cost $1.98 per pound. You buy 3.5 pounds of grapes. How much do you pay for the grapes?

16.1 Exponents
For use with Activity 16.1

Essential Question How can you use exponents to write numbers?

The expression 3^5 is called a *power*. The *base* is 3. The *exponent* is 5.

$$\boxed{\text{base}} \longrightarrow 3^5 \longleftarrow \boxed{\text{exponent}}$$

1 ACTIVITY: Using Exponent Notation

Work with a partner.

a. Complete the table.

Power	Repeated Multiplication Form	Value
$(-3)^1$		
$(-3)^2$		
$(-3)^3$		
$(-3)^4$		
$(-3)^5$		
$(-3)^6$		
$(-3)^7$		

b. REPEATED REASONING Describe what is meant by the expression $(-3)^n$.

How can you find the value of $(-3)^n$?

Name _____ Date _____

2 ACTIVITY: Using Exponent Notation

Work with a partner.

a. The cube at the right has $3 in each of its small cubes. Write a power that represents the total amount of money in the large cube.

b. Evaluate the power to find the total amount of money in the large cube.

3 ACTIVITY: Writing Powers as Whole Numbers

Work with a partner. Write each distance as a whole number. Which numbers do you know how to write in words? For instance, in words, 10^3 is equal to *one thousand*.

a. 10^{26} meters:
   diameter of observable universe

b. 10^{21} meters:
   diameter of Milky Way galaxy

c. 10^{16} meters:
   diameter of solar system

d. 10^7 meters:
   diameter of Earth

e. 10^6 meters:
   length of Lake Erie shoreline

f. 10^5 meters:
   width of Lake Erie

16.1 Exponents (continued)

4 **ACTIVITY:** Writing a Power

Work with a partner. Write the number of kits, cats, sacks, and wives as a power.

As I was going to St. Ives
I met a man with seven wives
Each wife had seven sacks
Each sack had seven cats
Each cat had seven kits
Kits, cats, sacks, wives
How many were going to St. Ives?

Nursery Rhyme, 1730

What Is Your Answer?

5. **IN YOUR OWN WORDS** How can you use exponents to write numbers? Give some examples of how exponents are used in real life.

16.1 Practice
For use after Lesson 16.1

Write the product using exponents.

1. $4 \cdot 4 \cdot 4 \cdot 4 \cdot 4$

2. $\left(-\dfrac{1}{8}\right) \cdot \left(-\dfrac{1}{8}\right) \cdot \left(-\dfrac{1}{8}\right)$

3. $5 \cdot 5 \cdot (-x) \cdot (-x) \cdot (-x) \cdot (-x)$

4. $9 \cdot 9 \cdot y \cdot y \cdot y \cdot y \cdot y \cdot y$

Evaluate the expression.

5. 10^3

6. $(-7)^4$

7. $-\left(\dfrac{1}{6}\right)^5$

8. $3 + 6 \cdot (-5)^2$

9. $\left| -\dfrac{1}{3}\left(1^{10} + 9 - 2^3\right) \right|$

10. A foam toy is 2 inches wide. It doubles in size for every minute it is in water. Write an expression for the width of the toy after 5 minutes. What is the width after 5 minutes?

16.2 Product of Powers Property
For use with Activity 16.2

Essential Question How can you use inductive reasoning to observe patterns and write general rules involving properties of exponents?

1 ACTIVITY: Finding Products of Powers

Work with a partner.

a. Complete the table.

Product	Repeated Multiplication Form	Power
$2^2 \cdot 2^4$		
$(-3)^2 \cdot (-3)^4$		
$7^3 \cdot 7^2$		
$5.1^1 \cdot 5.1^6$		
$(-4)^2 \cdot (-4)^2$		
$10^3 \cdot 10^5$		
$\left(\dfrac{1}{2}\right)^5 \cdot \left(\dfrac{1}{2}\right)^5$		

b. INDUCTIVE REASONING Describe the pattern in the table. Then write a *general rule* for multiplying two powers that have the same base.

$$a^m \cdot a^n = a \text{——}$$

c. Use your rule to simplify the products in the first column of the table above. Does your rule give the results in the third column?

d. Most calculators have *exponent* keys that are used to evaluate powers. Use a calculator with an exponent key to evaluate the products in part (a).

16.2 Product of Powers Property (continued)

2 ACTIVITY: Writing a Rule for Powers of Powers

Work with a partner. Write the expression as a single power. Then write a *general rule* for finding a power of a power.

a. $\left(3^2\right)^3 =$

b. $\left(2^2\right)^4 =$

c. $\left(7^3\right)^2 =$

d. $\left(y^3\right)^3 =$

e. $\left(x^4\right)^2 =$

3 ACTIVITY: Writing a Rule for Powers of Products

Work with a partner. Write the expression as the product of two powers. Then write a *general rule* for finding a power of a product.

a. $\left(2 \bullet 3\right)^3 =$

b. $\left(2 \bullet 5\right)^2 =$

c. $\left(5 \bullet 4\right)^3 =$

d. $\left(6a\right)^4 =$

e. $\left(3x\right)^2 =$

16.2 Product of Powers Property (continued)

4 ACTIVITY: The Penny Puzzle

Work with a partner.

- The rows y and columns x of a chess board are numbered as shown.

- Each position on the chess board has a stack of pennies. (Only the first row is shown.)

- The number of pennies in each stack is $2^x \cdot 2^y$.

a. How many pennies are in the stack in location $(3, 5)$?

b. Which locations have 32 pennies in their stacks?

c. How much money (in dollars) is in the location with the tallest stack?

d. A penny is about 0.06 inch thick. About how tall (in inches) is the tallest stack?

What Is Your Answer?

5. IN YOUR OWN WORDS How can you use inductive reasoning to observe patterns and write general rules involving properties of exponents?

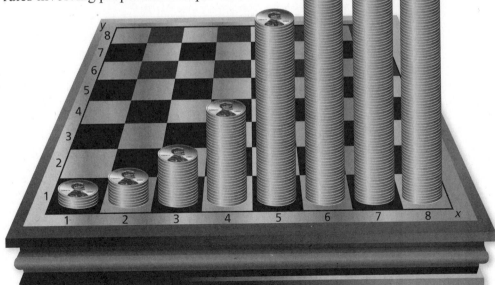

16.2 Practice
For use after Lesson 16.2

Simplify the expression. Write your answer as a power.

1. $(-6)^5 \cdot (-6)^4$

2. $x^1 \cdot x^9$

3. $\left(\dfrac{4}{5}\right)^3 \cdot \left(\dfrac{4}{5}\right)^{12}$

4. $(-1.5)^{11} \cdot (-1.5)^{11}$

5. $\left(y^{10}\right)^{20}$

6. $\left(\left(-\dfrac{2}{9}\right)^8\right)^7$

Simplify the expression.

7. $(2a)^6$

8. $(-4b)^4$

9. $\left(-\dfrac{9}{10}p\right)^2$

10. $(xy)^{15}$

11. $10^5 \cdot 10^3 - \left(10^1\right)^8$

12. $7^2\left(7^4 \cdot 7^4\right)$

13. The surface area of the Sun is about $4 \times 3.141 \times \left(7 \times 10^5\right)^2$ square kilometers. Simplify the expression.

16.3 Quotient of Powers Property
For use with Activity 16.3

Essential Question How can you divide two powers that have the same base?

---

1 ACTIVITY: Finding Quotients of Powers

Work with a partner.

a. Complete the table.

Quotient	Repeated Multiplication Form	Power
$\dfrac{2^4}{2^2}$		
$\dfrac{(-4)^5}{(-4)^2}$		
$\dfrac{7^7}{7^3}$		
$\dfrac{8.5^9}{8.5^6}$		
$\dfrac{10^8}{10^5}$		
$\dfrac{3^{12}}{3^4}$		
$\dfrac{(-5)^7}{(-5)^5}$		
$\dfrac{11^4}{11^1}$		

b. INDUCTIVE REASONING Describe the pattern in the table. Then write a rule for dividing two powers that have the same base.

$$\frac{a^m}{a^n} = a^{\underline{\quad}}$$

16.3 Quotient of Powers Property (continued)

c. Use your rule to simplify the quotients in the first column of the table on the previous page. Does your rule give the results in the third column?

2 ACTIVITY: Comparing Volumes

Work with a partner.

How many of the smaller cubes will fit inside the larger cube? Record your results in the table on the next page. Describe the pattern in the table.

a.
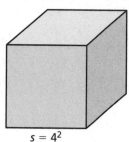
$s = 4$ $s = 4^2$

b.
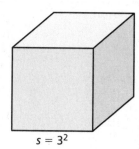
$s = 3$ $s = 3^2$

c.
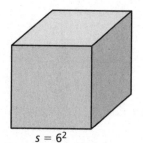
$s = 6$ $s = 6^2$

d.
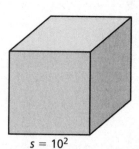
$s = 10$ $s = 10^2$

16.3 Quotient of Powers Property (continued)

	Volume of Smaller Cube	Volume of Larger Cube	$\dfrac{\text{Larger Volume}}{\text{Smaller Volume}}$	Answer
a.				
b.				
c.				
d.				

What Is Your Answer?

3. **IN YOUR OWN WORDS** How can you divide two powers that have the same base? Give two examples of your rule.

Name_____ Date_____

16.3 Practice
For use after Lesson 16.3

Simplify the expression. Write your answer as a power.

1. $\dfrac{7^6}{7^5}$

2. $\dfrac{(-21)^{15}}{(-21)^9}$

3. $\dfrac{(3.9)^{20}}{(3.9)^{10}}$

4. $\dfrac{t^7}{t^3}$

5. $\dfrac{8^7 \bullet 8^4}{8^9}$

6. $\dfrac{(-1.1)^{13} \bullet (-1.1)^{12}}{(-1.1)^{10} \bullet (-1.1)^1}$

Simplify the expression.

7. $\dfrac{k \bullet 3^9}{3^5}$

8. $\dfrac{x^4 \bullet y^{10} \bullet 2^{11}}{y^8 \bullet 2^7}$

9. The radius of a basketball is about 3.6 times greater than the radius of a tennis ball. How many times greater is the volume of a basketball than the volume of a tennis ball? $\left(\text{Note: The volume of a sphere is } V = \dfrac{4}{3}\pi r^3. \right)$

16.4 Zero and Negative Exponents
For use with Activity 16.4

Essential Question How can you evaluate a nonzero number with an exponent of zero? How can you evaluate a nonzero number with a negative integer exponent?

1 ACTIVITY: Using the Quotient of Powers Property

Work with a partner.

a. Complete the table.

Quotient	Quotient of Powers Property	Power
$\dfrac{5^3}{5^3}$		
$\dfrac{6^2}{6^2}$		
$\dfrac{(-3)^4}{(-3)^4}$		
$\dfrac{(-4)^5}{(-4)^5}$		

b. REPEATED REASONING Evaluate each expression in the first column of the table. What do you notice?

c. How can you use these results to define a^0 where $a \neq 0$?

16.4 **Zero and Negative Exponents** (continued)

2 **ACTIVITY:** Using the Product of Powers Property

Work with a partner.

   a. Complete the table.

Product	Product of Powers Property	Power
$3^0 \cdot 3^4$		
$8^2 \cdot 8^0$		
$(-2)^3 \cdot (-2)^0$		
$\left(-\dfrac{1}{3}\right)^0 \cdot \left(-\dfrac{1}{3}\right)^5$		

   b. Do these results support your definition in Activity 1(c)?

3 **ACTIVITY:** Using the Product of Powers Property

Work with a partner.

   a. Complete the table.

Product	Product of Powers Property	Power
$5^{-3} \cdot 5^3$		
$6^2 \cdot 6^{-2}$		
$(-3)^4 \cdot (-3)^{-4}$		
$(-4)^{-5} \cdot (-4)^5$		

   b. According to your results from Activities 1 and 2, the products in the first column are equal to what value?

16.4 **Zero and Negative Exponents** (continued)

c. **REASONING** How does the Multiplicative Inverse Property help you to rewrite the numbers with negative exponents?

d. **STRUCTURE** Use these results to define a^{-n} where $a \neq 0$ and n is an integer.

4 **ACTIVITY:** Using a Place Value Chart

Work with a partner. Use the place value chart that shows the number 3452.867.

Place Value Chart

	thousands	hundreds	tens	ones	and	tenths	hundredths	thousandths
	10^3	10^2	10^1	$10^\square$		$10^\square$	$10^\square$	$10^\square$
	3	4	5	2	.	8	6	7

a. **REPEATED REASONING** What pattern do you see in the exponents? Continue the pattern to find the other exponents.

b. **STRUCTURE** Show how to write the expanded form of 3452.867.

What Is Your Answer?

5. **IN YOUR OWN WORDS** How can you evaluate a nonzero number with an exponent of zero? How can you evaluate a nonzero number with a negative integer exponent?

16.4 Practice
For use after Lesson 16.4

Evaluate the expression.

1. 29^0

2. 12^{-1}

3. $10^{-4} \cdot 10^{-6}$

4. $\dfrac{1}{3^{-3}} \cdot \dfrac{1}{3^5}$

Simplify. Write the expression using only positive exponents.

5. $19x^{-6}$

6. $\dfrac{14a^{-5}}{a^{-8}}$

7. $3t^6 \cdot 8t^{-6}$

8. $\dfrac{12s^{-1} \cdot 4^{-2} \cdot r^3}{s^2 \cdot r^5}$

9. The density of a proton is about $\dfrac{1.64 \times 10^{-24}}{3.7 \times 10^{-38}}$ grams per cubic centimeter. Simplify the expression.

16.5 Reading Scientific Notation
For use with Activity 16.5

Essential Question How can you read numbers that are written in scientific notation?

---

1 ACTIVITY: Very Large Numbers

Work with a partner.

- Use a calculator. Experiment with multiplying large numbers until your calculator displays an answer that is *not* in standard form.

- When the calculator at the right was used to multiply 2 billion by 3 billion, it listed the result as

    $6.0\text{E}+18.$

- Multiply 2 billion by 3 billion by hand. Use the result to explain what $6.0\text{E}+18$ means.

- Check your explanation using products of other large numbers.

- Why didn't the calculator show the answer in standard form?

- Experiment to find the maximum number of digits your calculator displays. For instance, if you multiply 1000 by 1000 and your calculator shows 1,000,000, then it can display 7 digits.

16.5 **Reading Scientific Notation** (continued)

2 **ACTIVITY:** Very Small Numbers

Work with a partner.

- Use a calculator. Experiment with multiplying very small numbers until your calculator displays an answer that is *not* in standard form.

- When the calculator at the right was used to multiply 2 billionths by 3 billionths, it listed the result as

    6.0E−18.

- Multiply 2 billionths by 3 billionths by hand. Use the result to explain what 6.0E−18 means.

- Check your explanation by calculating the products of other very small numbers.

3 **ACTIVITY:** Powers of 10 Matching Game

Work with a partner. Match each picture with its power of 10. Explain your reasoning.

| 10^5 m | 10^2 m | 10^0 m | 10^{-1} m | 10^{-2} m | 10^{-5} m |

A.

B.

C.

D.

E.

F.

16.5 **Reading Scientific Notation** (continued)

4 **ACTIVITY:** Choosing Appropriate Units

Work with a partner. Match each unit with its most appropriate measurement.

inches	centimeters	feet	millimeters	meters

a. Height of a door:

2×10^0

b. Height of a volcano

1.6×10^4

c. Length of a pen:

1.4×10^2

d. Diameter of a steel ball bearing:

6.3×10^{-1}

e. Circumference of a beach ball:

7.5×10^1

What Is Your Answer?

5. **IN YOUR OWN WORDS** How can you read numbers that are written in scientific notation? Why do you think this type of notation is called "scientific notation"? Why is scientific notation important?

16.5 Practice
For use after Lesson 16.5

Tell whether the number is written in scientific notation. Explain.

1. 14×10^8

2. 2.6×10^{12}

3. 4.79×10^{-8}

4. 3.99×10^{16}

5. 0.15×10^{22}

6. 6×10^3

Write the number in standard form.

7. 4×10^9

8. 2×10^{-5}

9. 3.7×10^6

10. 4.12×10^{-3}

11. 7.62×10^{10}

12. 9.908×10^{-12}

13. Light travels at 3×10^8 meters per second.

   a. Write the speed of light in standard form.

   b. How far has light traveled after 5 seconds?

16.6 Writing Scientific Notation
For use with Activity 16.6

Essential Question How can you write a number in scientific notation?

---

1 ACTIVITY: Finding pH Levels

Work with a partner. In chemistry, pH is a measure of the activity of dissolved hydrogen ions (H^+). Liquids with low pH values are called *acids*. Liquids with high pH values are called *bases*.

Find the pH of each liquid. Is the liquid a base, neutral, or an acid?

a. Lime juice: $[H^+] = 0.01$

b. Egg: $[H^+] = 0.00000001$

c. Distilled water: $[H^+] = 0.0000001$

d. Ammonia water:
$[H^+] = 0.00000000001$

e. Tomato juice: $[H^+] = 0.0001$

f. Hydrochloric acid: $[H^+] = 1$

pH	$[H^+]$	
14	1×10^{-14}	
13	1×10^{-13}	
12	1×10^{-12}	Bases
11	1×10^{-11}	
10	1×10^{-10}	
9	1×10^{-9}	
8	1×10^{-8}	
7	1×10^{-7}	**Neutral**
6	1×10^{-6}	
5	1×10^{-5}	
4	1×10^{-4}	
3	1×10^{-3}	Acids
2	1×10^{-2}	
1	1×10^{-1}	
0	1×10^{0}	

16.6 **Writing Scientific Notation** (continued)

2 **ACTIVITY:** Writing Scientific Notation

Work with a partner. Match each planet with its distance from the Sun. Then write each distance in scientific notation. Do you think it is easier to match the distances when they are written in standard form or in scientific notation? Explain.

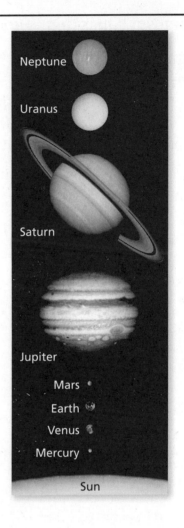

Neptune

Uranus

Saturn

Jupiter

Mars

Earth

Venus

Mercury

Sun

a. 1,800,000,000 miles

b. 67,000,000 miles

c. 890,000,000 miles

d. 93,000,000 miles

e. 140,000,000 miles

f. 2,800,000,000 miles

g. 480,000,000 miles

h. 36,000,000 miles

16.6 Writing Scientific Notation (continued)

3 ACTIVITY: Making a Scale Drawing

Work with a partner. The illustration in Activity 2 is not drawn to scale. Use the instructions below to make a scale drawing of the distances in our solar system.

- Cut a sheet of paper into three strips of equal width. Tape the strips together.

- Draw a long number line. Label the number line in hundreds of millions of miles.

- Locate each planet's position on the number line.

What Is Your Answer?

4. **IN YOUR OWN WORDS** How can you write a number in scientific notation?

16.6 Practice
For use after Lesson 16.6

Write the number in scientific notation.

1. 4,200,000

2. 0.038

3. 600,000

4. 0.0000808

5. 0.0007

6. 29,010,000,000

Order the numbers from least to greatest.

7. $6.4 \times 10^8, 5.3 \times 10^9, 2.3 \times 10^8$

8. $9.1 \times 10^{-3}, 9.6 \times 10^{-3}, 9.02 \times 10^{-3}$

9. $7.3 \times 10^7, 5.6 \times 10^{10}, 3.7 \times 10^9$

10. $1.4 \times 10^{-5}, 2.01 \times 10^{-15}, 6.3 \times 10^{-2}$

11. A patient has 0.0000075 gram of iron in 1 liter of blood. The normal level is between 6×10^{-7} gram and 1.6×10^{-5} gram. Is the patient's iron level normal? Write the patient's amount of iron in scientific notation.

16.7 Operations in Scientific Notation
For use with Activity 16.7

Essential Question How can you perform operations with numbers written in scientific notation?

---

1 ACTIVITY: Adding Numbers in Scientific Notation

Work with a partner. Consider the numbers 2.4×10^3 and 7.1×10^3.

a. Explain how to use order of operations to find the sum of these numbers. Then find the sum.

$$2.4 \times 10^3 + 7.1 \times 10^3$$

b. The factor _____ is common to both numbers. How can you use the Distributive Property to rewrite the sum $(2.4 \times 10^3) + (7.1 \times 10^3)$?

$(2.4 \times 10^3) + (7.1 \times 10^3) =$ _____   Distributive Property

c. Use order of operations to evaluate the expression you wrote in part (b). Compare the result with your answer in part (a).

d. **STRUCTURE** Write a rule you can use to add numbers written in scientific notation where the powers of 10 are the same. Then test your rule using the sums below.

- $(4.9 \times 10^5) + (1.8 \times 10^5) =$ _____

- $(3.85 \times 10^4) + (5.72 \times 10^4) =$ _____

---

2 ACTIVITY: Adding Numbers in Scientific Notation

Work with a partner. Consider the numbers 2.4×10^3 and 7.1×10^4.

a. Explain how to use order of operations to find the sum of these numbers. Then find the sum.

$$2.4 \times 10^3 + 7.1 \times 10^4$$

16.7 **Operations in Scientific Notation** (continued)

b. How is this pair of numbers different from the pair of numbers in Activity 1?

c. Explain why you cannot immediately use the rule you wrote in Activity 1(d) to find this sum.

d. **STRUCTURE** How can you rewrite one of the numbers so that you can use the rule you wrote in Activity 1(d)? Rewrite one of the numbers. Then find the sum using your rule and compare the result with your answer in part (a).

e. **REASONING** Does this procedure work when subtracting numbers written in scientific notation? Justify your answer by evaluating the differences below.

- $\left(8.2 \times 10^5\right) - \left(4.6 \times 10^5\right) =$ _____

- $\left(5.88 \times 10^5\right) - \left(1.5 \times 10^4\right) =$ _____

3 **ACTIVITY:** Multiplying Numbers in Scientific Notation

Work with a partner. Match each step with the correct description.

Step		Description
$\left(2.4 \times 10^3\right) \times \left(7.1 \times 10^3\right)$		**Original expression**
1.	$= 2.4 \times 7.1 \times 10^3 \times 10^3$	**A.** Write in standard form.
2.	$= (2.4 \times 7.1) \times \left(10^3 \times 10^3\right)$	**B.** Product of Powers Property
3.	$= 17.04 \times 10^6$	**C.** Write in scientific notation.
4.	$= 1.704 \times 10^1 \times 10^6$	**D.** Commutative Property of Multiplication
5.	$= 1.704 \times 10^7$	**E.** Simplify.
6.	$= 17,040,000$	**F.** Associative Property of Multiplication

16.7 Operations in Scientific Notation (continued)

Does this procedure work when the numbers have different powers of 10?
Justify your answer by using this procedure to evaluate the products below.

- $(1.9 \times 10^2) \times (2.3 \times 10^5) =$

- $(8.4 \times 10^6) \times (5.7 \times 10^{-4}) =$

---

4 ACTIVITY: Using Scientific Notation to Estimate

Work with a partner. A person normally breathes about 6 liters of air per minute. The life expectancy of a person in the United States at birth is about 80 years. Use scientific notation to estimate the total amount of air a person born in the United States breathes over a lifetime.

What Is Your Answer?

5. **IN YOUR OWN WORDS** How can you perform operations with numbers written in scientific notation?

6. Use a calculator to evaluate the expression. Write your answer in scientific notation and in standard form.

   a. $(1.5 \times 10^4) + (6.3 \times 10^4)$

   b. $(7.2 \times 10^5) - (2.2 \times 10^3)$

   c. $(4.1 \times 10^{-3}) \times (4.3 \times 10^{-3})$

   d. $(4.75 \times 10^{-6}) \times (1.34 \times 10^7)$

Name _____ Date _____

Find the sum or difference. Write your answer in scientific notation.

1. $\left(2 \times 10^4\right) + \left(7.2 \times 10^4\right)$

2. $\left(3.2 \times 10^{-2}\right) + \left(9.4 \times 10^{-2}\right)$

3. $\left(6.7 \times 10^5\right) - \left(4.3 \times 10^5\right)$

4. $\left(8.9 \times 10^{-3}\right) - \left(1.9 \times 10^{-3}\right)$

Find the product or quotient. Write your answer in scientific notation.

5. $\left(6 \times 10^8\right) \times \left(4 \times 10^6\right)$

6. $\left(9 \times 10^{-3}\right) \times \left(9 \times 10^{-3}\right)$

7. $\left(8 \times 10^3\right) \div \left(2 \times 10^2\right)$

8. $\left(2.34 \times 10^5\right) \div \left(7.8 \times 10^5\right)$

9. How many times greater is the radius of a basketball than the radius of a marble?

Radius = 1.143×10^1 cm   Radius = 5×10^{-1} cm

Topic 1 **Practice**
For use after Topic 1

Solve the equation. Check your solution.

1. $3x - 11 = 22$

2. $24 - 10b = 9$

3. $2.4z + 1.2z - 6.5 = 0.7$

4. $\dfrac{3}{4}w - \dfrac{1}{2}w - 4 = 12$

5. $2(a + 7) - 7 = 9$

6. $20 + 8(q - 11) = -12$

7. Find the width of the rectangular prism when the surface area is 208 square centimeters.

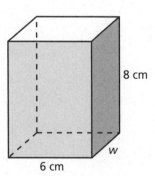

8 cm

6 cm

w

Topic 1 Practice (continued)

8. The amount A of money in your savings account after m months is represented by $A = 135m + 225$. After how many months do you have \$765 in your savings account?

9. A rectangular garden has a length of $(x + 8)$ feet and a width of 20 feet. The perimeter of the garden is 110 feet. How much greater is the length than the width?

10. A sponsor of a youth baseball team buys new hats and jerseys for the players on the team. Each hat costs \$10 and each jersey costs \$20. The sponsor also donates \$200 to help pay for umpires. The sponsor spends a total of \$650. How many players are on the team?

Topic 2 Practice
For use after Topic 2

Solve the equation. Check your solution.

1. $x + 16 = 9x$

2. $4y - 70 = 12y + 2$

3. $5(p + 6) = 8p$

4. $3(g - 7) = 2(10 + g)$

5. $1.8 + 7n = 9.5 - 4n$

6. $\dfrac{3}{7}w - 11 = -\dfrac{4}{7}w$

7. One movie club charges a \$100 membership fee and \$10 for each movie. Another club charges no membership fee but movies cost \$15 each. Write and solve an equation to find the number of movies you need to buy for the cost of each movie club to be the same.

Topic 2 **Practice** (continued)

Solve the equation. Check your solution, if possible.

8. $4x + 6 = 4x - 6$

9. $5y - 7 = 7 - 5y$

10. $3(p + 3) = 3p + 9$

11. $g - 2 = \dfrac{1}{4}(4g - 2)$

12. $12 - 4n = -12 - 4n$

13. $\dfrac{1}{3}(3w - 15) = -\dfrac{1}{5}(25 - 5w)$

14. Thirty percent of all the students in a school are in a play. All students except for 140 are in the play. How many students are in the school?

Topic 3 Practice
For use after Topic 3

Solve the equation for *y*.

1. $2x + y = -9$

2. $4x - 10y = 12$

3. $13 = \dfrac{1}{6}y + 2x$

4. The formula for the perimeter of a triangle is $P = a + b + c$.

   a. Solve the formula for *c*.

   b. Use the new formula to find the value of *c*.

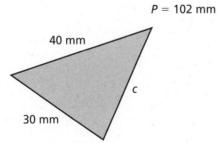

$P = 102$ mm

40 mm

30 mm

c

Big Ideas Math Red Accelerated **399**
Record and Practice Journal

Name_____ Date _____

Solve the formula for the bold variable.

5. $V = \ell wh$

6. $f = \dfrac{1}{2}(r + 6.5)$

7. $V = \dfrac{1}{3}Bh$

8. The formula for the area of a triangle is $A = \dfrac{1}{2}bh$.

   a. Solve the formula for h.

   b. Use the new formula to find the value of h.

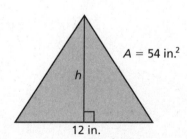

$A = 54$ in.^{2}

h

12 in.

Glossary

This student friendly glossary is designed to be a reference for key vocabulary, properties, and mathematical terms. Several of the entries include a short example to aid your understanding of important concepts.

Also available at *BigIdeasMath.com*:

- multi-language glossary
- vocabulary flash cards

---

absolute value

The distance between a number and 0 on a number line; The absolute value of a number a is written as $|a|$.

$$|-5| = 5$$
$$|5| = 5$$

Addition Property of Equality

Adding the same number to each side of an equation produces an equivalent equation.

$$
\begin{array}{rr}
x - 5 = & -1 \\
+5 & +5 \\
\hline
x = & 4
\end{array}
$$

Addition Property of Inequality

When you add the same number to each side of an inequality, the inequality remains true.

$$
\begin{array}{rr}
x - 3 > & -10 \\
+3 & +3 \\
\hline
x > & -7
\end{array}
$$

---

additive inverse

The opposite of a number

The additive inverse of 8 is -8.

Additive Inverse Property

The sum of an integer and its additive inverse is 0.

$$8 + (-8) = 0$$

---

adjacent angles

Two angles that share a common side and have the same vertex

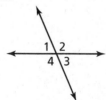

$\angle 1$ and $\angle 2$ are adjacent.

$\angle 2$ and $\angle 4$ are not adjacent.

---

algebraic expression	**angle**
An expression that contains numbers, operations, and one or more symbols $$8 + x, 6 \times a - b$$	A figure formed by two rays with the same endpoint 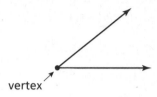 vertex

angle of rotation	**base (of a power)**
The number of degrees a figure rotates 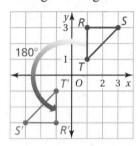 $\triangle RST$ has been rotated $180°$ to $\triangle R'S'T'$.	The base of a power is the common factor. *See power.*

biased sample	**center (of a circle)**
A sample that is not representative of a population; One or more parts of the population are favored over others. You want to estimate the number of students in your school who like to play basketball. You survey 100 students at a basketball game.	The point inside a circle that is the same distance from all points on the circle *See circle.*

center of dilation	**center of rotation**
A point with respect to which a figure is dilated *See dilation.*	A point about which a figure is rotated *See rotation.*

center of a sphere

The point inside a sphere that is the same distance from all points on the sphere

See sphere.

circle

The set of all points in a plane that are the same distance from a point called the center

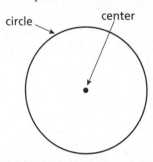

circumference

The distance around a circle

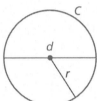

complementary angles

Two angles whose measures have a sum of 90°

complex fraction

A fraction that has at least one fraction in the numerator, denominator, or both

$$\dfrac{\dfrac{1}{4}}{\dfrac{1}{2}}$$

composite figure

A figure made up of triangles, squares, rectangles, semicircles, and other two-dimensional figures

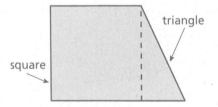

compound event

An event that consists of two or more events

Spinning a spinner and flipping a coin

concave polygon

A polygon in which at least one line segment connecting any two vertices lies outside the polygon

congruent angles

Angles that have the same measure

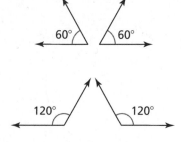

congruent figures

Figures that have the same size and the same shape

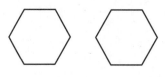

congruent sides

Sides that have the same length

Side *AB* and side *FG* are congruent sides.

constant of proportionality

The number k in the direct variation equation
$y = kx$

The constant of proportionality in the equation
$y = 2x$ is 2.

convex polygon

A polygon in which every line segment connecting any two vertices lies entirely inside the polygon

coordinate plane

A coordinate plane is formed by the intersection of a horizontal number line and a vertical number line.

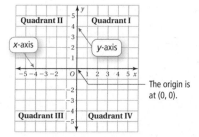

corresponding angles

Matching angles of two congruent figures

$\triangle ABC \cong \triangle DEF$

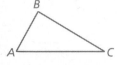

Corresponding angles: $\angle A$ and $\angle D$

$\angle B$ and $\angle E$

$\angle C$ and $\angle F$

corresponding sides

Matching sides of two congruent figures

$\triangle ABC \cong \triangle DEF$

Corresponding sides: side *AB* and side *DE*

side *BC* and side *EF*

side *AC* and side *DF*

cross products

In the proportion $\dfrac{a}{b} = \dfrac{c}{d}$, the products $a \bullet d$ and $b \bullet c$ are called cross products.

2 • 6 and 3 • 4

Cross Products Property

The cross products of a proportion are equal.

$2 \bullet 6 = 3 \bullet 4$

cross section

A two-dimensional shape formed by the intersection of a plane and a solid

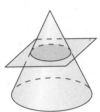

The intersection of the plane and the cone is a circle.

cube root

A number that, when multiplied by itself, and then multiplied by itself again, equals a given number

$$\sqrt[3]{8} = 2$$
$$\sqrt[3]{-27} = -3$$

degree

A unit used to measure angles

90°, 45°, 32°

dependent events

Two events such that the occurrence of one event affects the likelihood that the other event(s) will occur

A bag contains 3 red marbles and 4 blue marbles. You randomly draw a marble, do not replace it, then randomly draw another marble. The events "first marble is blue" and "second marble is red" are dependent events.

diameter (of a circle)

The distance across a circle through the center

See circumference.

dilation

A transformation in which a figure is made larger or smaller with respect to a fixed point called the center of dilation

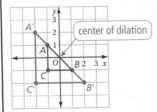

$A'B'C'$ is a dilation of ABC with respect to the origin. The scale factor is 2.

direct variation Two quantities x and y show direct variation when $y = kx$, where k is a number and $k \neq 0$. The graph of $y = kx$ is a line with a slope of k that passes through the origin. 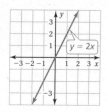	**discount** A decrease in the original price of an item The original price of a pair of shoes is \$95. The sale price is \$65. The discount is \$30.
distance formula The distance d between any two points (x_1, y_1) and (x_2, y_2) is given by the formula 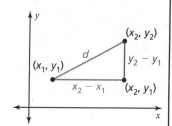 $d = \sqrt{(x_2 - x_1)^2 + (y_2 - y_1)^2}$.	**Division Property of Equality** Dividing each side of an equation by the same number produces an equivalent equation. $$-3y = 18$$ $$\frac{-3y}{-3} = \frac{18}{-3}$$ $$y = -6$$
Division Property of Inequality When you divide each side of an inequality by the same positive number, the inequality remains true. When you divide each side of an inequality by the same negative number, the direction of the inequality symbol must be reversed for the inequality to remain true. $$4x > -12 \qquad\qquad -5x > 30$$ $$\frac{4x}{4} > \frac{-12}{4} \qquad\quad \frac{-5x}{-5} < \frac{30}{-5}$$ $$x > -3 \qquad\qquad\quad x < -6$$	**enlargement** A dilation with a scale factor greater than 1 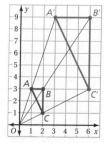 $A'B'C'$ is an enlargement of ABC.
equation A mathematical sentence that uses an equal sign to show that two expressions are equal $$4x = 16, \; a + 7 = 21$$	**equivalent equations** Equations that have the same solutions $$2x - 8 = 0 \text{ and } 2x = 8$$

event	**experiment**
A collection of one or more outcomes of an experiment	An investigation or procedure that has varying results
Flipping heads on a coin	Rolling a number cube

experimental probability	**exponent**
Probability that is based on repeated trials of an experiment	The exponent of a power indicates the number of times a base is used as a factor.
$$P(\text{event}) = \frac{\text{number of times the event occurs}}{\text{total number of trials}}$$	*See power.*
A basketball player makes 19 baskets in 28 attempts. The experimental probability that the player makes a basket is $\frac{19}{28}$, or about 68%.	

expression	**exterior angles**
A mathematical phrase containing numbers, operations, and/or variables	When two parallel lines are cut by a transversal, four exterior angles are formed on the outside of the parallel lines. 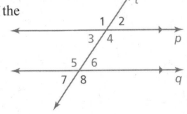
$12 + 6, 18 + 3 \times 4$ $8 + x, 6 \times a - b$	$\angle 3, \angle 4, \angle 5,$ and $\angle 6$ are interior angles. $\angle 1, \angle 2, \angle 7,$ and $\angle 8$ are exterior angles.

exterior angles of a polygon	**factor**
The angles outside a polygon that are adjacent to the interior angles	When whole numbers other than zero are multiplied together, each number is a factor of the product.
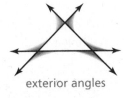 exterior angles	$2 \times 3 \times 4 = 24$, so 2, 3, and 4 are factors of 24.

factoring an expression	**favorable outcomes**
Writing an expression as a product of factors $$5x - 15 = 5(x - 3)$$	The outcomes of a specific event When rolling a number cube, the favorable outcomes for the event "rolling an even number" are 2, 4, and 6.
Fundamental Counting Principle	**graph of an inequality**
An event M has m possible outcomes and event N has n possible outcomes. The total number of outcomes of event M followed by event N is $m \times n$. You have 7 shirts, 5 pairs of pants, and 2 pairs of shoes. You can make $7 \times 5 \times 2 = 70$ different outfits.	A graph that shows all the solutions of an inequality on a number line $$x > -2$$ 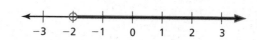
hemisphere	**hypotenuse**
One-half of a sphere 	The side of a right triangle that is opposite the right angle 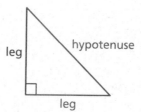
image	**independent events**
The new figure formed by a transformation *See translation, reflection, rotation, and dilation.*	Two events such that the occurrence of one event does not affect the likelihood that the other event(s) will occur You flip a coin and roll a number cube. The events "flipping tails" and "rolling a 4" are independent events.

indirect measurement Indirect measurement uses similar figures to find a missing measure when it is difficult to find directly. 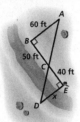 $$\frac{x}{60} = \frac{40}{50}$$ $$60 \cdot \frac{x}{60} = 60 \cdot \frac{40}{50}$$ $$x = 48$$ The distance across the river is 48 feet.	**inequality** A mathematical sentence that compares expressions; It contains the symbols $<$, $>$, $\leq$, or $\geq$. $$x - 4 < 14, \; x + 5 \geq -12$$
integers The set of whole numbers and their opposites $$\dots -3, -2, -1, 0, 1, 2, 3, \dots$$	**interest** Money paid or earned for the use of money *See simple interest.*
interior angles When two parallel lines are cut by a transversal, four interior angles are formed on the inside of the parallel lines. *See exterior angles.*	**interior angles of a polygon** The angles inside a polygon 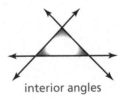 interior angles
irrational number A number that cannot be written as the ratio of two integers $$\pi, \sqrt{14}$$	**kite** A quadrilateral with two pairs of congruent adjacent sides and opposite sides that are not congruent 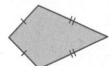

lateral surface area (of a prism)	**legs**
The sum of the areas of the lateral faces of a prism	The two sides of a right triangle that form the right angle
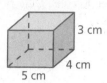	
Lateral surface area $= 2(4)(3) + 2(5)(3)$ $= 24 + 30 = 54 \text{ cm}^2$	*See hypotenuse.*
like terms	**line of reflection**
Terms of an algebraic expression that have the same variables raised to the same exponents	A line that a figure is reflected in to create a mirror image of the original figure
4 and 8, $2x$ and $7x$	*See reflection.*
linear equation	**linear expression**
An equation whose graph is a line	An algebraic expression in which the exponent of the variable is 1
$y = x - 1$ 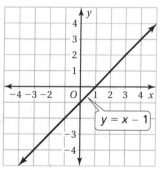	$-4x,\ 3x + 5,\ 5 - \dfrac{1}{6}x$
literal equation	**markup**
An equation that has two or more variables	The increase from what a store pays to the selling price
$2y + 6x = 12$	A store buys a hat for \$12 and sells it for \$20. The markup is \$8.

Multiplication Property of Equality

Multiplying each side of an equation by the same number produces an equivalent equation.

$$\frac{x}{3} = -6$$

$$3 \bullet \frac{x}{3} = 3 \bullet (-6)$$

$$x = -18$$

Multiplication Property of Inequality

When you multiply each side of an inequality by the same positive number, the inequality remains true.

When you multiply each side of an inequality by the same negative number, the direction of the inequality symbol must be reversed for the inequality to remain true.

$$\frac{x}{2} < -9 \qquad \qquad \frac{x}{-6} < 3$$

$$2 \bullet \frac{x}{2} < 2 \bullet (-9) \qquad -6 \bullet \frac{x}{-6} > -6 \bullet 3$$

$$x < -18 \qquad\qquad\qquad x > -18$$

negative number

A number less than 0

$$-0.25, -10, -500$$

opposites

Two numbers that are the same distance from 0, but on opposite sides of 0

-3 and 3 are opposites.

ordered pair

A pair of numbers (x, y) used to locate a point in a coordinate plane; The first number is the x-coordinate, and the second number is the y-coordinate.

The x-coordinate of the point $(-2, 1)$ is -2, and the y-coordinate is 1.

origin

The point, represented by the ordered pair $(0, 0)$, where the horizontal and vertical number lines intersect in a coordinate plane

See coordinate plane.

outcomes

The possible results of an experiment

The outcomes of flipping a coin are heads and tails.

parallel lines

Lines in the same plane that do not intersect;

Nonvertical parallel lines have the same slope. All vertical lines are parallel.

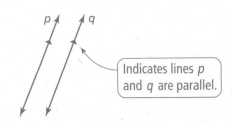

Indicates lines p and q are parallel.

percent A part-to-whole ratio where the whole is 100 $$37\% = 37 \text{ out of } 100 = \frac{37}{100}$$	**percent of change** The percent that a quantity changes from the original amount $$\text{percent of change} = \frac{\text{amount of change}}{\text{original amount}}$$ The percent of change from 20 to 25 is: $$\frac{25 - 20}{20} = \frac{5}{20} = 25\%$$
percent of decrease The percent of change when the original amount decreases percent of decrease $$= \frac{\text{original amount} - \text{new amount}}{\text{original amount}}$$ The price of a shirt decreases from \$20 to \$10. The percent of decrease is $\frac{20 - 10}{20}$, or 50%.	**percent error** The percent that an estimated quantity differs from the actual amount $$\text{percent error} = \frac{\text{amount of error}}{\text{actual amount}}$$ Estimated length: 16 feet Actual length: 21 Percent error: $\frac{21 - 16}{21}$, or 23.8%
percent of increase The percent of change when the original amount increases percent of increase $$= \frac{\text{new amount} - \text{original amount}}{\text{original amount}}$$ The price of a shirt increases from \$20 to \$30. The percent of increase is $\frac{30 - 20}{20}$, or 50%.	**perfect cube** A number that can be written as the cube of an integer $$-27, 8, 125$$
perfect square A number with integers as its square roots $$16, 25, 81$$	**perpendicular lines** Lines in the same plane that intersect at right angles; Two nonvertical lines are perpendicular when the product of their slopes is −1. Vertical lines are perpendicular to horizontal lines. 

pi (π)

The ratio of the circumference of a circle to its diameter

The value of π can be approximated as 3.14 or $\dfrac{22}{7}$.

point-slope form

A linear equation written in the form $y - y_1 = m(x - x_1)$ is in point-slope form.
The line passes through the point (x_1, y_1), and the slope of the line is m.

$$y - 1 = \frac{2}{3}(x + 6)$$

polygon

A closed figure in a plane that is made up of three or more line segments that intersect only at their endpoints

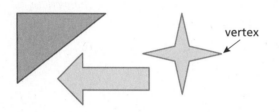

vertex

polyhedron

A solid whose faces are all polygons

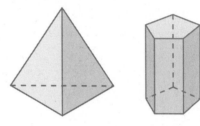

population

An entire group of people or objects

Population: All of the 14-year-old females in the United States

Sample: All of the 14-year-old females in your town

positive number

A number greater than 0

0.5, 2, 100

power

A product of repeated factors

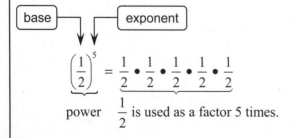

base   exponent

$$\left(\frac{1}{2}\right)^5 = \frac{1}{2} \cdot \frac{1}{2} \cdot \frac{1}{2} \cdot \frac{1}{2} \cdot \frac{1}{2}$$

power $\dfrac{1}{2}$ is used as a factor 5 times.

Power of a Power Property

To find a power of a power, multiply the exponents.

$$\left(3^4\right)^2 = 3^{4 \cdot 2} = 3^8$$

$$\left(a^m\right)^n = a^{mn}$$

Power of a Product Property To find a power of a product, find the power of each factor and multiply. $$(5 \cdot 7)^4 = 5^4 \cdot 7^4$$ $$(ab)^m = a^m b^m$$	**principal** An amount of money borrowed or deposited You deposit \$200 in an account that earns 4% simple interest per year. The principal is \$200.
prism A polyhedron that has two parallel, congruent bases; The lateral faces are parallelograms. 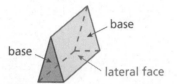	**probability** A number from 0 to 1 that measures the likelihood that an event will occur *See experimental probability and theoretical probability.*
Product of Powers Property To multiply powers with the same base, add their exponents. $$3^7 \cdot 3^{10} = 3^{7+10} = 3^{17}$$ $$a^m \cdot a^n = a^{m+n}$$	**proportion** An equation stating that two ratios are equivalent $$\frac{3}{4} = \frac{12}{16}$$
proportional Two quantities that form a proportion are proportional. Because $\frac{3}{4}$ and $\frac{12}{16}$ form a proportion, $\frac{3}{4}$ and $\frac{12}{16}$ are proportional.	**pyramid** A polyhedron that has one base; The lateral faces are triangles. 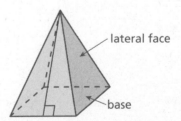

Pythagorean Theorem

In any right triangle, the sum of the squares of the lengths of the legs is equal to the square of the length of the hypotenuse.

$$a^2 + b^2 = c^2$$

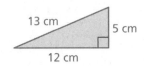

$$5^2 + 12^2 = 13^2$$

quadrilateral

A polygon with four sides

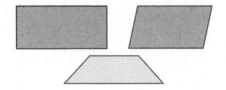

Quotient of Powers Property

To divide powers with the same base, subtract their exponents.

$$\frac{9^7}{9^3} = 9^{7-3} = 9^4$$

$$\frac{a^m}{a^n} = a^{m-n}, \text{ where } a \neq 0$$

radical sign

The symbol $\sqrt{}$ which is used to represent a square root

$$\sqrt{25} = 5$$
$$-\sqrt{49} = -7$$
$$\pm\sqrt{100} = \pm10$$

radicand

The number under a radical sign

The radicand of $\sqrt{25}$ is 25.

radius (of a circle)

The distance from the center of a circle to any point on the circle

See circumference.

radius of a sphere

The distance from the center of a sphere to any point on the sphere

See sphere.

rate

A ratio of two quantities with different units

You read 3 books every 2 weeks.

ratio	**rational number**
A comparison of two quantities using division; The ratio of a to b (where $b \neq 0$) can be written as a to b, $a : b$, or $\dfrac{a}{b}$. $$4 \text{ to } 1,\ 4 : 1,\ \text{or } \dfrac{4}{1}$$	A number that can be written as $\dfrac{a}{b}$ where a and b are integers and $b \neq 0$ $$3 = \dfrac{3}{1}, \qquad -\dfrac{2}{5} = \dfrac{-2}{5}$$ $$0.25 = \dfrac{1}{4}, \qquad 1\dfrac{1}{3} = \dfrac{4}{3}$$

real numbers	**reduction**
The set of all rational and irrational numbers $$4,\ -6.5,\ \pi,\ \sqrt{14}$$	A dilation with a scale factor greater than 0 and less than 1 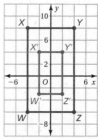 $W'X'Y'Z'$ is a reduction of $WXYZ$.

reflection	**regular polygon**
A transformation in which a figure is reflected in a line called the line of reflection; A reflection creates a mirror image of the original figure. 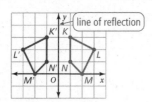 $K'L'M'N'$ is a reflection of $KLMN$ over the y-axis.	A polygon in which all the sides are congruent, and all the interior angles are congruent

regular pyramid	**relative frequency**
A pyramid whose base is a regular polygon 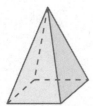	The fraction or percent of the time that an event occurs in an experiment You flip a coin 20 times. If you flip heads 11 times, the relative frequency of flipping heads is $\dfrac{11}{20}$, or 55%.

repeating decimal	**right angle**
A decimal that has a pattern that repeats $$0.555... = 0.\overline{5}$$ $$1.727272... = 1.\overline{72}$$	An angle whose measure is $90°$
right triangle	**rise**
A triangle that has one right angle 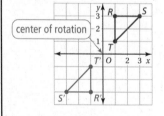	The change in y between any two points on a line *See slope.*
rotation	**run**
A transformation in which a figure is rotated about a point called the center of rotation; The number of degrees a figure rotates is the angle of rotation.  $\triangle RST$ has been rotated about the origin O to $\triangle R'S'T'$.	The change in x between any two points on a line *See slope.*
sample	**sample space**
A part of a population *See population.*	The set of all possible outcomes of one or more events You flip a coin twice. The outcomes in the sample space are HH, HT, TH, and TT.

scale A ratio that compares the measurements of a drawing or model with the actual measurements <div align="center">12 cm : 1 cm $\dfrac{2 \text{ in.}}{15 \text{ ft}}$</div>	**scale drawing** A proportional, two-dimensional drawing of an object <div align="center">A blueprint or a map</div>
scale factor (of a dilation) The ratio of the side lengths of the image of a dilation to the corresponding side lengths of the original figure *See dilation.*	**scale factor (of a scale drawing)** A scale without units *See ratio.*
scale model A proportional, three-dimensional model of an object	**scientific notation** A number is written in scientific notation when it is represented as the product of a factor and a power of 10. The factor must be greater than or equal to 1 and less than 10. <div align="center">8.3×10^{4} 4×10^{-3}</div>
semicircle One-half of a circle 	**similar figures** Figures that have the same shape but not necessarily the same size; Two figures are similar when corresponding side lengths are proportional and corresponding angles are congruent.

similar solids

Solids that have the same shape and proportional corresponding dimensions

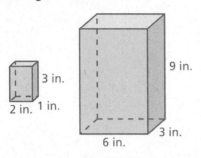

simple interest

Money paid or earned only on the principal

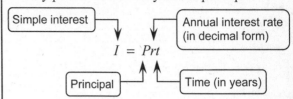

$$I = Prt$$

You put $200 into an account. The account earns 5% simple interest per year. The interest earned after 3 years is $200 × 0.05 × 3, or $30. The account balance is $200 + $30 = $230 after 3 years.

simplest form (of an algebraic expression)

An algebraic expression is in simplest form when it has no like terms and no parentheses.

$$6a + 9a^2, \; 3t + 5$$

simulation

An experiment that is designed to reproduce the conditions of a situation or process

slant height (of a pyramid)

The height of each triangular face of a pyramid

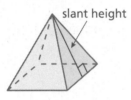

slant height

slope

The slope m of a line is a ratio of the change in y (the rise) to the change in x (the run) between any two points (x_1, y_1) and (x_2, y_2) on a line. It is a measure of the steepness of a line.

$$m = \frac{\text{rise}}{\text{run}} = \frac{\text{change in } y}{\text{change in } x}$$

$$= \frac{y_2 - y_1}{x_2 - x_1}$$

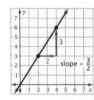

slope-intercept form

A linear equation written in the form $y = mx + b$ is in slope-intercept form. The slope of the line is m, and the y-intercept of the line is b.

The slope is 1 and the y-intercept is 2.

solid

A three-dimensional figure

See three-dimensional figure.

solution of an equation A value that makes an equation true 6 is the solution of the equation $x - 4 = 2$.	**solution of an inequality** A value that makes an inequality true A solution of the inequality $x + 3 > -9$ is $x = 2$.
solution of a linear equation All of the points on a line	**solution set** The set of all solutions of an inequality
sphere The set of all points in space that are the same distance from a point called the center 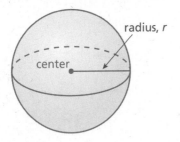	**square root** A number that, when multiplied by itself, equals a given number The two square roots of 100 are 10 and -10. $\pm\sqrt{100} = \pm10$
standard form The standard form of a linear equation is $ax + by = c$, where a and b are not both zero. $$-2x + 3y = -6$$	**Subtraction Property of Equality** Subtracting the same number from each side of an equation produces an equivalent equation. $$\begin{aligned} w + 5 &= 25 \\ \underline{-5} \quad &\underline{-5} \\ w &= 20 \end{aligned}$$

Subtraction Property of Inequality

When you subtract the same number from each side of an inequality, the inequality remains true.

$$x + 7 > -20$$
$$\underline{-7 \quad\quad -7}$$
$$x > -27$$

supplementary angles

Two angles whose measures have a sum of $180°$

terminating decimal

A decimal that ends

$$1.5, \ 2.58, \ -5.605$$

terms (of an algebraic expression)

The parts of an algebraic expression

The terms of $4x + 7$ are $4x$ and 7.

theorem

A rule in mathematics

The Pythagorean Theorem

theoretical probability

The ratio of the number of favorable outcomes to the number of possible outcomes when all possible outcomes are equally likely

$$P(\text{event}) = \frac{\text{number of favorable outcomes}}{\text{number of possible outcomes}}$$

When rolling a number cube, the theoretical probability of rolling a 4 is $\dfrac{1}{6}$.

three-dimensional figure

A figure that has length, width, and depth; also known as a solid

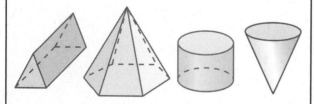

transformation

A transformation changes a figure into another figure.

See translation, reflection, rotation, and dilation.

translation

A transformation in which a figure slides but does not turn; Every point of the figure moves the same distance and in the same direction.

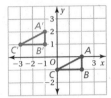

ABC has been translated 3 units left and 2 units up to *A'B'C'*.

transversal

A line that intersects two or more lines

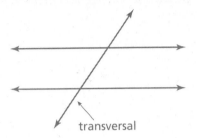

two-dimensional figure

A figure that has only length and width

unbiased sample

A sample that is representative of a population; It is selected at random and is large enough to provide accurate data.

You want to estimate the number of students in your school who like to play basketball. You survey 100 students at random during lunch.

unit rate

A rate with a denominator of 1

The speed limit is 65 miles per hour.

variable

A symbol that represents one or more numbers

x is a variable in $2x + 1$.

vertex (of an angle)

The point at which the two sides of an angle meet

See angle.

vertex (of a polygon)

A point at which two sides of a polygon meet; The plural of vertex is vertices.

See polygon.

vertical angles

The angles opposite each other when two lines intersect; Vertical angles are congruent angles.

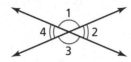

∠1 and ∠3 are vertical angles.

∠2 and ∠4 are vertical angles.

whole numbers

The numbers 0, 1, 2, 3, 4, …

---

x-axis

The horizontal number line in a coordinate plane

See coordinate plane.

x-coordinate

The first coordinate in an ordered pair, which indicates how many units to move to the left or right from the origin

In the ordered pair (3, 5), the x-coordinate is 3.

---

x-intercept

The x-coordinate of the point where a line crosses the x-axis

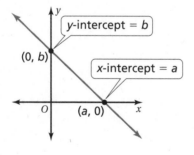

y-axis

The vertical number line in a coordinate plane

See coordinate plane.

---

y-coordinate

The second coordinate in an ordered pair, which indicates how many units to move up or down from the origin

In the ordered pair (3, 5), the y-coordinate is 5.

y-intercept

The y-coordinate of the point where a line crosses the y-axis

See x-intercept.

Photo Credits

100 Jean Thompson; **107** Baldwin Online: Children's Literature Project at www.mainlesson.com; **149** Scott J. Carson/Shutterstock.com; **189** *top left* ©iStockphoto.com/Luke Daniek; *top right* ©iStockphoto.com/Jeff Whyte; *bottom left* ©Michael Mattox. Image from BigStockPhoto.com; *bottom right* ©iStockphoto.com/Hedda Gjerpen; **210** ryasick photography/Shutterstock.com; **218** Warren Goldswain/Shutterstock.com; **221** *top right* John McLaird/Shutterstock.com; *center right* Robert Asento/Shutterstock.com; *bottom right* Mark Aplet/Shutterstock.com; **231** *Activity 1a left* ©iStockphoto.com/Shannon Keegan; *Activity 1a right* ©iStockphoto.com/Lorelyn Medina; *Activity 1b left* Joel Sartore/joelsartore.com; *Activity 1b right* Feng Yu/Shutterstock.com; *Activity 1c left* ©iStockphoto.com/kledge; *Activity 1c right* ©iStockphoto.com/spxChrome; *Activity 1d* ©iStockphoto.com/Alex Slobadkin; **261** *top* ©iStockphoto.com/Viatcheslav Dusaleev; *bottom left* ©iStockphoto.com/Jason Mooy; *bottom right* ©iStockphoto.com/Felix Möckel; **273** Elena Elisseeva/Shutterstock.com.; **276** Estate Craft Homes, Inc.; **312** ©iStockphoto.com/biffspandex; **333** ©Oxford Science Archive/Heritage Images/Imagestate; **368** ©iStockphoto.com/Franck Boston; **369** Stevyn Colgan; **383** ©iStockphoto.com/Kais Tolmats; **384** *top right* ©iStockphoto.com/Kais Tolmats; *Activity 3a and d* Tom C Amon/Shutterstock.com; *Activity 3b* Olga Gabay/Shutterstock.com; *Activity 3c* NASA/MODIS Rapid Response/Jeff Schmaltz; *Activity 3f* HuHu/Shutterstock.com; **385** *Activity 4a* PILart/Shutterstock.com; *Activity 4b* Matthew Cole/Shutterstock.com; *Activity 4c* Yanas/Shutterstock.com; *Activity 4e* unkreativ/Shutterstock.com; **388** NASA

Cartoon Illustrations Tyler Stout

Cover Image: Serg64/Shutterstock.com, ©Unlisted Images/Fotosearch.com, valdis torms/Shutterstock.com

1.25	0.75	$\dfrac{3}{4}$	0.6
-0.6	$\dfrac{19}{10}$	-0.4	$-\dfrac{2}{5}$
$-\dfrac{3}{4}$	-1.2	-0.75	1.6
$\dfrac{3}{10}$	$\dfrac{8}{5}$	1.9	$-\dfrac{3}{10}$
$-\dfrac{3}{2}$	$\dfrac{3}{20}$	1.5	$\dfrac{6}{5}$

*Available at *BigIdeasMath.com*.

-0.3	-1.6	$\dfrac{3}{5}$	$\dfrac{5}{4}$	-0.15
0.3	1.2	$-\dfrac{3}{5}$	$-\dfrac{6}{5}$	-1.5
$-\dfrac{19}{10}$	$-\dfrac{3}{20}$	$\dfrac{2}{5}$	-1.9	$-\dfrac{5}{4}$
$-\dfrac{8}{5}$	0.4	-1.25	$\dfrac{3}{2}$	0.15

*Available at *BigIdeasMath.com.*

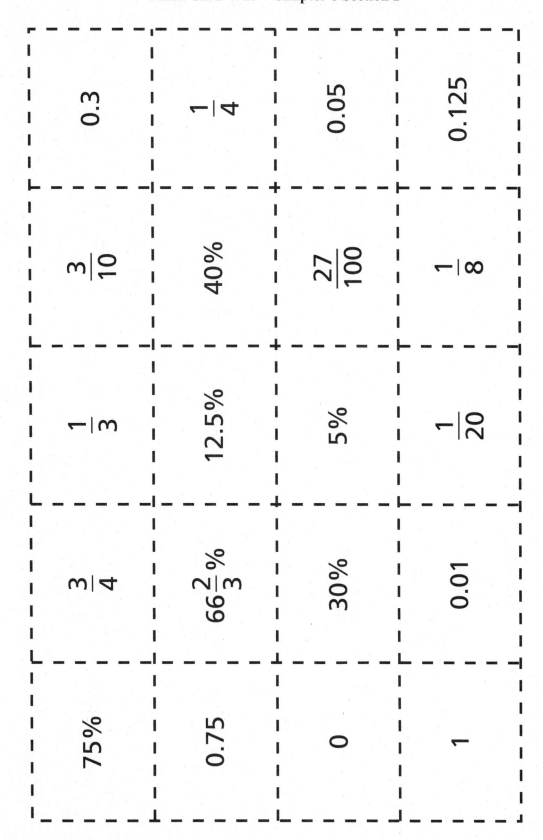

0.3	$\dfrac{3}{10}$	$\dfrac{1}{3}$	$\dfrac{3}{4}$	75%
$\dfrac{1}{4}$	40%	12.5%	$66\dfrac{2}{3}\%$	0.75
0.05	$\dfrac{27}{100}$	5%	30%	0
0.125	$\dfrac{1}{8}$	$\dfrac{1}{20}$	0.01	1

*Available at *BigIdeasMath.com.*

0.27	$\dfrac{2}{3}$	1%	0%
100%	$\dfrac{1}{100}$	27%	0.666...
0.25	0.04	0.333...	0.005
0.4	0.5%	$\dfrac{2}{5}$	$\dfrac{1}{200}$
25%	4%	$33\dfrac{1}{3}\%$	$\dfrac{1}{25}$

*Available at *BigIdeasMath.com.*

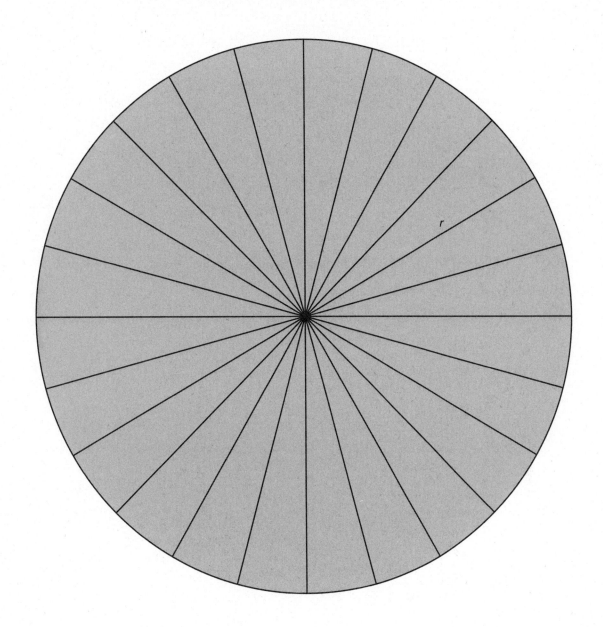

*Available at *BigIdeasMath.com*.

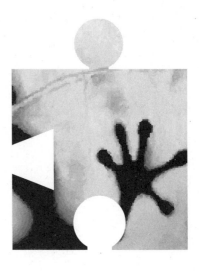

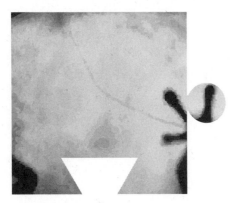

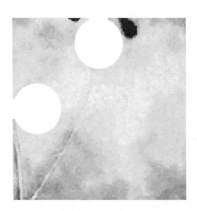

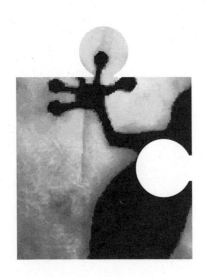

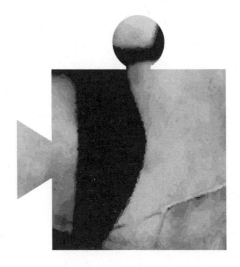

*Available at *BigIdeasMath.com*.

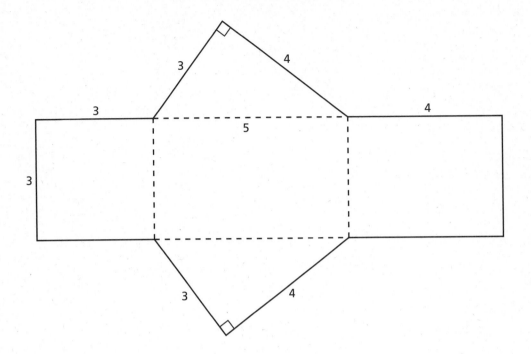

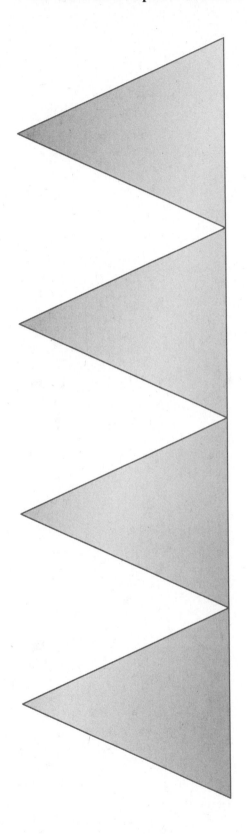

*Available at *BigIdeasMath.com.*

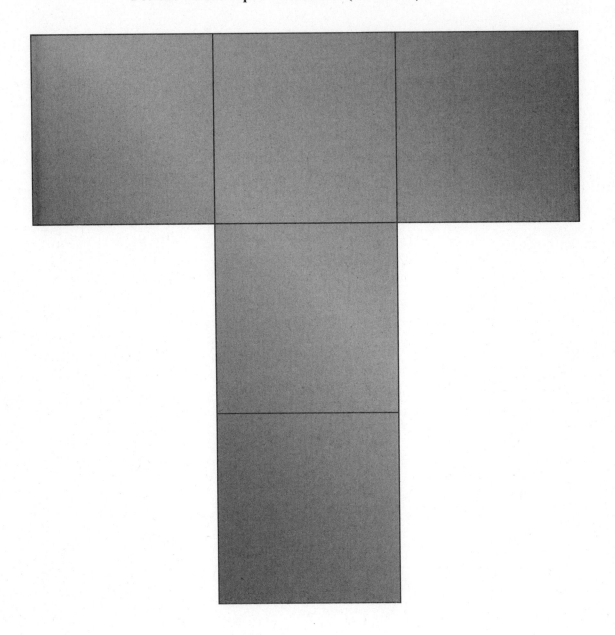

a.

d.

*Available at *BigIdeasMath.com.*

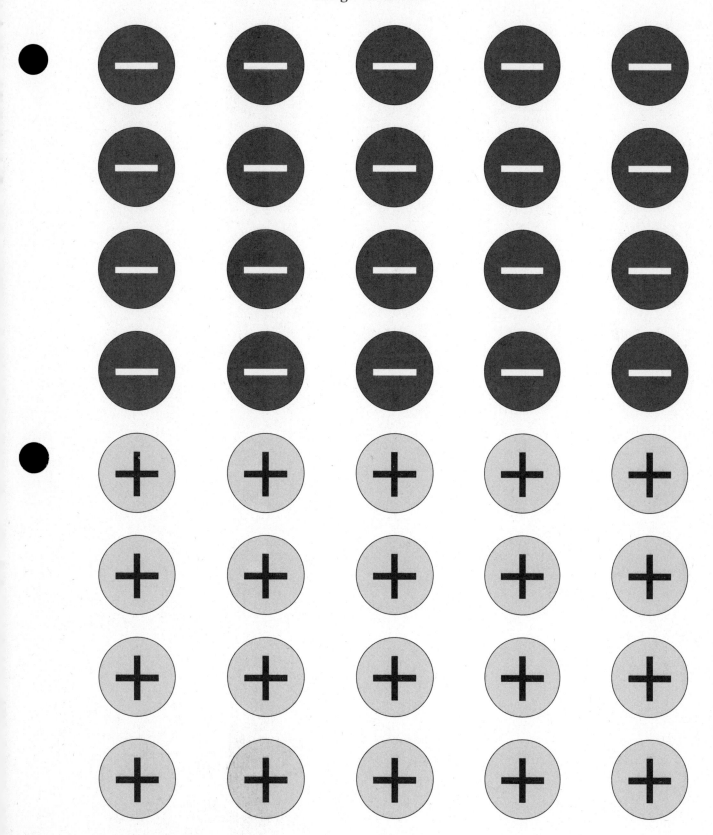

*Available at *BigIdeasMath.com.*

Algebra Tiles*

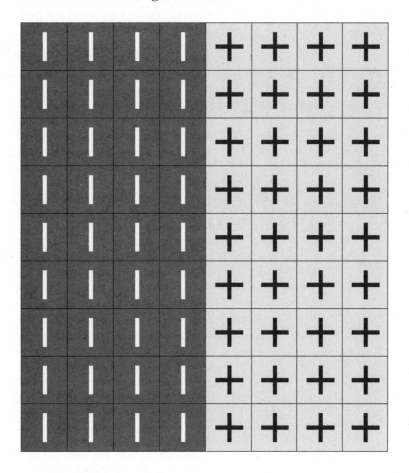

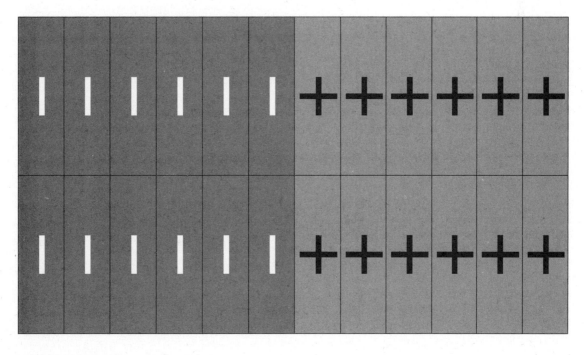

*Available at *BigIdeasMath.com*.